Advocacy, Inc.

ADVOCACY, INC.

INGOs and the Business of "Modern Slavery"

STEPHANIE A. LIMONCELLI

STANFORD UNIVERSITY PRESS
Stanford, California

Stanford University Press
Stanford, California

Library of Congress Cataloging-in-Publication Data

Names: Limoncelli, Stephanie A., author.
Title: Advocacy, Inc. : INGOs and the business of "modern slavery" / Stephanie A. Limoncelli.
Description: Stanford, California : Stanford University Press, 2026. | Includes bibliographical references and index.
Identifiers: LCCN 2025033673 (print) | LCCN 2025033674 (ebook) | ISBN 9781503640160 (cloth) | ISBN 9781503644823 (paperback) | ISBN 9781503644830 (ebook)
Subjects: LCSH: Forced labor—Prevention. | Slave labor—Prevention. | Human trafficking—Prevention. | Child labor—Prevention. | Antislavery movements. | Non-governmental organizations. | Social responsibility of business.
Classification: LCC HD4871 .L56 2026 (print) | LCC HD4871 (ebook)
LC record available at https://lccn.loc.gov/2025033673
LC ebook record available at https://lccn.loc.gov/2025033674

Cover art and design: Jan Šabach
Typeset by Newgen in 10/14.5 Capitolina Regular

The authorized representative in the EU for product safety and compliance is: Mare Nostrum Group B.V. | Mauritskade 21D | 1091 GC Amsterdam | The Netherlands | Email address: gpsr@mare-nostrum.co.uk | KVK Chamber of Commerce number: 96249943

Contents

Contents

Acknowledgments

Writing a book is a lengthy journey made possible with the support of others, and I extend my heartfelt appreciation to all of those who helped in myriad ways. I am thankful for the questions and comments I received from the Harvard History, Culture, and Society Workshop, where I presented the book project in March 2024, and I am grateful to Orlando Patterson and Ya-Wen Lei for the invitation to present. The book is surely stronger for the feedback and scholarly insights I received.

Thank you also to the Global Alliance Against Traffic in Women, Borislav Gerasimov, Jennifer Musto, and Mitali Thakor for organizing a special journal issue of the *Anti-Trafficking Review* and a related webinar on technology in anti-trafficking efforts, as well as an ancillary panel at the 14th United Nations Congress on Crime and Crime Prevention in Kyoto, Japan, which allowed me to present and publish work from the chapter on technology that became a separate article. I received helpful feedback on that chapter during a presentation of the work at Southern Utah University as well, and I am grateful to Shobha Gurung for arranging that talk. Emma Dunn provided impeccable research assistance for that part of the project.

Thanks also to all of the participants at the July 21–23, 2021 international workshop "Terms of Work – Shifting Boundaries of 'Free' and 'Un-Free' Work" organized by Marianne Braig, Léa Renard, Nicola Schalkowski, and

Theresa Wobbe of Freie Universität Berlin, where I presented a small piece of chapter 2. I especially appreciated the thoughts and suggestions of Barbara Brents and Orlando Patterson.

I received constructive feedback from the participants and organizers of the various conference sessions where I presented the work: the 2023 International Sociological Association RC44 Repertoires of Action session; the 2022 American Sociological Association Transnational Processes session; the 2022 Society for the Study of Social Problems Work and the Global Economy session; the 2022 Labor in Crisis Mini Conference, co-sponsored by the American Sociological Association Sections on Global and Transnational Sociology, Political Economy of the World System, and Labor and Labor Movements; the 2021 American Sociological Association Economic Sociology Section; and the 2018 International Sociological Association's RC09 Discourse, Power, and Development: Turning a Critical Lens on INGOs session at the World Congress. The discussions at each of these presentations helped me to further develop the project and clarify my thinking.

I would also like to thank Samantha Majic and Molly Clark-Barol for reading and providing helpful feedback during the earliest stages of the book. I have been especially lucky to benefit from Sam's prodigious knowledge of anti-trafficking work, keen analytic ability, and cheerful support even while she was busy with her own research and prolific scholarship.

Gail Kligman, Chris Tilly, and Rachel Washburn kindly made suggestions on the prospectus. The SUP reviewers provided extremely helpful comments and detailed suggestions that helped to strengthen the organization and arguments of the book. I hope that I have adequately addressed them.

Loyola Marymount University's Bellarmine College of Liberal Arts provided support through the 2016 Faculty Research Grant, the 2021 Daum Mid-Career Research Award, and the 2024 Research and Writing Grant, which enabled me to develop and complete the project. Aiza Santos, the Senior Administrative Coordinator in the Sociology Department, was also incredibly helpful with a variety of administrative tasks while I was both teaching and working to complete the book.

Finally, I would like to thank my editor, Marcela Cristina Maxfield, for helping to move the book forward in a timely manner; Mark Herwick and Sophia Limoncelli-Herwick for listening supportively to an array of "little Limoncelli lectures" and being thoughtful sounding boards; and all of those I interviewed, for their time and willingness to discuss their work.

INTRODUCTION

When I interviewed the director of the Western international nongovernmental organization (INGO) we'll call Global Slavery Fighters, he was
hopeful about the organization's activities and its future. In addition to the
nonprofit's core activities of supporting partner organizations in countries
of the global south, conducting media campaigns and awareness raising on
issues of "modern slavery," and advocating for new and better enforcement
of policies and laws, the organization now had a new opportunity for consulting. Headquartered in a country with recent legislation requiring large
for-profit companies to publicly report what, if anything, they were doing to
address issues of "modern slavery" meant that the INGO could provide expertise to companies crafting their responses. Global Slavery Fighters was
one of many nonprofits that had lobbied for the legislation, though they had
not gotten any purchase with government officials until businesses said
that they were also in favor of it.

The INGO had varied experiences working with the private sector. It
had endured a failed attempt to work with companies in a multistakeholder
initiative (MSI) to address forced labor and child labor happening in a South
Asian country, at first attempting to be discreet about the problems it found
in the companies' supply chains, but eventually resorting to naming and
shaming the Western brands when matters devolved and the firms threat-
ened to sue. Still, Global Slavery Fighters was involved in other MSIs, and

its ongoing relationship with a multinational company, which the director considered a positive one, remained strong.[1] Now the INGO was hoping to court other businesses, marketing itself to them on its website, which explained that they should contact the director for information about supply chain consultancy services. Global Slavery Fighters offered trainings and tailored services to companies, including systems to identify risks and monitor deficiencies in supply chains, advice on management responses within companies and in supplier relations, and support for developing company policies and procedures to address issues of "modern slavery."

Within a few years, Global Slavery Fighters was appealing to companies even more directly and with more explicit business language: they would act as a "critical friend," discuss cause-related marketing schemes for relevant products or services, and help facilitate collaborations with other businesses and civil society groups to help "leverage activities" and "scale up positive impact." Interested companies were no longer instructed to call the director of the INGO, who had left the organization, or its new leader, whose title had been changed to CEO; instead, they should contact Global Slavery Fighters' new corporate partnerships manager for further information.

Many scholars and activists, as proponents of increased business involvement and collaboration in the "modern slavery" field, would view this example positively (see, e.g., Bain 2017; Bain, Metallidis, and Shelley 2014; Foot 2015, 60–62). They are part of a broad trend lauding corporate leadership, business approaches, and multistakeholder collaborations in a variety of advocacy fields, including health, the environment, humanitarianism, and international development, as well as issues of "modern slavery" (Dale and Kyle 2016). "Modern slavery" scholars Shelley and Bain (2015, 140), for example, argue that, in addressing human trafficking:

> Current and emerging business leaders have a crucial role to play, whether as the head of major corporations and imparting social value or embarking on social enterprises or applying business-thinking to non-governmental organizations.

One can also find this sentiment echoed on "anti-slavery" INGO websites and in their written materials. It is not uncommon to see claims that "business[es] [have] an immense power to prevent trafficking globally" and are "the most trusted entity for change within society," or that they

are "incubators of innovative and continued learning" and "uniquely positioned to build understanding of what human trafficking is and how it
can be addressed." There are several underlying assumptions at work in
this view: that business leadership is necessary and helpful, that markets
provide the key to addressing issues of "modern slavery," and that the application of business-thinking will help to make nonprofits better able to
address problems.

Collaborations between businesses, governments, international governmental organizations (IGOs), and nonprofit organizations are also seen
as key. As "modern slavery" scholars Nolan and Boersma (2019, 181) argue,
"collaboration with companies is vital," because "they can act as influential
change agents." Such collaborations may involve an INGO and one or more
companies or it can take the form of an MSI, which voluntarily brings together IGOs, governments, companies, and civil society groups to address
a broad array of human rights and environmental harms linked to business
activity, including "modern slavery" (Baumann-Pauly et al. 2016; Foot 2020).
In short, proponents believe that business innovation and expertise will help
end issues of "modern slavery," that the public sector and civil society organizations need to collaborate with the private sector, and that all parties
should have faith in capitalism and market solutions as the best way forward.

This book explores and critiques these assumptions. It examines business influence in "anti-slavery" advocacy; the role of companies and INGOs
and relations between them; and the best ways to help address unfree
labor in the global economy. How have businesses been conceptualized in
"anti-slavery" advocacy? What does their increasing involvement mean for
other organizational actors in the field, particularly INGOs, and for the ability of the movement to fight issues of "modern slavery?" Based on interviews
with involved organizations in the west, and an analysis of their written documents and online content, I find that INGOs have been pressed to become
increasingly like for-profit businesses in their strategies, communications,
and operations, and their actions are doing little to address the driving
forces that have created conditions for unfree labor in the global economy.

Businesses benefit from this, becoming the "heroes" of "anti-slavery"
efforts without having to engage in substantial change. Accepting business
dominance minimizes what INGOs and activists can press companies to do
and helps to replicate the status quo. A faith in business paradigms, market

solutions, and corporate partners promises flexible, efficient, and immediate solutions to issues of "modern slavery," but perpetuates surface-level and ultimately ineffective strategies that do little to actually help ameliorate labor exploitation in the global economy, challenge neoliberal capitalist practices, or engage the very people that the movement purports to help.

"Modern slavery" is often used as an umbrella term for issues of forced labor, human trafficking, and child labor, referring to processes by which people are compelled to work against their will and exploited by others for gain.[2] Those in the advocacy field regularly use the term, reiterate it in their communications, and incorporate it into the names of their programs, initiatives, and organizations. I note from the outset that it is a problematic term for a number of reasons, including the need for more specificity in legal contexts (Chuang 2015, Jordan 2011, Prasad 2015), better analytic clarity in academic work on servitude (Patterson and Zhuo 2018), the way it can perpetuate simplified notions of chattel slavery and/or conflate historical systems of slavery with the forms of exploitation happening today (Davidson 2015; LeBaron, Pliley, and Blight 2021; Brace and O'Connell Davidson 2018), and the political implications of using the term, which can result in policies and programs that impede progress on labor and migrant rights and reinforce the idea that people lack agency (Brace and O'Connell Davidson 2018; Davidson 2010; Demetriou 2015; Lewis and Waite 2015; Palumbo and Sciurba 2015; Fudge 2015).

Many academics, myself included, prefer the term "unfree labor" to encompass all of the issues of "modern slavery" noted above and to explicitly denote a continuum of labor exploitation tied to capitalist systems and processes (LeBaron 2013; LeBaron and Phillips 2018; Fudge 2017). It is a term I use throughout the book. However, I also use "modern slavery" in quotes to denote that it is a contested term, along with the more specific iterations of forced labor, human trafficking, and child labor when it is possible to specify them, because those in the advocacy field use them. Whether they refer to "modern slavery," human trafficking, forced labor, child labor, or a combination of these, the organizations are part of the same national and transnational networks, attend the same meetings and working groups, compete for the same funding, and see themselves as working in the same advocacy arena. I conceptualize "anti-slavery" advocacy as a heterogeneous field, per sociologists Watkins, Swidler, and Hannan (2012) and Bartley (2007), with organizational actors embedded in social contexts that are complex and shifting, creating implications for the ways in which issues are understood and acted upon.

BACKGROUND: THE MOVEMENT AGAINST "MODERN SLAVERY"

Activists, governments, and international governmental organizations (IGOs) have all vowed to ameliorate issues of "modern slavery" in the last few decades, developing laws, governmental agencies, nonprofit organizations, programs, and collaborative initiatives at local, national, and international levels (Foot, Sworn, and Alejano-Stelle 2019; Foot 2015, 2010; Reed 2013). Initially focused on human trafficking for sexual exploitation, the field has expanded to emphasize labor exploitation in a variety of sectors, including agriculture, construction, apparel, hospitality, mining, food processing, transportation, domestic service, and caring work (see, e.g., Ditmore 2023). Exploitation in global supply chains is also now a prominent concern, with issues of "modern slavery" found in resource extraction, production, and manufacturing processes tied to export, as well as in the transnational recruitment, transportation, and management of workers via labor brokers (Plant 2015, 155).

The Evolution of Business Involvement: Along with this expanded focus, the movement against "modern slavery" has seen a change in the participation of businesses, who have moved from the sidelines, as funders, to an increasingly active role as partners and collaborators (Hoff and McGauran 2015, 72; Yaziji and Doh 2009). IGOs and wealthy governments, particularly the United States, Norway, and Japan, were the main financial supporters at the beginning of the movement, but private sector funding has been significant and increasing (Ucnikova 2014; Suhr 2016; Dottridge 2021; Hoff 2014; Gallagher 2021).[3] In contrast, support from national governments has begun to wane (Dottridge 2021).

Businesses have also become more central as the focus of funding and as recipients. In the past, government funding has gone mainly toward programs and projects involving INGOs, IGOs, and other governments, and much of it has been targeted toward public awareness; trainings; research, identification, and prosecution of those perpetuating exploitation; and detection of and assistance to people who experience issues of "modern slavery" (Rossoni 2024; Hebert 2024). Very little government funding went to or involved private sector companies (Hebert 2024).[4] However, new initiatives aim to support and engage companies in MSIs and technology-focused projects that are increasingly popular (Rossoni 2024; OSCE Office of the Special Representative and Coordinator for Combating Trafficking in Human Beings and Tech Against Trafficking 2020).

The companies that have gotten involved in the movement against "modern slavery" tend to be large corporations. Those taking leadership roles have included, for example, the large staffing and recruiting agency Manpower, wealth management and hospitality companies such as Carlson and Marriott, the food and beverage company Coca-Cola, the cosmetics company Body Shop International Limited, the clothing company Gap, Inc., retailers such as Walmart and C&A, various airlines, and technology companies such as Microsoft, Google, and Amazon.

A few billionaires have also gained outsized leverage in the field, developing foundations to support "anti-slavery" work (Chuang and Shih 2021). Some argue that these wealthy donors now have an effective monopoly over the field (cf. Dottridge 2021, Grono 2021). There is, for example, Humanity United, founded in 2008 and wholly funded by Pierre Omidyar, the billionaire entrepreneur, software engineer, and eBay founder. The Walk Free Initiative is another important example, founded in 2010 by Australian billionaire Andrew Forrest, who made his fortune in metals/minerals. Forrest is also the person behind the Freedom Fund, which provides support for global initiatives against "modern slavery" and for "hotspot" projects in Nepal, Ethiopia, India, and Thailand. It was established in 2013, with $30 million U.S. dollars in initial contributions from the Walk Free Foundation, Humanity United, and the Legatum Foundation, which is associated with New Zealand financier Christopher Chandler and the Legatum Group.[5]

Prompted by and following the lead of IGOs and states of the global north, companies have supported highly visible anti-slavery public awareness efforts, provided training and employment for those who experienced or were at risk of unfree labor, developed their own nonprofit membership organizations to work on issues of "modern slavery," and become part of MSIs. The United Nations Global Initiative to Fight Trafficking (UN.GIFT), is one example, launched in 2007 and managed by UNODC (United Nations Office on Drugs and Crime 2016a). Now defunct, UN.GIFT's goals were to develop public-private partnerships; promote corporate social responsibility (CSR) measures; develop a database of good practices; work with companies in the travel and tourism sectors on awareness campaigns; publish resources on human trafficking for businesses; and develop a "Business Leader's Award" in conjunction with UN Global Compact, a global CSR initiative (United Nations Office on Drugs and Crime 2016b; United Nations Global Initiative to Fight Human Trafficking et al. 2010). Another prominent and current MSI is Alliance 8.7, a voluntary initiative that seeks to share knowledge, coordinate actions, and mobilize resources to help eradicate forced labor, "modern slavery" and human trafficking, and child labor as part of the UN Sustainable Development Goal on Decent Work and Economic Growth.[6]

The growth of MSIs involving issues of "modern slavery" is part of a broader move from public to private governance, understood by proponents as the solution for problems that escape the reach of individual states (cf. Baumann-Pauly et al. 2016; LeBaron et al. 2021). As such, they promote voluntary self-regulation to address issues of "modern slavery." Efforts like these have helped bring issues of "modern slavery" firmly into the realm of CSR, which is itself a movement and a field of practice involving companies working voluntarily to incorporate greater responsibility for social and environmental concerns beyond what they are legally required to do (Vogel 2005; Scherer and Palazzo 2011; Tsutsui and Lim 2015; Crane et al. 2008).

The Growth of Nonprofits: Nonprofits that directly identify themselves as "anti-slavery" or anti-human trafficking organizations or that have dedicated programs and projects to address issues of "modern slavery" grew tremendously from the early 1990s (Limoncelli 2016).[7] There were nonprofits working on these issues in at least 168 countries by 2015, with most headquartered primarily in Western Europe and the United States as well as in South and Southeast Asia.

Large, specialized "anti-slavery" INGOs tend to be prominent voices in the field; in some cases, they are the lead or main "anti-slavery" nonprofit in their country, and in others, they are one of many. Other large INGOs that focus more broadly on poverty and economic development, human rights, and/or migration are also prominent organizational actors, having long-standing projects or programs on issues of "modern slavery." They are active within and across countries and most often have partner organizations in the places where they are working. Smaller nonprofits, national and international, have also proliferated in the field and they have tended to focus on research and policy advocacy, public awareness, identification and rescue of people in "modern slavery" and/or services to them at the client level. This is particularly true in the United States, where small grassroots organizations have grown (Schnable 2015).

The current field thus includes a diverse set of nonprofits, varying in size and focus, including grassroots, faith-based, and specialized "anti-slavery" and/or anti-trafficking nonprofits, and large humanitarian and development organizations that have "anti-slavery," forced labor, child labor, and anti-human trafficking programs. These organizations have been joined by MSIs involving INGOs and companies; nonprofits that operate for-profit components as part of their approach; and nonprofits that are operated by businesses.

What all of the nonprofit organizations have in common is that they engage in advocacy to prevent or address issues of "modern slavery." Advocacy organizations have as their goals social or political/policy changes, and they engage in a variety of tactics to achieve them (Mosley, Suárez, and Hwang 2022). In "anti-slavery" advocacy, this often entails working on public awareness campaigns, developing and implementing trainings and workshops and/or providing consultations on "modern slavery," and supporting programs and projects to address these issues in countries with developing economies. It also involves pressing governments for new laws, policies, or practices and working to hold officials accountable to existing ones, and it can include assisting in the prosecution of traffickers or "slaveholders." While some nonprofits that provide services to people who experience issues of "modern slavery" can be faced with restrictions to lobbying or involvement with political campaigns due to funding and/or governmental partnerships, they, too, find ways to engage in advocacy, such as challenging existing policies and advocating on behalf of their constituents (Berry and Arons 2005; Majic 2014).

THEORIZING BUSINESSES AND INGOS IN THE "ANTI-SLAVERY" FIELD

The academic literature pertaining to businesses and INGOs in transnational advocacy is expansive and cuts across the social sciences, law, business, and nonprofit, social movement, and labor studies. It includes scholarship on globalization and corporations, the nonprofit sector, social movements, and global governance, defined as systems to manage transnational issues that involve multiple organizational actors beyond states. Depending on theoretical and disciplinary concerns, the literature offers very different conceptualizations of the roles of businesses and INGOs in global governance, including different understandings of their power.

For scholars who are optimistic about the ability of global governance to address difficult issues such as labor exploitation, companies are key stakeholders. Companies act when governments cannot or will not, respond to issues raised by INGOs, help set ethical standards through private regulation and CSR, and take part in deliberative democracy (Scherer and Palazzo 2011, 2007). The optimists similarly view INGOs as stakeholders in global governance, with power to press states and companies for changes on behalf of their constituencies and keep states and companies accountable for their actions.

There is ample literature to support this view about INGOs. They do advocate for new regulations and benchmarks to improve existing practices; engage in service provision to vulnerable or marginalized groups; help to set national and global agendas; assist in framing issues; represent societal interests; design and implement programs for the public good; and advocate for social change and action being promoted by social movements (Stroup and Wong 2017). They also support domestic civil society groups by placing pressures on states in a boomerang effect (Keck and Sikkink 1998) and team up with companies to challenge or bypass state power when governments are unwilling to guarantee rights (Bair, Anner, and Blasi 2020). They can also, as organizations, provide employment, professionalization, and leadership opportunities for marginalized groups within countries and spaces to influence IGOs, states, and companies (Bernal and Grewal 2014; Garwood 2011).

Those who are optimistic about global governance tend to also have an underlying pluralist vision, in which states, nonprofits, and companies are seen as equal stakeholders in collaborations addressing global issues, each able to have a say in the responses decided and actions taken. Differences of position or opinion may occur and contestation can happen, but there is no assumed imbalance of power. Businesses fill in where regulatory vacuums have occurred and respond to INGOs' authority and legitimacy, which they

derive from their commitment to the common good and their representation of the people they are trying to help (Baur and Palazzo 2011; Baur 2011;
Scherer and Palazzo 2011).

A separate body of sociological literature, looking at international organizations and transnational social issues, complicates this pluralist vision,
but it, too, downplays power differentials between the public, private, and
nonprofit sectors (see, e.g., Powell and Bromley 2020; Maier, Meyer, and
Steinbereithner 2016). Drawing from new institutionalist theory, these
scholars stress the convergence they believe is happening between the sectors. They see global cultural norms and, in particular, processes of rationalization driving changes among businesses, nonprofits, and states alike,
leading them to organize themselves similarly and blur the lines between
them (Bromley and Meyer 2014; Pope et al. 2018; Allin and Thomas 2023).
From this perspective, nonprofits professionalize and become more like
for-profits, including becoming increasingly reliant on commercial components (Smith 2014; Powell 2020, 17; Horwitz 2020). At the same time,
companies are said to become more "nonprofit-like," seeking legitimacy
by committing to more ethical social and environmental practices, such as
what we see with private regulation and efforts like MSIs and the CSR movement (Lim 2017; Meyer, Pope, and Isaacson 2015; Hofferberth et al. 2011).[8]

New institutionalists argue expressly against those who suggest that
corporations are using collaborations to vie for power or coopt other organizational actors in advocacy fields. They view world culture as comprising
and providing "discursive frames to support, legitimate, and constitute the
actors involved" in direct opposition to the view that companies are constructing discourses as "smokescreens to hide, with manipulated frames,
raw interests" (Meyer, Pope, and Isaacson 2015, 28). By focusing on cultural diffusion and characterizing that process as one of mutual change,
however, these scholars discount power relations within advocacy fields
(Downey et al. 2020).

In contrast to pluralist or new institutionalist perspectives, an array of
critical scholars raise concerns about the roles of companies and INGOs in
global governance, emphasize the power of business, and tie these issues to
neoliberalism, as both a paradigm and set of policy directives in contemporary global capitalism. Coming from political economy, post-structuralist,
and feminist approaches, and often indebted to Marx, Gramsci, or Foucault,

these scholars place corporations and INGOs firmly within the context of shrinking states, the growing influence of market liberalism, and corporate power. Though they have varying ontological and epistemological assumptions, these scholars, as I am grouping them here, share a focus on the intersection of culture, politics, and the economy; an interest in the production and reproduction of dominant ideologies; and a critique of existing power structures in global governance.

Companies in Critical Perspective: Critical scholars have good reason to be skeptical about the role of companies in global governance, including efforts to fight unfree labor: business practices play a role in contributing to labor exploitation in the first place. What happens in factories and on farms, mining and construction sites, with migrant and other workers, in formal and informal work situations, involves employers, labor recruiters, labor brokers, producers, and suppliers (Jenkins forthcoming; Sexsmith and Tarlau forthcoming). Businesses small and large, in the global north and south, can be directly or indirectly involved (Crane 2013, 2017). Globalization has also contributed to the conditions that exacerbate issues of "modern slavery," with Western companies sourcing from states reliant on export sectors populated with internal or international migrant workers and little enforcement of labor rights. Countries with a "business-friendly" regulatory climate (i.e., policies promoting market deregulation) have an increased likelihood of being a source and destination country for labor trafficking as well as having domestic trafficking (Peksen, Blanton, and Blanton 2017). Moreover, Western companies' subcontracting and purchasing practices exacerbate the possibilities of exploitation in supply chains via a lack of oversight and cost and time pressures on suppliers (LeBaron et al. 2018; Anner 2019b, 2019a).

Unfree labor predated neoliberalism, but it is currently happening in a time period characterized by the movement away from governments as regulators of market forces, the rise of privatization measures and private actors taking on what had previously been in the realm of governments in the west, and the belief that the private sector can do it better and more efficiently (see, e.g., Birch and Siemiatycki 2015). As a philosophy that espouses free markets as the most effective means of organizing political, social, and economic life, the influence of neoliberalism goes far beyond the economic realm and extends to all facets of social life, including social action to address ongoing societal problems (Brown 2015).[9] While the success of neo-liberal policy proscriptions has not been uniform across Western countries (Prasad 2006; Ferguson 2017), the economic implications of neoliberalism, as well as the increasing normalization of ideas that reinforce the individ-ualization of social problems and promote privatized, market-based, and consumption-based solutions, have nonetheless had broad impacts glob-ally. It has also certainly had a strong impact in the "anti-slavery" field since there is a concentration of INGOs headquartered in the west where neoliberalism has been embraced and the privatization agenda promoted by IGOs, states, and companies.

Within this context, critical scholars have raised concerns about the ways in which for-profit companies increasingly dominate political, cul-tural, and economic areas of social life, including social activism (Dau-vergne and Lebaron 2014; King and Busa 2017; King 2008). Academic studies on the ways corporations affect social movements remains somewhat lim-ited (Davis and Kim 2017), but scholars have often written about corporate actors intentionally seeking to commandeer advocacy movements by en-gaging with their ideas and practices and shaping the discourses and activ-ities of the field in their interests (King and Busa 2017; Busa and King 2015). Companies, then, may take part in MSIs and private governance "solutions" like CSR as a means of cooptation, and business interests can dominate movement activities and weaken efforts toward corporate accountability (Dauvergne and Lebaron 2014; Williams 2020; LeBaron et al. 2021; Soeder-berg 2007). Furthermore, some companies actively enter fields with orga-nizations of their own as part of that process: "MNCs have learnt to deploy and mold the nonprofit sector to fit a hegemonic neo-liberal version of civil society" with "nominally nonprofit organizations that blur the lines be-tween the old categories of state, market and civil society" and alliances that MNCs create (Shamir 2004, 684).

Critical scholars also point to the way private funding and "philan-throcapitalism," i.e., the application of business approaches to conducting charitable activities, facilitate cooptation (Bloom and Rhodes 2018, 92–93; Thompson 2017; Chuang and Shih 2021; Soskis 2020; Nickel and Eikenberry 2010). It centralizes control and gives elites power over states; allows them to leverage public resources toward private goals and gains; and moves foundations into more directive, controlling, metric-focused directions

(Thompson 2017; Gallagher 2021).[10] It also gives a small number of people the ability to make decisions that affect millions without checks on this power (Nickel and Eikenberry 2010). In the "modern slavery" field, for example, Walk Free's Global Fund to End Modern Slavery has gotten substantial funding from national governments and has been criticized by some scholars for promoting market-based solutions and business leadership (Fudge 2022, 20–21; Dottridge 2021).

INGOs in Critical Perspective: Critical scholars have often questioned the role of INGOs in global governance; rather than seeing them as vital building blocks of global civil society, they point out the ways that INGOs reinscribe state power in new ways. In the context of transnational advocacy fields, especially, INGOs can be engaged in neocolonial agendas, perpetuating the interests of global north states and exacerbating racial, ethnic, gender or other social inequalities (Bernal and Grewal 2014; Choudry and Kapoor 2013). They can drain resources, including people who would otherwise be involved in the state, undermine the governance capacity of states in the global south, and the high-paying jobs that large INGOs bring can create inequalities and divisions within countries (Schuller 2009). They also lack accountability except to funders and their boards, may or may not reflect the needs and wishes of their constituents, and can work in ways that can undermine other civil society groups and unions (Eade and Leather 2005).

When it comes to companies and INGOs in global governance, critical scholars, like new institutionalists, see a blurring among the public, private for-profit, and nonprofit sectors, but they see it in the context of cooptation. This leads to problems for INGOs and advocacy fields: a "deradicalizing" effect by which INGOs take part in incremental and reformist strategies rather than more extensive challenges to either corporate power or systemic problems caused by processes of global capitalism (Dauvergne and LeBaron 2014; Stroup and Wong 2017; Subramaniam 2007). In addition, INGOs become more "business-like" in their operations and activities, whether due to funder requirements, a wish to gain influence and promote change as "insiders," or because it is what INGO leadership and staff believe is feasible in today's political and economic climate (Williams 2020; Stroup and Wong 2017; Soule 2009). This goes beyond the rationalization of INGOs to processes involving the adoption of corporate-like structures, operations, management, and communication, as well as market-based and consumer-driven revenue generation (Joachim and Schneiker 2018).

Cooptation can be a matter of intentional corporate action; that businesses deploy their power politically, in order to stave off regulation, is a routine observation made by scholars (Walker and Rea 2014; LeBaron and Rühmkorf 2017; Kaplan 2014). So, too, is the point that private governance initiatives can be used as a smokescreen to legitimate companies and help them maintain the status quo (Hanlon 2008; Hanlon and Fleming 2009; Soederberg 2007; Banerjee 2020; Banerjee 2008).[11] However, cooptation can also be something more pervasive: helping to set the agenda, the rules of the game, the language used, and the conceptualizations or framing of issues in ways that favor business interests. As sociologists Walker and Rea (2014, 283) suggest, business power is not dependent on business unity; it is ideological and institutional, not just economic, and it is great and growing.

If INGOs are increasingly being coopted by business, they start to speak the same language, employing similar methods of justification and strategies of action. They become more reliant on commercial revenue and accede to pressure to become more business-like in actions, rhetoric, and operations (Eikenberry and Kluver 2004; Maier, Meyer, and Steinbereithner 2016). They begin to adopt market-oriented strategies as part of ". . . a hegemonic business-oriented model concerning the 'right way of doing things'" (Shamir 2004, 685). They may even become intermediaries for corporations, advancing their interests and advocating for policies that benefit them (Walker and Oszkay Febres-Cordero 2020, 514–515).

Modern Slavery Literature: Critical scholars writing specifically about "anti-slavery" advocacy have often called attention to the ways the movement bolsters and reinscribes state power. They have routinely critiqued "anti-slavery" policies and programs based on criminal justice frameworks that harm migrants and sex workers; are used by governments to justify increasing surveillance within and across borders; and reinforce the norms, values, and political agendas of governments of the global north (see, e.g., Lerum and Brents 2016; Kempadoo, Sanghera, and Pattanaik 2005; Davidson 2006; Chapkis 2005; Bernstein 2007; Showden and Majic 2014; Musto 2016). Studies of "anti-slavery" nonprofits have also focused on the ways they reinforce or challenge state power in their framing of issues, representations of constituents, methods of political participation, and the actions they take within or outside of parameters set by states (Limoncelli 2010; Musto 2016; Shih 2016; van Doorninck 2018; Musto 2010; Majic 2023).

While critical scholars have routinely explored the politics of "anti-slavery" advocacy, they have paid less attention to the private sector and its intersection with INGOs. There have been calls for more attention to "corporate humanitarianism" and "redemptive capitalism" as neoliberalism has intertwined with efforts to combat sex trafficking, in particular, but scholarship on this has been limited (Bernstein 2014, 2016; Shih 2023). One notable exception is Shih (2023), who has critiqued Western anti-sex trafficking INGOs' vocational training programs in Thailand and China, arguing that they fail to offer social mobility or economic independence and that they reinforce dependence on Western aid and capitalist markets via "racialized redemptive labor." Additional research can help to further our understandings of the intersection of capitalism and "anti-slavery" advocacy and this book is one attempt to do just that. It takes a critical perspective of "anti-slavery" advocacy and explores business influence and INGO activities in the field. It focuses on the ways business leadership is being constructed and how INGOs are responding to this trend, paying particular attention to their actions, communications, and operations.

THE EMPIRICAL CASE

I treat contemporary "anti-slavery" advocacy as a site for empirical investigation to explore private sector involvement, the ways INGOs navigate it, and the implications for INGOs as well as the potential success of the movement.[12] It is a case study that adds to others such as food, recycling, breast cancer, and environmental activism, as well as activism more generally (King and Busa 2017; Busa and King 2015; King 2008; Dauvergne and Lebaron 2014). Movements working on issues that attract a wide range of people, are compatible with a focus on individuals, and that provide marketable technological solutions or potential commodities seem particularly susceptible to business influence (Busa and King 2015). "Anti-slavery" advocacy fits these criteria.

It is a case study that adds a focus on labor exploitation to the above examples, something important in light of the neoliberalism that has dominated global capitalism, leading to precarity, informalization, and widespread challenges to decent work (Preminger et al. forthcoming; Tilly forthcoming). In addition, "anti-slavery" efforts have had much attention and resources directed to them in recent decades, in some sense supplanting interest in other forms of labor exploitation and labor rights; in conjunction with union decline and the deregulation of labor, it is all the more important to critically examine a field that has become influential in addressing labor exploitation.

Rather than accepting the optimist case for business solutions and assuming the positive influence of corporate leadership or presuming an apolitical diffusion of rationalization affecting businesses and INGOs similarly, I look with a critical lens at the "anti-slavery" field as a case study to trace what is happening and how those involved make sense of it. I pay particular attention to framings of labor exploitation and the actions of INGOs. The goal is to understand the discourses of the field and the way the organizational actors, especially INGOs, view their organizations, their work, and their collaborations, to shed light on whether and how change is being fostered and what that change looks like, and also whether and how progress is being made. Attending to the interactions of INGOs and corporations can help to illuminate the ways they re-configure or create fields and logics (de Bakker et al. 2013).

I do not assume that INGOs are a uniform group, nor that they are either pristine arbiters of the global good or passive tools of northern states. They are varied, can be engaged in internal and external conflicts and competition to ensure their own survival, and can work toward goals that have both positive and negative consequences for the people they are trying to help and the issues that they are trying to address. INGOs act but are also acted upon as they collaborate and compete with other organizations within a field (see, e.g., Krause 2014; Watkins, Swidler, and Hannan 2012).

My approach is critical in that it attends to power in transnational advocacy fields. Like sociologist Tim Bartley (2021), I assume that businesses are one type of organizational actor among many, but that they occupy a privileged position in relation to INGOs. I seek to understand if and how business influence results in "field stabilization" or hegemony, and the economic, organizational, and discursive processes that can align in ways that secure business interests (Levy and Egan 2003; Levy and Kaplan 2009). I therefore analyze these aspects of the field with attention to the ways they reinforce or challenge corporate interests and existing state practices, press for reform or business as usual, and affect INGOs as advocates in the field. I do this by considering funding, discourses of "modern slavery," and the actions, communications, and operations of INGOs.

Toward this end, from 2016 to 2019, I interviewed leaders and staff working at INGOs as well as other organizations in the "modern slavery" field and I analyzed the documents and online content they produced (see the Appendix for further details). To ensure some representation of the heterogeneity of the field, as well as a broad overview, I conducted interviews with a purposive sample of fifty people in forty organizations in nine countries: Austria, Belgium, Canada, Germany, Greece, the Netherlands, Switzerland, the United Kingdom, and the United States. The focus on organizations based in the west was a reflection of the geographic locations where business influence, states, and INGOs have been concentrated.[13]

Half of the organizations were in the United States with the other half distributed among the other eight countries mentioned. Twenty-nine of the organizations were INGOs that self-identified as working on issues of "labor trafficking," "forced labor," and/or "modern slavery" as the sole or main focus of the organization. In addition to these organizations, I interviewed staff at one business-led INGO, one survivor-led nonprofit, four IGO offices, three unions, and two academic centers working on "modern slavery" and labor issues. The diversity of interviews was to ensure that I included the views of market-oriented INGOs and business-led INGOs, as well as to broaden my knowledge of the field and triangulate information between IGOs, INGOs, and others in the advocacy field.

In addition to interviews, I also collected and analyzed 524 documents and 1,900 pages of online texts from these organizations including transcriptions of video content that they produced. Combining the texts with interviews allowed me to consider both the ways the organizations represented themselves and what they were doing in practice. Because I collected the texts at two points in the research process—once at the time that I conducted the interview, and once in 2020 after the interviews were completed—I was able to trace changes in the INGOs' representations over time. This meant that I could often see, as with the case of Global Slavery Fighters, business-related discourses and actions being adopted by the INGOs during the research process.

The INGOs reflected the diversity in the advocacy field. They included organizations large and small, well-established and new (most had originated in the 1990s or 2000s, but some had been in operation much longer), secular and faith-based, and varied in their activities and advocacy strategies. They reflected a number of different frameworks for understanding unfree labor, including criminal justice, human rights, development, gender, and labor perspectives. They were located in a variety of urban areas, with a few smaller ones in shared spaces with other organizations or in co-working sites, but the majority were in large, modern office buildings.

Led mainly by highly educated, white men and women who had made careers out of advocacy, they had between $250,000 in annual revenue to more than $75 million for "anti-slavery work;" they averaged about $8 million, with only five INGOs having less than a million in annual revenue.[14] The overwhelming majority of them were successfully maintaining or growing their organizations during the course of the research; only two of the smaller INGOs were struggling to maintain funding. A few were growing rapidly, and one was an absolute juggernaut, increasing its revenue by millions year after year. Most were getting their funding from multiple sources, including government and private grants, donations, IGO funding, and to a much lesser extent, fees and commercial revenue, including for-profit social enterprises.

OUTLINE OF THE BOOK

In the remainder of the book, I examine the business of "anti-slavery" advocacy, and the implications for both INGOs and the amelioration of unfree labor in the global economy. First, I explore the framings of "modern slavery" and "anti-slavery" advocacy in chapters 1 and 2, respectively, followed by a focus on the way INGOs are navigating business influence in chapters 3 through 6.

Chapter 1, "Framing 'Modern Slavery' as a Business Enterprise," presents and critically analyzes the conceptualization of unfree labor as a new type of criminal business. This characterization promotes misconceptions about those perpetuating issues of "modern slavery;" reinforces the idea that unfree labor is an aberration of normal business practices; obfuscates the political economy of unfree labor; and avoids critiques of current forms of capitalism and business practices that might contribute. INGOs, faced with framings that emphasize individualized and criminalized action rather than ones that address political, economic, and social structures, struggle with these characterizations. Some adopt law and order approaches to "anti-slavery" advocacy, and others try to juggle crime and development approaches, but very few connect their work to either corporate accountability efforts or the work of unions and labor groups. Framing unfree labor in this way undermines the potential for a stronger and multifaceted civil society response.

Chapter 2, "Using 'Good' Business to Fight 'Bad' Business," questions the premise that issues of "modern slavery" can best be solved with the help of legitimate businesses in advanced capitalist economies. Discourses advocating the use of "good business" to fight "bad business" reflect a number of problematic features. They place business interests at the center of the problem rather than the workers that "anti-slavery" advocacy is intended to help—the 'victims' of "modern slavery" become the businesses themselves. They characterize businesses as victims of suppliers, partners, labor brokers, governments, and INGOs. They also suggest that "good" businesses are "heroes" uniquely suited to voluntarily solve the problems of unfree labor, even though there is little evidence that past voluntary measures have been successful in ameliorating labor abuses. Framing "anti-slavery" advocacy from a business-centered perspective reinforces neoliberalism, allows Western businesses to maintain a veneer of vulnerability and innocence in labor exploitation, and, as critical scholars suggest, perpetuates business as usual.

Chapter 3, "Fraught Collaborations and Business-Friendly Strategies," provides examples of the ways INGOs' actions and advocacy strategies are becoming more business-friendly. INGO staff are aware of the power differentials between civil society organizations and large companies, so they walk a thin line whereby they seek to engage companies but retain credibility. The solutions have been to develop "anti-slavery" strategies involving market-based and voluntary schemes (codes or certifications), incentives for businesses, trainings and consultation, and consumption-oriented strategies, such as transparency laws. Some NGOs are hoping to compete in the newly emerging market of consultants/specialists by helping businesses with their "anti-slavery" efforts and providing research and services to them, introducing the idea of businesses as INGO constituents. I argue that these trends and strategies are not just business-friendly; they are actually shifting the responsibility for monitoring businesses from nonprofits to consumers, in effect "outsourcing" it, just as some governments had previously outsourced their monitoring to nonprofits. To some extent, INGOs are seeking to act as business service organizations rather than corporate watchdogs.

Extending that argument, chapter 4, "Technological 'Fixes' for Complex Problems," examines technological initiatives increasingly touted by businesses and INGOs as solutions to unfree labor. It questions technological "fixes" for addressing issues of "modern slavery" and their ability to ameliorate labor exploitation, and it considers the potential problems that such initiatives may entail, including privacy issues and potential harm to workers. Even where technological innovation is leading to tools that can be used to better monitor supply chains, the social conditions in which they are to be used and the possible misuse or unintended consequences of the tools need to be carefully considered and the role of INGOs and workers clarified. Failing that, technological initiatives will continue to perpetuate the idea that company expertise will solve issues of "modern slavery," divert attention and resources away from other needed advocacy strategies, provide a superficial sense of action, and do little to hold businesses accountable for unfree labor, even in their own tech supply chains.

Chapter 5, "Communicating Like a Business: Branding and Marketing 'Anti-Slavery' INGOs," looks at the way INGOs adopt business-like rhetoric and communications in representing themselves to audiences. Those working in INGOs are aware of competition in the advocacy field and experience pressure to brand the organizations and specialize. They emphasize their efficiency with outcomes, testimonials, and statistics; seek to engage donors through media marketing techniques involving the "celebritization" of INGO founders; appeal for funds by constructing donors as heroes and consumers; and market people who have experienced unfree labor. All of this moves the INGOs toward the language, ideas, and goals of corporate communication, reinforcing the belief that markets are the solution to issues of "modern slavery" and that individual donor-heroes who buy into the actions of INGOs are what it takes to address unfree labor.

Chapter 6, "Making INGO Operations and Structures More Business-Like," shows that hybridization has happened along a continuum. INGOs have adopted business titles, added business representatives to their boards, hired professionalized staff including business liaisons, and generated revenue through merchandise sales, co-branding, cause-related marketing, the promotion of goods produced by "survivor entrepreneurs," and the development of for-profit social enterprise companies. While most of the INGOs are maintaining their missions, these changes to INGO operations and structures raise questions about their ability to advocate for changes to exploitative labor conditions. They become sellers of goods and services, employers of clients, and business entrepreneurs, further disconnected from, or possibly in a contradictory position to, the people they are intending to help. INGOs that have substantial for-profit components can introduce their own set of inequalities and perpetuate existing capitalist systems with no guarantee of changing them.

The concluding chapter revisits the main questions and arguments of the book, suggests further research, and discusses potential ways to channel the power of INGOs in the "anti-slavery" field toward corporate accountability and the involvement of workers.

One

FRAMING "MODERN SLAVERY" AS A BUSINESS ENTERPRISE

[Our organization is working] to ultimately put an end to the
fastest growing criminal enterprise of the twenty-first century
  —Text from the website of a U.S.-based "anti-slavery" INGO

The conceptualization of "modern slavery" as a business is ubiquitous, often repeated on websites and in reports of "anti-slavery" organizations. We see it on INGO websites that tell us, for example, that human trafficking has grown to be one of the largest criminal enterprises globally, that it is a global criminal industry estimated to be worth billions of dollars annually, and that it is thriving. Similar characterizations are found on government websites, such as the U.S. Department of Justice, which claims that "human trafficking is the world's fastest growing criminal enterprise, valued to be an estimated $32 billion-a-year global industry"[1] and among international governmental organizations (IGOs), such as UNICEF, which suggests that human trafficking and forced labor generate an estimated $150 billion in yearly profits.[2] If one simply opens a web browser to ask the question "What is the fastest growing criminal industry?" the answers that pop up first will reference human trafficking.

Is "modern slavery," which involves the coercive exploitation of others for gain, also a business? And why should we be concerned with this characterization? This chapter presents and critically analyzes the conceptualization of "modern slavery" as a type of new criminal business activity that can best be solved with the help of "legitimate" businesses in advanced capitalist economies. This conceptualization is problematic for several reasons, including one that is important to our interest in INGOs. It discounts a long history of labor exploitation in countries around the world in favor of rhetoric that suggests the problem is new and different rather than a continuation of exploitive labor processes that have been used in the past. It promotes unhelpful generalizations about those who perpetuate labor exploitation and individualizes the problem. It reinforces the idea that issues of "modern slavery," as criminal business activities, are an aberration of normal business practices, thus avoiding critiques of current forms of capitalism and the practices of "legitimate" companies that might contribute. In addition, the conceptualization influences nonprofit organizations that see themselves and their work as separate from other organizational actors working on labor rights and/or corporate accountability, perpetuating silos between groups who could otherwise be collaborating on the worst forms of labor exploitation in the global economy. Portraying issues of "modern slavery" as criminal business activities obfuscates the political economy of unfree labor and stymies the potential for a more robust and broad-based civil society response.

UNFREE LABOR AS BUSINESS: ACADEMIC DISCOURSES

The notion of "modern slavery" as a type of business—that is, an activity involving the production, buying, or selling of goods or services for profit—is not only perpetuated by "anti-slavery" organizations. It is also repeated by academics in economics, business schools, and the social sciences, who emphasize the calculated activity of criminal actors and entrepreneurs (Spapens 2018). Criminologist Louise Shelley (2003), for example, has written about the practices of transnational crime groups engaged in sex trafficking, characterizing them as relying on particular business models that vary by cultural and regional differences. There is a post-socialist "natural resource model" that focuses on short-term profit with little concern for the long-term durability of the business; a Chinese "trade and development model" which involves expensive smuggling sums and is long-term and tightly controlled; a Mexican "supermarket model" that involves moving large numbers of people on the cheap; a Balkan "violent entrepreneur model;" a Nigerian and West African "traditional slavery with modern technology model;" and a Dutch "rational actor model."

The conflation of smuggling and human trafficking is problematic in Shelley's classification, as are the cultural attributions that can reinforce racial, ethnic, and national stereotypes,[3] but what is relevant for our purposes is the understanding of trafficking as a type of business. People are characterized as being just like other commodities and traffickers as rational actors; "traditional patterns of trade and investment shape the trade in human beings as they do the trade in other commodities" (Shelley 2003, 122).

Similarly, business scholars such as Crane et al. (2018) see issues of "modern slavery" as part of "dark organizations" in the unregulated or unexplored parts of the economy and a form of "economic rationality" that prompts and sustains the use of slavery-like practices. They suggest that "modern slavery" entails new business models involving control rather than ownership, and like Shelley, they also develop a classification scheme by which to categorize them: (1) a risk reduction model, in which coercion is used to reduce labor costs and lower the risks of detection; (2) asset leveraging, such as charging workers for the use of the trafficker's assets or using the workers' assets, such as identity cards, to make fraudulent benefits claims or to sell them for extra money; (3) an evading legal minimum model, which uses intermediaries to avoid legal requirements and/or re-categorizes workers as self-employed to exploit loopholes and still control them; and (4) workers as consumers, in which contracts are used to make workers indebted and to get revenue from them (Crane et al. 2021).

Such classification efforts show how disciplinary divisions can work to limit rather than broaden knowledge. Sociologists, political scientists, historians, and labor scholars from all of these disciplines have written extensively on all of the above processes, which have historically been a part of capitalism. From the exploitation of miners in U.S. company towns in the late 19th and early 20th centuries, to the role of employment agencies in the exploitation of women internationally during the interwar period, to historical and contemporary scholarship on the experiences of workers in informal economies around the world, we already have *vast* amounts of scholarship on processes of labor exploitation in the past as well as in the present.

The forms of exploitation described above have been used in agriculture, mining, construction, restaurants, and manufacturing work for many decades; the elements of what is now called "modern slavery," human trafficking, forced labor, and child labor have very long histories, indeed. Yet many scholars and activists still stress that "modern slavery" issues are new; it is not uncommon to see them asserting that "modern day slaves" are different because they are disposable, that the trade in people is particularly lucrative because they can be repeatedly "bought and sold," and that people are more profitable than drugs or guns because they can be used over and over again and bought and sold at will (Bales 1999; Kara 2010).[4] Unfree labor is far more complicated than that; it fundamentally involves social relations, not just economic ones, and it belies a simple "new entrepreneur" narrative (Patterson 2012; Patterson and Zhuo 2018).

INDIVIDUALIZING THE PROBLEM: EXPLOITERS AS RATIONAL ACTORS

The danger in characterizing "modern slavery" as business is not limited to simple rebranding and duplication in the production of scholarly knowledge, or even the possibility of contributing to the mischaracterization of contemporary problems under study. It is a matter of ontological importance as well. It evokes the image of canny, rational actors making instrumental decisions to exploit others as "business people and entrepreneurs," leading to economic responses. For example, the Organization for Security and Co-operation in Europe (OSCE) and the United Nations Global Initiative to Fight Human Trafficking (UN.GIFT) sponsored a project to analyze the business model of trafficking with the goal of better preventing it (Aronowitz, Theuermann, and Tyurykanova 2010). If one better understands the business model, the logic goes, one can take measures to target particular markets that are the most prone to "modern slavery" and increase the costs and risks for traffickers to reduce their profits. This leads to recommendations such as better international cooperation on criminal investigations, tracing assets and money flows, and the seizure and confiscation of assets.

The goal of making unfree labor less profitable was evident among several of the organizations that I interviewed and it is also found in a variety of their texts and in scholarship on "modern slavery." Employing an economic perspective, IGOs have attempted to estimate the profits of human trafficking (Belser 2005) and "modern slavery" scholars have sought to enumerate the costs to "run the business" of sex trafficking, which is thought to have "a profit margin greater than almost any industry in the world, illicit or otherwise" (Kara 2010, 16–17).[5] As one U.S.-based INGO affirmed on its website:

> Increasing knowledge about and enforcement of anti-trafficking laws can reduce the profitability of slavery, making it too risky a gamble for criminal gangs and business owners.

For many INGOs, "modern slavery" is seen as a choice that people make because, in economic terms, it is high profit and low risk.

In thinking of "modern slavery" as a logical decision-making process in which individual actors intentionally consider payoffs and risks, however, we are drawing from a theoretical perspective with severe limitations in explaining social behavior:

> When the analysis is exclusively focused on an individual's rationality, the macro variables such as the role of the state, ideology, historical legacies, collective memories and so on are completely left out of the picture. Because of its overemphasis on an individual's rationality, rational choice theories very often do not see the wood for the trees (Malešević 2010).

Rational choice theory has therefore been criticized for its methodological individualism, micro-level analysis, assumptions about motivation, neglect of emotion and values, lack of attention to structural constraints of individual choice, and tautological tendency to explain social behavior, post hoc, as rational. Economic processes are social constructions, and economic action needs to be studied sociologically (Bourdieu 2005).

In addition, when all individual choices are treated as equal but the structural conditions of choices are very unequal, power is obscured and we end up with a skewed perception of who exploiters are and why they are involved in "modern slavery." From the vantage point of many economists and business professionals, "modern slavery" is reduced from a complex, multifaceted social phenomenon to a "management practice" of "slave operators" who persist in the interstices of otherwise regulative and normative business operations (Crane 2013, 63). A rational choice perspective may be employed for analyzing the decision-making processes of organized crime groups that are involved in issues of "modern slavery," but there are indications that only a portion of those involved fit this characterization.

I discussed this issue with two members of an IGO who worked specifically on human trafficking and related issues; both questioned the prevalence of organized crime in "modern slavery" and the profits involved:

> Interviewee #1: We kind of wanted to do an analysis on how much money can be collected from this crime. We found, actually to a very large extent, it's not big money. . . . These big criminal organizations, of course, are bringing in some money, but I think the big criminal organizations represent probably 30 percent of all traffickers.
>
> Interviewee #2: But even for an individual trafficker, no [not big money]. I do think there are some people, individually, I do guess, [that can] make a lot of money, even if it's just one person. Then it [the money] goes back to the country of origin in that case, where they [do things with it like] build houses, but still it doesn't amount to anything.

I note this exchange in detail here because these particular interviewees worked with governments on issues of criminalizing issues of "modern slavery;" the IGO helps countries draft, develop, and review their laws, policies, and action plans to combat human trafficking and trains and mentors those who work to apprehend, prosecute, and convict traffickers. These particular staff members are well-placed, on the basis of their work, to have some sense of who exploiters are globally, at least those whom states are prosecuting and convicting.

Studies do exist that seem to corroborate the views of the staff members. Scholars point out that those perpetuating issues of "modern slavery" may be individual friends, family members, acquaintances, and/or crucially, people who have experienced unfree labor themselves. In China, for example, some labor brokers are themselves indebted and may be only slightly better off than the construction workers they are recruiting from the same rural areas in which they live (Chuang 2014). In the Netherlands, some human traffickers are women who have themselves experienced trafficking (Siegel and de Blank 2010). In India, rural farmers are often indebted and struggling to keep the bonded laborers they "employ" (Choi-Fitzpatrick 2017). In various European countries, trafficking in domestic work occurs mostly within families or individual networks rather than criminal ones, and is not associated with high profits (Ricard-Guay and Maroukis 2017). In the United States, youth who trade sex may have romantic partners, roommates, or friends as facilitators (Showden and Majic 2018).

People may also be involved in unfree labor out of specific forms of duress rather than for calculated benefit. In some cases, it may be the result of a direct threat of violence; for example, women who experience human trafficking are sometimes forced to recruit new women or girls, blurring the lines between who is considered a trafficker and who is considered a victim or survivor of trafficking. In other cases, political and economic processes create the duress. The rural farmers or "slaveholders" that Choi-Fitzpatrick (2017) studied in India had trouble surviving after the implementation of neoliberal International Monetary Fund (IMF) interventions, including structural adjustment programs, export-oriented agriculture, and cuts in government subsidies along with increased prices for equipment and seeds patented by the multinational corporation Monsanto. Many farmers were forced to take loans in order to survive, and their increasing indebtedness led some to commit suicide. Others, seeking jobs abroad to help pay their debt, experienced trafficking themselves, paying companies for transportation and accommodations but ending up in highly exploitive and coercive working conditions.

Likewise, Chuang's (2014) ethnography of rural labor brokerage processes in China highlights the way that the country's residence-based citizenship creates a complex and highly exploitive system of labor recruitment in rural areas. It is one in which laborers agree to coercive arrangements in hopes of cultivating good relations and becoming brokers themselves. As she concludes, "trafficking, never simply a binary relation between trafficked people and their traffickers, implicates and entangles entire communities" (Chuang 2014, 67).

These examples draw attention to the ways that macroeconomic policies, migration regimes, and corporate practices contribute to unfree labor, and they show us that the line between who is considered a trafficker/"slaveholder" and who is considered a person experiencing trafficking/"slavery" is not always clear. IGOs and governments of the global north have not been deterred by this problem, with many developing campaigns to target criminal recruiters and labor brokers in supply chains. This can help to address the problem of employees being charged recruitment fees that leave them in situations of debt bondage and possibly rein in some individuals who coerce workers, but it can also lead to the criminalization of larger numbers of already marginalized groups, including people who have experienced unfree labor (Gordon 2017; Andrees 2009).

AVOIDING CRITIQUE OF CAPITALISM

Emphasizing "modern slavery" as an offshoot or harm occurring in the otherwise non-exploitive organization of labor in the global economy also diverts attention from structural analyses of capitalist processes. Instead of seeing exploitation as a continuum that occurs in the organization of work relations that vary from less exploitive to fully exploitive—and understanding that people who experience trafficking can become involved in exploitation at any point along such a continuum—the problem is instead portrayed in a binary fashion as free or unfree (Davidson 2010; LeBaron 2013; Barrientos, Kothari, and Phillips 2013).

This framing perpetuates the idea that only workers who experience violence and physical coercion are "real victims" while "free" workers are not, despite circumstances such as a lack of other job options, desperate poverty, and/or social relationships and expectations that compel them to stay in situations that in no way meet the criteria for decent work—i.e., work done in conditions of freedom, equity, security and human dignity.

One of the INGO interviewees that I spoke with in the United States discussed this issue. She recounted her evolving understanding of unfree labor as she began working on a project to combat child labor in Afghanistan:

> It's funny, when I started, I thought, this is the most black and white issue ever. Who doesn't want [to stop] child labor, right? Then the more you get into it, there's so many shades of gray on almost every level, particularly in Afghanistan, where it's all home-based labor and they are like fifteen-year-olds and there is no other source of income for the family. Then getting into, now, bonded labor issues, particularly on the brick kilns and what line do you draw when, in terms of the debt to wages ratios and stuff, it's just so gray.

She had earlier explained to me that workers in Nepal depend on advances from brick kiln owners to be able to weather the interim periods between brick seasons because the work is not year-round. The rates were high, but the workers:

> . . . actually want these advances, they need them. . . . They've got no other option. And they don't have any other employment options either, so they're going to come back anyway, so these advances are fine, but it ties them, like, they can't not go back. So, it's obviously bonded labor, but then how do you deal with that when everybody wants it?

This example illustrates the difficulties of categorizing workers as "free" to enter or leave a work situation when they may have "severe and/or multiple constraints on negotiating the terms of work" or have to work out of economic coercion or social obligation (McGrath, Rogaly, and Waite 2022; Howard 2018; Parreñas 2022). Consequently, many scholars have questioned the use of the "modern slavery" framework and its related terminology for addressing labor exploitation in the global economy (cf. Cockbain 2020; Ollus 2015; Quirk, Robinson, and Thibos 2020; Taylor 2020).

In addition to reifying a binary view about exploitation, the framing of unfree labor as an aberration of normal capitalist business practices reinforces the idea that capitalism normally tends toward non-exploitive forms of labor and that issues of "modern slavery" somehow exist outside of it (Howard 2018). Social scientists and historians have debated the relationship between unfree labor and capitalism and their compatibility (Brass and van der Linden 1997; Brass 2011; Lerche 2007). However, the general tendency among scholars and activists in the "anti-slavery" movement has been to see neoliberal forms of capitalist practices as context but not causal in exacerbating the problems of unfree labor (Bales 2000, 1999, 2007b; van den Anker 2007).

For situations of unfree labor that happen downstream in global supply chains, such a view is problematic: it sidesteps root causes tied to economic globalization and leaves the door open for privatization proponents to tout market strategies as solutions rather than causes (LeBaron et al. 2018). When companies in the global north choose to source from countries with vulnerable populations, weak or poorly enforced labor laws, high levels of poverty and unemployment, and/or restrictions on worker organizing, they both benefit from and contribute to these problems (Banerjee 2020; LeBaron et al. 2018; Jenkins forthcoming 2025). Many scholars have pointed to direct and indirect business complicity in forced labor and human trafficking; they are embedded in legitimate markets as active, passive, or involuntary participants; they may be strongly or weakly connected by geography, suppliers, or partners, or their own position in the supply chain (Van Buren, III, Schrempf-Stirling, and Westermann-Behaylo 2019; De Vries 2019; Crane 2017; de Vries, Jose, and Farrell 2020).

There is wide agreement among academics about specific business practices that exacerbate exploitation in global supply chains. Brands/retailers in the global north pressure suppliers in the global south and pay them so little that they subcontract to others. The cost cutting and monopolies of some lead brands, their subcontracting practices with short-term contracts and quick turnaround times that squeeze suppliers, and their ability to pass responsibility for labor rights to others in supply chains create structural conditions for unfree labor (New 2015; Boersma and Nolan 2022; Caspersz et al. 2022; LeBaron 2020; Anner 2019b, 2019a). This fragmented system facilitates conditions in which some intermediaries engage in the abuse of workers (LeBaron 2020).

Some of those I interviewed at INGOs picked up on this point, emphasizing that abuses in supply chains have been well-known to brands that choose to overlook them. Responding to the idea that companies are unable to map supply chains, a director of a UK-based INGO said:

> To me, it's on an intuitive level and felt like manifesting nonsense. We produced, however, many years ago, eight, nine years ago, a document born out of a conversation I had with a very senior and very experienced person in the industry who had been buying for many years. He said to me, "It is *absolute nonsense* that you cannot tell where your cotton is coming from if you want to". . . . If you are one of the large buyers and institutional businesses that have the power of the money, you can do it. More importantly, you should do it. Sure, there's always a cost for it and no one pretends there isn't, but you can do it at a totally achievable and realistic cost burden in the marketplace.

Similarly, an interviewee at Global Slavery Fighters, the INGO cited at the beginning of this book, echoed that sentiment, even using the same exclamation:

> Everybody talks about how impenetrable the supply chains are. . . . I'm like, well, if Gap, or Primark, or, and whoever, H&M, want a new T-shirt on their shelves in four weeks, it can happen. . . . People say, "No, it can't be done." No, it can, we just need to pay for it. "No, it's too expensive." No, no, it's just more expensive than you're willing to pay for. If you look at the big garment industry. . . look at the profits that they make for them to be able to say that they can't afford to properly investigate, and properly open up, and properly take responsibility. You're just like, "It's just *absolute nonsense*."

In both of these examples, the interviewees stressed that businesses do know about the problems in their supply chains and can afford to address them but choose not to act.

Based on this understanding, there are views that try to merge a criminalization approach with corporate accountability. For example, criminologists Davies and Ollus (2019) argue that, since corporations and their regular business practices facilitate both the worst forms of labor abuse as well as more common forms of labor exploitation, a corporate crime framework would be useful. In this way, they push for legal action, even if the difficulties of establishing corporate criminal liability are myriad and well-known, such as discrepancies over forced labor and human trafficking definitions and disputes over jurisdiction when it comes to cases (Schumann 2020).

Criminal actors in global supply chains, including employers, suppliers, and labor intermediaries, absolutely need to be addressed, and Western buyers and brands held to account for their part in contributing to their actions. The danger in such an approach, however, is that the focus will still be mainly on finding and criminalizing "bad actors" without much change in the structure, operations, or regulation of global supply chains. All criminalization approaches seek punishment and redress after the fact, while the macro political economy of unfree labor and the structures contributing remain unaddressed, whether they relate to rules concerning finance, trade, migration, or local labor conditions (Mende and Drubel 2020). This is also why a focus on the outsourcing and purchasing practices of

Western companies, while vitally important, is only one part of the problem. Business actions and decisions are made within broader contexts whereby companies consider market and financial pressures: "short-term profit expectations of shareholders combined with pricing pressure from consumers propel the ongoing search for lower costs of production" (Nolan and Boersma 2019, 157).

A corporate crime lens may help focus attention on business activities, supply chain practices, and the regulatory context at the center of harmful practices for workers (Davies and Ollus 2019), but it does not address the way states may be willing to allow labor exploitation so as to ensure foreign investment and safeguard exports, or the way state migration regimes may work to benefit businesses while harming migrants, or the trade agreements and practices that can exacerbate persistent poverty and leave people without viable options for decent work (Howard 2012). Focusing on the issue of problematic actors will not ensure migrant labor regimes that empower workers, and rooting out individual "bad" employers while incorporating vulnerable people into global production networks may end up creating further exploitation, reproduce poverty, and/or result in increased inequalities among groups within and between countries (Phillips and Mieres 2014).

INGO FRAMINGS OF "MODERN SLAVERY"

INGOs working on "modern slavery" have to navigate their places within a field that characterizes "modern slavery" as a criminal business and focuses on organized crime groups and individual perpetrators. Some INGOs have embraced this framing, as the epigraph at the beginning of the chapter illustrates. There were many other examples as well. For example, the CEO of a UK-based INGO, introducing their impact report, wrote:

> We continue to learn, and we believe that the way we see trafficking is the right one. The criminal business of trafficking relies on: the recruitment of vulnerable people, the ability to move the proceeds of crime and to maintain a global demand for exploited labour and services.

This particular INGO was seeking collaborations with law enforcement and with businesses to pinpoint where crime was happening.

The website of an INGO based in the United States also demonstrated its acceptance of the criminal justice framing of "modern slavery," describing its model in the following way:

> We relentlessly pursue justice in court. We ensure that traffickers, rapists, and other criminals go to jail so they cannot abuse, exploit, or enslave others.

The INGO has done so by partnering with law enforcement to conduct raids and rescues of people being exploited. The interviewee from this organization, a senior and long-term advisor, succinctly described the INGO:

> When it comes to labor trafficking, we're really focused and we want our law enforcement to focus on sting operations that go after the human traffickers. That's where we're at.

Their website corroborates the interviewee's view, emphasizing that the INGO finds "victims of violence, forced labor, or sex trafficking. We then support local police in rescue operations and help meet the victims' urgent needs. . . ." The goal is to "bring criminals to justice" and work with "local law enforcement in investigating, arresting, and charging slave owners with crimes."

Only a few of the INGOs were relying on raids and rescues as a central strategy, but they often did coordinate and/or partner with law enforcement in some way, as part of service provision, training and public awareness, and/or legal advocacy. For example, during the course of the research, one INGO based in the United States partnered with law enforcement to form a task force on human trafficking and co-located with them in the same building in order to strengthen their relationship. At the time I met with the interviewee, the INGO was engaged in developing protocols for working together to create a survivor-centered approach for those who have experienced issues of "modern slavery." It was challenging work:

> . . . in the past, law enforcement was arresting individuals and not really knowing where to bring in service providers. There's been tension. . . we would find that our clients are getting re-traumatized and also really bullied in some ways to go to court. . . and the roles, we have found in working with our clients, sometimes go back and forth. They [those experiencing trafficking] are also part of enforcement [trafficking others].

Here we again see the blurred lines between "trafficker" and "person who was trafficked" along with the problem of criminalizing people engaged in human trafficking who have themselves been trafficked.

There *were* INGOs with a different approach to issues of "modern slavery," one that focused primarily on community and economic development rather than the disruption of criminal entrepreneurs. As one director of an INGO in the United States explained:

> . . . there's a group of organizations that really focus on trying to deter trafficking through [the] use of the criminal justice system. And then there are organizations like ours, which specialize more in a community-based approach to that. What we're really trying to do is build resistance and resilience in vulnerable communities.

INGOs in Europe were more likely to take this approach, emphasizing unfree labor as an outcome of poverty, inequality, and unequal development. One UK-based INGO, coming from a development perspective, exemplified the difference in their project to help child domestic workers in a South American country. Most of the children worked for neighbors or close family members, and rather than seeking to criminalize these "employers," the INGO worked with parents and communities for the improvement of child domestic workers' positions.

Because of the dominance of the crime perspective, however, even development-oriented INGOs grappled with the overlap between their organization's approach and a criminal justice one, particularly when it came to their work in countries of the global south. This was a problem across the INGOs in the study. As one "anti-slavery" INGO director recounted:

> Often the lines are a little blurry. For example, in the course of our community-based work, part of what we're also trying to do is enhance the rule of law. So, we do work with. . . local authorities, with the police, with local judges that actually try to get the law enforced so that the communities are protected. To build bridges between the communities and local law enforcement, because of course, those are the communities likely to be most alienated from the protection of the law. And part of the community empowerment is to attack that part of the problem. So, the lines are a little, in the real world, are a little fuzzy.

While this organization worked explicitly on issues of "modern slavery" using a development approach, they focused also on the criminalization of perpetrators. The relationship between law enforcement and people in poor communities, and the possibility of further marginalizing the people they were trying to help, were issues that the INGO director and staff had to carefully consider.

Some INGOs working from a development approach focused on cultural explanations for exploitation, something that is an important consideration but can detract attention from the political economy of unfree labor and the roles of businesses and states if considered separately. For example, bonded labor is found in many countries with developing economies, yet one interviewee from an INGO that deals specifically with this problem explained to me that it was the result of historical traditions in the country where his organization worked. Local practices are an important factor in working conditions and work relations within countries, but in defining the problem as primarily cultural, he did not view the people he was helping as workers producing for domestic markets or the supply chains of retailers in Europe and the United States. This particular INGO did not think of debt bondage as a form of criminal violence, but it did not see it as an issue of political economy either (see, e.g., Howard 2018).[6]

Another INGO employing a development approach was interesting in that it clearly framed labor exploitation as a problem tied to globalization. Examining bonded labor in a Southeast Asian seafood industry, for example, the INGO reported in great detail about the structural adjustment programs imposed by the IMF and World Bank leading to pressure for the country to produce seafood for export. The problem was described in the following way: processing factories place orders for seafood with intermediaries, and the intermediaries, in turn, collect the seafood from numerous unregistered small-scale farmers. Exporters, who have a monopoly over the national market and processing factories, put pressure on the farmers to sell cheaply (i.e., they engage in price fixing).

Without recourse to sell elsewhere, the small farmers are regularly forced to accept amounts of money that are well under the value of what they produce, so they take loans to cover their costs and wind up accruing debt. Intermediaries also take loans when the processing factories do not pay them in full, compounding the problem, and some become lenders who take advantage of the farmers with high interest rates. The cycle of debt continues. Meanwhile, workers in the processing factories, many of whom are subcontracted, are routinely underpaid. They lack health and safety equipment, are subjected to hazardous working conditions, experience verbal abuse, are required to work overtime without pay, are denied toilet breaks, are made to work seven days a week, and are not given holidays. The factories have also engaged in union busting when workers attempted to organize, threatening, beating, and firing them.

Even with this in-depth accounting of the processes leading to labor exploitation in the seafood industry, the INGO was firmly wedded to an incremental or reformist strategy to address it. The organization recommended that businesses allow independent third-party audits to enhance transparency, a certification scheme for producers, more regular payments be made to intermediaries, and more awareness-raising for factory and farm workers about their rights. This INGO, one of only a few that provided an analysis of the political economy of unfree labor and the role of businesses in an export industry, nonetheless suggested little that would alter business practices and nothing in the way of systemic change. It retained a faith in free markets and globalization as solutions to the very problems that they had helped to create.

FRAMING "MODERN SLAVERY" AND ORGANIZATIONAL SILOS

INGOs with varying approaches to issues of "modern slavery" are sometimes part of networks and working groups with other nonprofits and/or businesses, facilitated by states, IGOs, and funders, but there is a notable lack of engagement with unions and labor rights groups as well as organizations working on corporate accountability. In discussing her organization's project on forced labor in an Asian country, the senior advisor of an INGO based in the United States explained the reasons that they have not historically worked with labor organizations:

> Labor trafficking is our biggest [focus] by far. But we look at it as forms of violence... it's a very different crime [from sex trafficking] and the perps are different, and the motivations are different. But on the police side, because we work on the criminal side, which is the beginning of the explanation for why we don't work so much with ILO and some of the other labor [groups],

we're doing criminal law. These are in the penal codes. And there's also, of course, all manner of labor standards in the labor codes, but we don't have much to do with that because we're trying to put people in jail, in a word.

"Anti-slavery" INGOs have often seen themselves, their constituents, and their advocacy strategies as separate from those that address labor issues. This is the perception shared by some unions and labor groups as well. A long-time union activist in the United States saw it this way:

Even though in certain cases the issue ["modern slavery"] does overlap with union interests, such as in construction or home care, the issue is really narrowly defined as violence and criminal activity and it is such a small population of people affected that they [unions] prefer to work on broader employment conditions and issues such as wage theft.

I found a similar sentiment in Europe. As the interviewee at an international union explained:

. . . in the EU, where we're working and there's a lot of trade unions working as well. . . the whole sphere is in criminal justice, which administratively gives some kind of a disconnect to the whole labor side and sphere in administration. . . in many, many countries, you have anti-trafficking legislation, anti-trafficking bodies, anti-trafficking networks, but it's all linked to criminal justice, and it focuses on police, border guards, and bringing cases to court and then having compensation for those victims. . . it's maybe a bit of a chicken and egg story, but it means that trade unions don't really relate to some of the anti-trafficking work, as soon as the word trafficking is in there, and vice versa.

This does not mean that the interviewee did not see a role for trade unions in addressing forced labor and labor trafficking. He went on to explain:

. . . for trade unions, it's not really important whether it's called anti-trafficking, what they do. Our perspective is that in the continuum that gets people to a state of forced labor or human trafficking, which we see as always a process over time and degree of exploitation, the work for trade unions is actually on the prevention side. It's not when you actually have victims and when you have a crime and then remedy; it's prevention. That's just normal labor work, that's making sure that there's no discrimination, seeing that there's equal treatment, that there's no unpaid salaries, that there's no contract substitution. It's all those specific elements that, when all of those occur together, they lead to a situation of forced labor.

For both unions and INGOs, then, the framing of "modern slavery" issues as crimes separates them out from a continuum of labor exploitation and divides groups that could potentially partner.

There have been ad hoc collaborations between INGOs and unions or labor groups on occasion, showing that alliances can be fruitful for workers despite myriad challenges that go beyond the framing of issues (Eade and Leather 2005; Connor 2007).[7] A number of interviewees cited efforts to help domestic workers. For example, one UK INGO supported domestic workers in India with training sessions on migration and labor rights and helped them to obtain a minimum wage. It also helped Nepalese migrant domestic workers in Western Asia to self-organize. Another INGO worked on issues of forced labor and the trafficking of migrant domestic workers within the UK.

Interviewees also mentioned an NGO in Hong Kong that helped migrant domestic workers become affiliated to the Hong Kong Confederation of Trade Unions. In this example, unionizing allowed the domestic workers to engage in collective bargaining with the Hong Kong government to get minimum standards in place, including days off, minimum wages, and other protections. It had the advantage of providing a common baseline for domestic workers from multiple sending countries, rather than leaving minimum standards to the individual negotiations of sending countries in bilateral agreements with the Hong Kong government.

There were also a couple of examples tied to export industries. One INGO helped to put pressure on a multinational corporation to negotiate a collective bargaining agreement with an agricultural union in a West African country to help reduce child labor. Another played a mediator role between a Western brand and local authorities in a Philippines export processing zone (EPZ) where authorities were violently repressing factory workers. As the INGO interviewee recounted:

> [We] almost played a peacemaker role to connect the dots for people because there were a lot of people talking past each other. . . the thing that stood out in my mind was that the EPZ authorities would say things like, we have to use the batons to crack over the heads of the union people, the Americans won't want to invest here anymore. Then we go to the brand and

they say, are you crazy? No, we don't want that. We don't want the unions, yes, but we don't want you doing that. . . it's like nobody has connected the dots to say to some of these American brands. . . [that there are] measures that could take place that would facilitate a more peaceful situation, which then also leads to people being able to exercise their rights.

Examples such as these, especially those in which INGOs working on "modern slavery" support unionization efforts, freedom of association, and collective bargaining, are not the norm. However, there was a sense among the interviewees that more collaborations could develop, especially in Europe.

As the co-founder of a newer, small, and scrappy UK anti-trafficking INGO explained:

We've reached out to unions and have found that there's often a couple of people within unions who are interested and engaged with the issue, but trying to get it to go union-wide is a bit more of a challenge. There's obviously tensions within unions about what's in the best interests of their members, which is always going to be a bit problematic. Some unions are a bit more advanced in the way that they cope with that than others.

Nonetheless, she was optimistic about making more connections in the future:

What we'd quite like to do is do more work on bringing this labor rights perspective into the trafficking framework, and include standards of prevention within the trafficking framework. . . . I think there's been quite a lot of discussion amongst academics about how those frameworks fit, and I think we're starting to see a bit of it in practice, as well. . .

I did not find the same optimism among interviewees in the United States, who cited anti-union sentiment, union-busting tactics, and continued distance on the part of both INGOs and unions. Only one INGO where I interviewed was actively addressing the division:

We work in a number of countries to get both NGOs to see why unions can be important and for unions to see why they need to care about this issue. We've had success in a lot of places, and I think there's some really good models out there about how this can work.

This INGO was unique in emphasizing the need for synergy between unions and INGOs in fighting "modern slavery."[8]

Aside from working only sporadically with unions and labor groups, INGOs addressing "modern slavery" tended to also work in isolation from social movements and civil society organizations fighting for corporate accountability (Bendell 2004). Social movement activity directed at corporations rose from the 1970s on with efforts to address the human rights and environmental abuses of multinational corporations (Soule 2009; Mac Sheoin 2014). While campaigns have come and gone depending on public awareness and corporate activities, one of the more recent efforts, the corporate accountability movement, has been aimed at challenging corporate power and holding companies to account for their social and environmental actions. Peter Utting, former Deputy Director of the United Nations Research Institute for Social Development, argued that this happened because legal and governance institutions have prioritized and strengthened corporate rights rather than obligations, leading people to see them as the primary beneficiaries of economic globalization even while they reproduce social exclusion and inequalities; he also suggested that it was a response to the limitations of the CSR's voluntary self-regulation (Utting 2008).

Corporate accountability campaigns are relevant for issues of "modern slavery" because they address traditional regulatory organizations and institutions, including state enforcement and inspection agencies. They promote stronger legal and regulatory frameworks that have "teeth," push for better enforcement of existing laws that hold companies accountable for illegal activities, and engage in lawsuits on behalf of those harmed by corporate actions (Utting 2008, 969). They also emphasize the need for companies to be accountable to workers, and they support worker empowerment.

Despite the potential for overlap, there were few connections between "anti-slavery" INGOs and those working on corporate accountability. The co-founder of a UK-based INGO noted the gap:

> ... in terms of encouraging or increasing corporate accountability, I think there needs to be a lot more action against those who are not treating their workers properly.

Another INGO interviewee in Europe pointed to one potential reason for it. She noted the tendency for corporate accountability nonprofits to be focused on the environment:

> Those who work on businesses, and feel that businesses do harm, work not so much on labor exploitation, but on environmental harm. . . so you see very much that it is not connected.

Scholars and activists have sometimes connected environmental degradation and "modern slavery" issues, particularly in fishing, farming, forests, and factories (Bales 2016; Brown et al. 2019), but this has not usually been in conjunction with corporate accountability campaigns. The Corporate Justice Coalition (formerly the CORE Coalition) is one exception. It is a nonprofit formed to ensure that corporations are held accountable for human rights and environmental abuses, and it has brought together INGOs and trade unions around issues of "modern slavery" in a campaign addressing the UK Modern Slavery Act. It argued that the legislation failed to achieve what it intended and campaigned for reforms to strengthen it.[9]

Many of the "anti-slavery" INGOs I interviewed were engaged in MSIs to address issues of labor exploitation in the supply chains of Western brands and retailers, but they were not involved in projects or campaigns that explicitly or directly targeted those companies. Only one INGO in the United States did so. It called out two powerful multinational corporations for their industry-governed voluntary certification system for palm oil, explaining that it had found the continued existence of child and forced labor in their supply chains. This INGO had a long record of corporate accountability efforts, suing companies on behalf of workers. As it stated in one of its annual reports:

> So many of these companies that we've sued claim to be good corporate citizens. They point to their "codes of conduct," purporting to provide their workers and others affected by their operations with a menu of rights. But when [our INGO] and other activists point out concrete injuries that people have suffered, these companies point to the fine print and hide behind various exclusions that demonstrate the reality that the codes are nothing but a public relations ploy.

The INGO was therefore working toward corporate accountability rather than CSR:

Today, we are pushing for a sea of change in corporate accountability: to move away from the voluntary, confidential "corporate social responsibility" programs that have repeatedly sidelined workers' voices, towards transparent, legally-binding agreements negotiated between corporations and unions. And we are pursuing multi-layered strategies to advance labor law reforms. In today's time of increased migration, debt bondage, and human trafficking, we must push back against laws that make it illegal for migrant workers to organize and bargain collectively.

This INGO was notable for its unusual efforts to combine direct legal action against companies with support for worker organizing and tying these actions to issues of "modern slavery."

Surprisingly, one of the interviewees most enthusiastic about direct action against companies was from a business-led INGO working on issues of "modern slavery." The INGO itself hewed closely to international legal definitions of forced labor, human trafficking, and child labor in its work, seeing them as criminal issues placing businesses at risk. When I asked the interviewee what he thought was the best way to motivate businesses to act on issues of "modern slavery," I anticipated an answer that would stress the importance of helping companies understand the threats they were facing and the need to protect themselves. Instead, he answered:

> . . . what I want to end up doing is just go start my own shop and draw on my legal background and just start suing companies that are not there. I think that's what does it. . . . I ran. . . [a] working group, it grew to be about forty companies from around the world that were working on human rights issues. . . we just did a show of hands, who's here because your company has been involved in a major human rights lawsuit, or some kind of major front page exposé. Everybody raised their hand. *Everybody* raised their hand. So you want to get companies to the table? Sue them. Yeah, every time one of these suits comes out, it's a great. . . it's going to be a victory for the space.

The interviewee had worked in CSR and on issues of business and human rights throughout his career, becoming more convinced over time that direct legal action against companies was the best way to make progress. That few "anti-slavery" INGOs were collaborating with campaigns or partners working on corporate accountability shows the continued fragmentation of "modern slavery" framings and the ways that the crim-inalization and development approaches, which are dominant, have cre-ated silos in the field.

CONCLUSION

The prominent framing of "modern slavery" as a new type of criminal busi-ness obfuscates the political economy of unfree labor, reinforces the idea that labor exploitation is a problem of individual bad actors, be they strang-ers or business partners, and falsely separates businesses from issues of "modern slavery." This is a problem not only because it influences public sentiment and scholarly research on unfree labor, but also because it helps to set parameters for "anti-slavery" organizations, the strategies that they pursue, and the partnerships they see as viable. When faced with this dom-inant framing, many of the INGOs I interviewed worked within it, treating unfree labor as a criminal issue. Those that did not, typically coming from a development approach, nonetheless had to respond to, and in some cases combine, their activities with a criminal business framing.

When "anti-slavery" INGOs remain focused on the idea of criminal en-trepreneurs, they see themselves as separate from unions, activists and organizations working on labor issues, and those fighting for corporate ac-countability who engage in more contentious action. Collaborations with those groups remain ad hoc. The framing also limits opportunities to press for changes to business practices that will help prevent exploitation, to lobby for labor rights, or to push for more substantial regulatory changes to current capitalist systems. Framing issues of "modern slavery" as crim-inal business operations also leaves open the door to claims that "good" businesses are the best qualified organizations to understand and fix what "bad" businesses are doing, which is the subject of the next chapter.

Two

USING "GOOD" BUSINESS TO FIGHT "BAD" BUSINESS

Business has always been a key driver of social change, shaping modern life through innovation and new technology. If corporate giants. . . prioritize the abolition of modern slavery as their next major innovation, we could quickly deal a major blow to the slavery industry in this generation.
—CEO of the Walk Free Foundation[1]

As the above quote illustrates, the widely accepted characterization of unfree labor as a criminal business enterprise is paralleled by the idea that the private sector is the solution to the problem. This chapter explores these discourses, which are being promoted by IGOs, INGOs, academics, CSR proponents, and businesses themselves. It finds that they place business interests at the center of concern rather than the workers that "anti-slavery" advocacy is intended to help—the "victims" of "modern slavery" become the businesses. They also blame suppliers, partners, labor brokers, governments of countries with developing economies, and demanding Western consumers instead of acknowledging the role of Western companies and business practices that might be contributing to unfree labor. INGOs enter into these discourses as another perceived threat to businesses, and they are typically portrayed in one of two ways: as ill-informed and unrealistic antagonists who create problems for companies due to their ignorance, or as savvy and powerful foes that purposely set out to harm companies.

At the same time, the discourses frame Western businesses as "heroes" uniquely suited to voluntarily solve "modern slavery," even though there is little evidence that past voluntary measures have been successful in ameliorating unfree labor in global supply chains. The idea that "good" businesses can take care of "bad" ones has set the stage for the for-profit sector to enter the advocacy field and compete with "anti-slavery" nonprofits as well. INGOs, along with governments, are now positioned as one of many types of organizational actors fighting "modern slavery."

These trends have important implications for governance, reinforcing neoliberalism by reaffirming a limited role for states, casting doubt on the ability of INGOs to be legitimate proponents of the public good, and shifting responsibility to consumers through market-based strategies. The success of framing "anti-slavery" advocacy from a business-centered perspective allows Western businesses to maintain a veneer of vulnerability and innocence in labor exploitation and, as critical scholars suggest, perpetuates business as usual.

THE BUSINESS CASE FOR FIGHTING "MODERN SLAVERY"

As IGOs and governments of the global north have helped to incorporate issues of "modern slavery" into CSR efforts, they, along with other organizations in the advocacy field, have regularly articulated the business case for addressing unfree labor. Why should companies get involved in fighting "modern slavery?" Because it is smart business.[2] Companies will capture the allegiance of ethical consumers, strengthen business partnerships, build strong investor relations, ensure market access, help create new business opportunities, be leaders in their industries, and gain a competitive advantage (Hoff and McGauran 2015; United Nations Global Compact and Maplecroft 2013a; United Nations Global Compact et al. 2018). They will enhance brand value and enable "knowledge transfer and spillover" (Bain, Metallidis, and Shelley 2014). Companies will also have greater access to business opportunities, positive recognition, more productivity, and better market stability, because cheap labor equates to lower spending power by consumers, and because when children are in school and complete their education rather than working full-time, the workforce will become more skilled and productive for companies (United Nations Global Compact et al. 2018, 16).

Businesses As Victims: Alongside the optimistic prognostications about the benefits for business are also dire warnings that businesses are in danger of legal, brand, and reputational risk from issues of "modern slavery" (United Nations Global Initiative to Fight Human Trafficking et al. 2010; United Nations Global Compact et al. 2018; United Nations Global Compact and Maplecroft 2013a, 2013b). For example, in 2013, the World Economic Forum launched a Global Agenda Council Network-Wide Human Trafficking Task Force. In a subsequent related report, they introduce the topic of human trafficking by warning businesses that: (1) all forms of illicit trade cost the legitimate private sector money; (2) an unregulated workforce and its recruiters and employers make no contribution to taxes, healthcare systems, or other services, leaving legitimate businesses to carry a larger share of the burden; and (3) there is a very real threat of reputational damage to businesses (Bain, Metallidis, and Shelley 2014, 3). The focus of these discourses is on prevention and protection from harm—but for businesses, not workers.

The language of risk avoidance is universal: without addressing issues of "modern slavery," businesses can be subject to legal risk, trade-related risk, threats to brand value and reputation, or threats to investment/investor relations if they pull out of a company (Hunter and Kepes 2012; International Labour Organization 2015). "Modern slavery" is said to jeopardize operations, supply chains, business partner relations, and credibility (United Nations Global Initiative to Fight Human Trafficking 2010a; United Nations Global Compact et al. 2018:16). Companies are urged to avoid complacency and warned that they can still be considered complicit even if others commit the crime (see, e.g., United Nations Global Compact and United Nations Office of the High Commissioner of Human Rights 2004). The potential result could be costly class action lawsuits or criminal prosecutions; one bad company can hurt an entire sector, and millennial investors are starting to care about human trafficking (Friedman 2014).

Businesses are also said to be under threat from consumers upset about "modern slavery." For example, in a presentation to businesses organized through the United Nations Global Compact Human Rights and Business Dilemmas Forum, a prominent "anti-slavery expert" and scholar warned:

One of the difficulties we face with the consumption side, with consumers, is that consumers absolutely do believe that there is a moral watershed that separates them from the people they buy from. So somehow many consumers believe that the moment they take something and buy it in a shop, they have at that moment achieved some form of innocence, but the people who sold them that good or that article of clothing are in fact guilty. . . . If you don't do it [get to the bottom of your supply chain], even if you are completely innocent, there is a chance that you will be perceived as a villain. (United Nations Global Compact and Maplecroft 2013b)

The statement is striking not only because it seems to exonerate businesses from being complicit in trafficking but also because it seems to reframe the problem as the fault of consumers.

At the same presentation, an INGO founder turned entrepreneur who now sells a for-profit software platform for companies to assess "modern slavery" risks was even more direct about the problem of judgmental consumers. He stated that his organization's intention was to "break the false assumption that consumers can blame businesses with impunity because at the end of the day, they share the responsibility" (United Nations Global Compact and Maplecroft 2013b). Shifting the blame to other actors has characterized corporate denials of responsibility for numerous issues, from the harms of tobacco to climate change, so perhaps it is not surprising to see consumers implicated here. Redirection is a common strategy used by corporations who criticize consumers, along with governments, for contributing to problems (Freese 2020).

Another way that issues of "modern slavery" are presented as a threat to "good" businesses is in the way "bad" businesses can use exploited labor to undercut competitors. Global Slavery Fighters, the INGO described in the opening of the book, provides one example. Its website explains:

Responsible businesses are often undermined by competitors who adopt exploitive labor practices. Which is why we campaign for national and international laws that would make businesses legally responsible for preventing human rights abuses in their supply chains and provide access to justice for victims.

The INGO goes on to say that the competitors "reap the profit" of exploitive labor and that "it is only right that a level playing field is created." The central message of all this is that "modern slavery" is a problem *for* businesses and that INGOs have a role in helping to ensure fair competition in the marketplace (Bales 2007a, 201).

These discourses also imply that issues of "modern slavery" are non-Western problems since it is the countries with emerging and developing economies that are routinely highlighted as being the greatest risk to Western companies; global brands and retailers are often presented as though they are outside of the economic processes they help to create and are being victimized by states and "bad" businesses elsewhere (Howard 2018; McGrath and Watson 2018). No mention is made of the fact that some Western companies choose to source from "high risk" countries due specifically to the features that lead them to be labeled as such, whether it is weak or poorly enforced labor laws, high levels of unemployment, or restrictions on worker organizing. Western firms are also assumed to have little risk in their direct operations, except for third parties or an occasional errant employee who may use their products or premises to commit crimes.[3]

Given the characterization of Western businesses as victims of "modern slavery," one theme that came out of the interviews and texts of the "anti-slavery" organizations, as well as academic literature by proponents of business leadership in the field, is that companies being affected by these issues need to be treated gently and carefully. This parallels a common assertion in "anti-slavery" advocacy that individuals who have been exploited need a safe space and assistance to help them recover from their ordeal; it is a means of garnering sympathy and support for those who experience unfree labor. In applying a similar characterization to companies, this trope reinforces ideas about their vulnerability. Companies, like people, need safety, support, and assistance as opposed to confrontation, pressure, or punishment.

For example, in promoting business initiatives to fight human trafficking, scholars Shelley and Bain (2015, 143) argue:

> Companies must be comfortable with launching these initiatives, free from fear of litigation, negative consumer response, or future backlash from competition. . . there also needs to be a public shift of conscious: the public must give corporations *the chance* and allow for this *safe space* to engage in the anti-trafficking movement [italics theirs]. . . it is important that the business sector voluntarily become more visibly engaged in this issue

before they are pressured. Those companies that are already doing much and are unrecognized for their actions must be encouraged to come forth through public-private partnerships.

We see here the language of ensuring a safe space as well as a call for voluntary action on the part of companies.

"Anti-slavery" INGOs frequently repeat this message. A UK "anti-slavery" nonprofit offers businesses "a safe space for discussing the complex, critical issues you face, with like-minded people from similar-sized companies." A business-led anti-trafficking INGO in the United States promises companies a "safe space" to "collaborate with peers" and "develop solutions to combat modern slavery." We even see it repeated by INGOs headquartered outside of Europe and the United States. For example, the Mekong Club, which uses a business-to-business approach to fighting slavery in Asia "to empower businesses to create a slave-free world," explains that they create a "safe space" for companies to come together to share best practices in a "positive, collaborative and non-naming and shaming way" (Mekong Club 2018).

IGOs reiterate the message in various programs, projects, and initiatives, as well, such as in the United Nations (UN) Global Compact (Limoncelli 2024). Billing itself as the world's largest voluntary corporate sustainability initiative, it seeks to influence companies to follow ethical principles by requiring its business participants to pledge to implement ten principles in the areas of human rights, labor, the environment, and anti-corruption. Participating companies are provided with networks, best practice guidance, tools, resources, and trainings to help them with their engagement; they then self-report on their progress. The initiative offers what it calls a safe space to learn about and discuss "modern slavery" in its Human Rights and Business Dilemmas Forum, which provides common scenarios, case studies, and recommended actions for businesses to pursue (United Nations Global Compact and Maplecroft 2013a).[4] Likewise, the World Economic Forum assures businesses that its Task Force on Human Trafficking, mentioned above, is a "safe space within which the trafficking conversation may continue" (Bain, Metallidis, and Shelley 2014, 4).

Related to the need for a safe space is the idea that businesses are innocent bystanders to labor exploitation. An interviewee of a business-led INGO reiterated this idea to me, explaining that the problem is that businesses are simply lacking information:

. . . businesses that are now at the table. . . have a lot of things and they lack a lot of things. They lack understanding of what the issue is. They lack understanding of where it exists in their supply chain, although it exists in every supply chain for every company. So, they need some help on that. And they also kind of lack what do we do about it? What's our scope of responsibility?

The organization he worked for reflected this view in their reports and website text as well:

. . . a business may not be aware that actions they have taken—even those that are considered common practice in their country or industry—are making their workers more vulnerable to conditions of modern slavery.

Assertions such as these are found routinely in "anti-slavery" documents and presentations aimed at businesses. "Senior officials may not know what. . . the recruitment and employment practices [are] in outsourced operations." So it is "difficult for them to know what to do," and suppliers "may not understand what forced labor is" (United Nations Global Compact and Maplecroft 2013a). "Companies may unwittingly become involved" in "modern slavery" and need a primer covering "what business needs to know." (Walk Free Foundation and University of Nottingham no date).[5] The problem is portrayed as a matter of education, and once a business knows about it, it can develop codes of conduct or train employees who are "failing to act responsibly or proactively in this area" (Shelley and Bain 2015, 141).[6]

Business Heroes: Alongside language emphasizing businesses as innocent victims of traffickers and "slaveholders," information aimed at businesses often seeks to engage them by emphasizing their role as leaders whose expertise is necessary to solve the problem. This casts businesses as the heroes of the narrative: "whether leading major corporations or starting a new nongovernmental organization, business students are now trained through an entrepreneurial lens to solve the world's most difficult and pressing global dilemmas" (Shelley and Bain 2015, 141). Business leadership in anti-trafficking work portends a "redemptive capitalism" intended to seamlessly merge social responsibility and economic profitability (Bernstein 2016, 52–55).

Some business schools have supported this trend. In the United States, for example, Babson College's Initiative on Human Trafficking and Modern

Slavery aimed to "produce practical entrepreneurial ideas and innovations to help end human trafficking and promote human rights through business expertise. . . ."[7] The director of the initiative stressed the importance of training the next generation of "entrepreneurs" who will combat human trafficking, noting that:

> . . . entrepreneurship education and entrepreneurs focused on addressing human trafficking are emerging globally. In recent years, entrepreneurs have developed a number of start-ups, nonprofits, and ventures to tackle this egregious human rights abuse (Bain 2017, 82).

Likewise, the Harvard Kennedy School has highlighted the "vital" role of the private sector and the need to "combine knowledge, experience, and skills of the private sector with public sector organizations in order to combat human trafficking" (Harvard University Ash Center's Government Innovators Network 2012).

For many of the organizations in the "anti-slavery" field, the idea of business heroes is used liberally and literally. For example, in a video aimed at "helping businesses see slavery," an "anti-slavery" INGO in the United States tells businesses that they can become slavery-free:

> You can do it, and become a global hero. . . . The fact of the matter is, businesses can be the heroes, the heroes of anti-slavery in the twenty-first century.

The Mekong Club likewise uses the term, providing examples of such "private sector heroes" fighting "modern slavery."[8] INGOs promise businesses that they are "in a unique position to deliver freedom to people across the world" and create awards to acknowledge corporate heroes, from the now defunct United Nations/End Human Trafficking Now! Campaign's Business Leaders Award to the Thomson Reuters Foundation Stop Slavery Award, which launched in 2015 to commend businesses that have set a "gold standard in efforts to eradicate forced labour from their supply chains."[9] As the Mekong Club CEO has stated:

> . . . at present, we have the NGOs and we have the governments and we have the United Nations, but what we are trying to do now is to add the private sector. Why? Because the private sector has. . . the skills, the means, the problem-solving ability, the resources, the networks to make a

difference. . . . The business sector is critical to freeing millions from slavery and to prevent any more men, women, and children from being enslaved (Mekong Club 2018).

Business is said to be best suited to lead the "anti-slavery" movement because it:

> . . . knows exactly how to root out bad business practice and already has the necessary skills and capabilities to tackle the problem, e.g., through their legal department, compliance codes, accounting methodologies, communications departments, and financial expertise (Friedman 2014).

Why the problems have persisted despite this expertise is not addressed in these narratives.

The optimism about business heroes solving issues of "modern slavery" did run up against a more complex reality expressed by some INGO interviewees. For example, an interviewee from a business-led INGO described his realization that businesses perhaps did not have all of the answers necessary and could in fact encounter challenges. His organization intended to provide jobs for people who had experienced sex trafficking with the goal of preventing re-trafficking, a problem he had seen on an American news program:

> How do you take a Nepalese survivor of labor trafficking who's living in Chennai and get them a job at [a multinational company]. . . . That's our vision, but that is just. . . to go from point A to point B there is really, really, really complicated. And trying to make sure that the company has the right jobs available and that they're working within their policy structure. . . a lot of the companies prohibited any criminal record, prohibited working with. . . survivors of sex trafficking in a lot of ways. I mean, these things are so easy to dream up, and so even as I was watching the *Frontline* documentary, I just thought. . . just sitting there, I was like, why doesn't big business give these people jobs? It's like, yeah, of course, you know how hard that is?

As a business association seeking to help businesses address issues of "modern slavery," the organization was nonetheless promoting the idea that businesses know best.

In general, the presumed efficiency of businesses and business heroes remains a strong message from IGOs, some INGOs, academics, and many business leaders. In setting up the Walk Free Foundation, billionaire Andrew

Forrest, the Australian mining magnate and "anti-slavery" crusader, out-lined the importance of his organization's business expertise: "This is set up like a high-achieving, measurement-driven, totally target-oriented company," Forrest said. "It's like a hard-edged business. We are out to defeat slavery" (Miller 2014). The characterizations of Western businesses, whether as victims or heroes, work to erase them as potential contributors to issues of "modern slavery."

BUSINESS LEADERSHIP AND VOLUNTARY ACTION

Discourses aimed at business heroes recommend voluntary action on their part; proponents of business leadership assume that private regulation will solve issues of "modern slavery" (Aronowitz, Theuermann, and Tyu-rykanova 2010, 12; de Vries, Jose, and Farrell 2020). As has happened with CSR more generally, businesses seem to have evolved a counter narrative that allows them to evade, oppose, or coopt unwanted political and civil society pressure (Shamir 2004, 670). It has worked. Sociologist Richard Ap-pelbaum tells us that the old tripartite structure of government/business/labor regulation has been dismantled and that there is consensus that pri-vate enforcement is the way forward (Appelbaum 2016). When globalization led to the loss of American manufacturing firms to low-waged countries, it also shifted the power in capitalism to the big buyers/brands/retailers that rule global supply chains, and they are setting the terms with actions that make them seem ethical and responsible while changing little in terms of practices (Soederberg 2007).

In private rather than public regulation, organizational actors other than states set and enforce labor standards through MSIs, voluntary guide-lines, codes, certifications, and transparency laws meant to provide the public with information about what companies are doing to address issues of "modern slavery" so that they can reward "good" companies with ethi-cal purchases and investments (LeBaron 2020, 3–4). While debates about private regulation are still being had among scholars, criticisms have been widespread.[10] Many scholars, social scientists, in particular, have been skeptical, arguing that voluntary strategies are not adequate solutions for improving labor conditions in global supply chains (Amengual, Distelhorst, and Tobin 2019; Esbenshade 2004b, 2012; Appelbaum and Lichtenstein 2016;

Bartley 2018; Nova and Wegemer 2016; Seidman 2008, 2007; Limoncelli 2017; LeBaron 2020; Phillips 2015; Williams 2020).

At best, voluntary strategies result in small scale and individual firm change; at worst, the efforts become marketing and branding tools for businesses, as well as an extension of corporate power (Hanlon and Fleming 2009; Shih, Rosenbaum, and Kyritsis 2021). "Typically business agrees to concessions that modify corporate practices at the margin, but which do not challenge the fundamentals of managerial authority or market rationality" (Levy and Kaplan 2009, 445; Williams 2020). In addition, scholars argue that roles that were once considered the realm of the state or unions, including responsibility for employee welfare, are now being assumed by corporations and can become a means of appropriating innovation and opposition (Hanlon and Fleming 2009, 8).[11]

The high-profile example of child labor on West African cocoa farms is instructive. In 2000 and 2001, the issue garnered widespread media attention, including a documentary by the BBC and a series of reports by an American media company. In response, the United States House of Representatives approved an amendment to an agricultural bill for the development of a federal labeling system for chocolate products, indicating that no child slave labor was used in the growing and harvesting of cocoa. The cocoa industry strenuously opposed this, lobbied against it, and agreed to voluntarily address the problem before the bill could go to the Senate. The 2001 Harkin-Engel Protocol was the outcome: a voluntary public-private agreement that brought together major chocolate brands (e.g., Hershey, Mars, and Nestle USA), cocoa processors, civil society groups, and national governments with the goal of eliminating child labor and forced labor in cocoa production in West Africa. The Protocol stopped the momentum for federal regulation and established the nonprofit International Cocoa Initiative (ICI) in 2002 to coordinate company efforts as part of the agreement (Whoriskey, Siegel, and Georges 2019).

ICI completed an impressive array of activities: working at the national level to back relevant policies, supporting capacity building for local partners, implementing community-based projects to change attitudes and practices related to child labor, supporting social protection for those exploitated, and sharing lessons learned to promote effective, wider engagements. The initiative was highlighted by the UN Global Compact for its "good practice" of "integrated [programs] to combat trafficking and promote thriving communities" in response to the business dilemma of "combating trafficking without demonizing the sector and damaging livelihoods."[12]

The big companies that started the initiative turned to third-party nonprofit certification organizations to help with monitoring and labeling chocolate products produced according to their ethical standards: the Rainforest Alliance, Fairtrade, and Utz. Certification schemes such as these rely on third-party and/or in-house auditors, rather than government labor inspectors, to check that worksites are meeting labor standards. The certifying organizations then provide labels or seals for export products with the assumption that consumers in the West will purchase certified products rather than others.

The companies involved in ICI buy only part of their cocoa through these certifiers, however, and they are no panacea in any case. Visits to the cocoa farms are limited in scope, infrequent (covering few of the hundreds of thousands of farms each year), and announced in advance, meaning that child laborers can be moved elsewhere during audits and returned to the farms afterward (Whoriskey, Siegel, and Georges 2019). Eighteen years after starting to work on the issue, the companies had spent about 150 million (out of 1.8 trillion in sales) and built schools, supported some cooperatives, and bought some of their cocoa (25–49 percent) through the certification groups mentioned above (Whoriskey, Siegel, and Georges 2019). Child labor, including hazardous work and forced labor, have continued, and activists are still putting forward lawsuits alleging that conditions have not changed (NORC 2020; Verité 2019).

Political scientist Genevieve LeBaron (2021b) corroborates the failure of certification schemes for cocoa and documents problems in the production of tea as well. With in-depth interviews of 121 tea and cocoa workers in India and Ghana and a survey of more than 1,000 workers as well as visits to plantations and farms (some certified by the Rainforest Alliance, Fairtrade, and Utz), she found similar amounts of exploitation and forced labor in both certified and uncertified worksites. Certification schemes have been undermined by numerous loopholes and gaps for the most vulnerable workers.

One major issue is that the focus is on working conditions and rights for cocoa farmers rather than the workers they hire, yet it is precisely these seasonal, temporary, informal, and contract workers at the base of the supply chain who are most likely to be subject to forced labor (LeBaron 2020, 59).[13] Other problems plagued certification schemes as well: producers who cannot afford to meet certification standards, confusion at the base of global supply chains about the arrangements and practices of certification schemes, audit fraud, and weak and limited verification systems (LeBaron 2018a, 2021a, 2020, 2021b, 2018b).

Scholars have noted similar problems in other industries as well. More than fifteen years ago, sociologist Gay Seidman (2007, 2008) found that the certification system of the nonprofit Rugmark, now named Goodweave, did not reduce child labor in the carpet industry of India. The issue had come to the fore as a result of international and national campaigns to eliminate child labor. With threats by the United States and campaigns by German churches and trade unions to prohibit the importation of products produced by child labor, the industry "clearly shifted to support a monitoring system to ward off state actions" (Seidman 2007, 90). The initiative involved the nonprofit implementing a monitoring system to visit registered looms looking for children and developing a label to place on carpets meeting the organization's standard.

While the organization regularly helps children—removing them from work settings and providing education, shelter, and rehabilitation services—it is not clear that the certification strategy has made much difference in the incidence of child labor in the carpet industry. Seidman cites many reasons for this, including that buyers in some countries were not interested in the label, so exporters used licensed looms only part of the time; there were too few and infrequent inspections of the many thousands of looms in India's carpet belt; and that carpet exporters and retailers came up with alternative and weaker labeling schemes that undercut Rugmark by not requiring monitoring (Seidman 2007, 94–95). Child labor has persisted.

Other examples abound. Barrientos and Smith (2007) found that the UK-based nonprofit Ethical Trading Initiative's Base Code, which is supposed to ensure member companies' compliance with international labor standards in global supply chains, had done little to improve process rights (such as freedom of association or freedom from discrimination) for workers.[14] High profile cases of labor exploitation in Gap and Nike factories have likewise resulted in CSR efforts with little actual change (Nadvi 2008).

Aside from certifications, businesses have also been leading the way with legislative responses, particularly around transparency laws that require companies to voluntarily report what they are doing to address "modern slavery." They include laws such as the California Transparency in Supply Chains Act of 2010; the UK Modern Slavery Act 2015; the Dutch Child Labor Due Diligence Law of 2019; the Australian Modern Slavery Act of 2018; and the French Vigilance Law of 2017. The laws vary in their specific obligations, but they typically, at minimum, ask that companies self-report what they are doing to combat "modern slavery" in supply chains.

Businesses were supportive of the UK Modern Slavery Act 2015, which has a Transparency in Supply Chains (TISC) provision that relies on self-reporting. As the director of a UK "anti-slavery" organization explained to me, businesses were key to moving the legislation forward:

> The thing that was decisive with getting the supply chain provision within that [the UK Modern Slavery Act] was businesses themselves. . . . I wasn't at the meeting; it was being described to me, saying it took a solid hour before the government representatives realized that the businesses were asking for it. Subsequent to that, this has become the great government idea, but it would not have happened if businesses [had] not said so. It would not have happened if NGOs had said so and unions said so, as we had been. It was the interference of business which was decisive on that.

Scholars have argued that this enthusiasm on the part of businesses was instrumental; companies were able to water down a more stringent model of proposed legislation to one that was more in keeping with their interests in voluntary disclosure (LeBaron and Rühmkorf 2017, 2019). Similar dynamics have been found in other case studies as well: just as we saw with the cocoa example above, businesses proactively turn to CSR strategies when facing the possibility of increased regulation (Kaplan and Kinderman 2019, 2017; Kaplan 2014; Jaffee 2012).

Support for transparency laws has been strong in countries of the global north, but they have a host of limitations, not least that, in many cases, businesses are not required to take any actual steps to address "modern slavery;" they only have to report whether or not they do anything at all

(Limoncelli 2017; Phillips 2015; Hess 2019). That means a company can report that it does not address "modern slavery" and it will have abided by the law. Many companies fail to do even that. Studies of the California Transparency in Chains Act, for example, have found that less than half of the companies examined adhered to it by posting disclosures, and that disclosures, when provided, tended to be symbolic rather than substantive (Ma, Lee, and Goerlitz 2015; Birkey et al. 2018). Other limitations are that unfree labor can be prevalent in sectors that produce for domestic markets (China and India are two important examples) or that produce for export to countries with developing economies rather than those in the global north (Hobbes 2017).

There are also problems with the underlying assumptions about consumption upon which transparency laws are based, particularly that consumers will make ethical purchasing decisions based on what companies report, buying products from "good" companies and punishing the "bad" ones by withholding their purchasing power. Consumers may not have the knowledge or resources to collect, view, compare, and assess companies' "anti-slavery" statements or the income to purchase more expensive products and services. Those consumers that do aspire to make informed decisions face a mountain of challenges: distinguishing the reliability of companies' self-reported information; gaining at least some knowledge of company business practices, the operations of supply chains, and the conditions of work in other countries; deciding between competing social issues (such as the environment or animal rights) that could complicate purchasing decisions; and a lack of other theoretically more ethical products and services to choose from (Limoncelli 2017, 2020).

There is also some evidence that consumers looking at disclosures rate companies with low levels of due diligence just as highly as those with high levels—in other words, consumers are not able to distinguish the difference between "good" and "bad" companies based on their statements (Chilton and Sarfaty 2016). These challenges, along with companies failing to comply with transparency laws or reporting little to no viable action, have been tempering some of the earlier enthusiasm (International Corporate Accountability Roundtable and Focus on Labour Exploitation 2019; Focus on Labour Exploitation 2018).

GOVERNMENT AND INGO ROLES IN THE BUSINESS LEADERSHIP PARADIGM

The supposed failures of governments and civil society groups are often highlighted in corporate leadership discourses; these other actors are said to be either unwilling or unable to solve the problems. For example, Ben Skinner, "anti-slavery" crusader and the founder and President of Transparentum, a United States-based nonprofit that investigates global supply chains, has had this to say about corporations and governments:

> Five years ago, out of the largest 175 economic entities in the world, 50 percent were corporations, 50 percent were countries. Today, 65 percent are corporations, and that trend line isn't going down. Corporations, increasingly in the world, are the most important actors. And, critically, and this should give us all some hope, corporations can do in forty-eight hours what it takes governments ten years to think about doing, to debate doing, and then never enforce at the district and local levels (Tandon 2018).

Likewise, the Mekong Club CEO asserts that "governments and NGOs have not been able to do it themselves" (Mekong Club 2018).

Governments are therefore advised that their role is to support businesses, providing them with incentives for job creation, human rights due diligence, and better technology in order to move forward in addressing "modern slavery" (Jägers and Rijken 2014; Lloyd 2020). They are counseled to make sure businesses have an equal playing field because "it is difficult for businesses to operate responsibly where laws, policies, and regulations are weak and there are no clear rules or consequences for companies that exploit and abuse workers" (United Nations Global Compact et al. 2018, 13). Concomitant with this, governments are also expected to enable consumer activism via the transparency laws described above (O'Brien and Macoun 2021).

Like governments, INGOs are assumed to be unable to address unfree labor and in need of business leadership. On one hand, nonprofits are accused of lacking an understanding of what the private sector does and how they do it, including lacking knowledge about supply chains.[15] On the other, INGOs are portrayed as a threat to businesses, out to name and shame them. This is consistent with scholarship that has found businesses lack trust in nonprofits, viewing them as ideological and intent on furthering their own interests (Arenas, Lozano, and Albareda 2009).

INGOs themselves sometimes repeat these tropes. One UK-based INGO provides a good example: it is a membership-based nonprofit with a code that its members follow; it provides trainings and assistance to companies as part of its work. It specifically advertises itself to potential members by highlighting both the ignorance and the threat that other nonprofits pose. As it states on its website:

> We recognise that some less sophisticated campaigning NGOs are often media darlings because they love to name and shame companies albeit often with little in the way of sound remedial recommendations. They're masters of clicktivism.

It reiterates this position in its training documents for companies as well, calling other nonprofits "poorly informed or unrealistic" with little understanding of "how long it takes to see real change." This INGO is giving a clear message that its market-oriented approach and its empathy for business distinguish itself from others in the "anti-slavery" field, and it vilifies other INGOs for their traditional watchdog role of monitoring and publicizing "modern slavery" abuses and pressing companies for change.

Other INGOs struggled with corporate-led efforts and the characterization of INGOs as well as governments. One INGO interviewee in the United States relayed the following thoughts about the role of governments and businesses in addressing forced labor in a West African country with rubber plantations:

> I was in [the country] and [a multinational corporation] kept building hospitals and they'd built a high school and they built new housing and I just kept thinking to myself, "What if you paid them a living wage?" Then they would pay the taxes to the government; they'd have a functioning government. The government could build schools. Why couldn't you just do that, instead of getting tax breaks for being there and then you build a hospital? I'm sure it must be cheaper in the calculation to build a hospital than it is to pay the workers a decent wage, but I really don't understand it.

Many of the INGOs continued to view governments as key actors in addressing issues of "modern slavery," but not in relation to corporate accountability or labor rights. Instead, the focus was mainly on governments taking responsibility for better identification and prosecution of traffickers and "slaveholders," as a criminal justice perspective would suggest, and for increased support for services for people who experience unfree labor.

THE MARKET IN FIGHTING "MODERN SLAVERY"

Along with the rise in discourses promoting business leadership and the incorporation of "modern slavery" into the CSR field, there has been a boom in "anti-slavery" entrepreneurship. One interviewee in the UK summed this up neatly, explaining her impression that "suddenly everyone is an expert in human trafficking, suddenly everyone is an expert in human rights risk analysis." A statement on another UK INGO's website corroborates her impression. Writing in 2016, after the passage of the UK Modern Slavery Act, the organization states:

> Over the past months, there has been a proliferation of consultancies offering businesses quick and simple solutions. It is important to note that unfortunately there is no quick and easy solution to a complex problem like modern slavery and many of those offering quick fixes lack credibility and have minimal knowledge of the issue.

This INGO was grappling with its place among a growing group of for-profit consultants claiming expertise on "modern slavery" and offering risk assessments, help with monitoring, and technological solutions, including software platforms to help companies identify risk (Theron 2019). It is a trend found in CSR more generally:

> . . . a whole commercial market develops around shaping, assessing, and consulting on the desired dimensions of social responsibility. A new breed of strategic consultants is also emerging in this new potentially lucrative field. . . these experts sell strategic CSR models and advise corporations on how to develop CSR campaigns, to monitor them, and to end up with "impact assessment" reports. Thus, the field emerges as non-profit and for-profit entities begin to compete among themselves over the selling of various CSR models. . . (Shamir 2004, 678)

This observation is true of the "anti-slavery" field as well. There are now business associations with specialized human trafficking or "modern slavery" arms, providing resources, tools, and platforms for their members.

There are also lucrative for-profit multinational auditing companies, and small and large law firms providing specialized consulting and purporting to have solutions (Theron 2019; LeBaron 2020). For example, Deloitte, one of the largest global professional services firms, has an "Anti-Human Trafficking" team that "convenes, advises, and delivers services to public and private sector entities to reduce human trafficking and provide dignified support to survivors."[16] Other global firms, such as PwC, KPMG, and EY, have offices that also offer consulting, particularly around risk management and transparency law compliance.

The newer entrants to the "anti-slavery" field do not necessarily offer anything innovative or different, and it is not always clear what expertise their staff have beyond general business or law knowledge (see, e.g., Sarfaty 2020). They may lack transparency, provide formulaic reports, have staff or leadership with little expertise in labor issues, and be unclear in their methodologies, such as the indicators of forced labor or human trafficking that are used, or the means by which determinations of forced labor are made (Sarfaty 2020). One of the directors I interviewed at a long-term INGO that provides consulting and assessment to companies on issues of "modern slavery" also made the point that they are less likely to be objective:

> . . . the for-profit consulting firms, and the auditing firms, and so on, are very good at giving the companies what they want, and even though cynically I could say for decades they've missed the forced labor that was right in front of their noses, now they're quickly able to provide all sorts of services to companies on their Modern Slavery statements or their work for forced labor and that kind of thing. The emphasis on forced labor trafficking has been a real boon to this sector. But it's more of the same groups that are getting the work, again for a lot of [those] reasons.

This INGO had found a niche by being willing to work with companies that had already used other consulting groups, including the big for-profit firms, but continued to have problems with issues of "modern slavery" in their supply chains. It was in a unique position in the "anti-slavery" field and was considered by other INGOs to be a credible organization providing research, assessment, and consulting.

While the global auditing firms, with their tens of thousands of employees across numerous countries and billions in revenue, may have found extra business in consulting and auditing related to issues of "modern slavery," their efforts have not been working. Political scientist Genevieve LeBaron (2020) bolsters the view of the INGO interviewee and his criticisms above, explaining that the big firms design and implement their auditing tools and programs to please companies, not to prevent and address labor exploitation. They engage in superficial actions, such as pre-announced audits, and focus on only the first tier of supply chains, though unfree labor occurs more often farther down. They provide their reports to the companies soliciting them only, so information about problems remains private, and issues persist when companies decide not to take action. In addition, the big auditing firms subcontract out inspections, which can lead to little accountability when problems do publicly arise in supply chains. The companies that hire the auditing firms blame them for missing the problems, and the auditing firms blame the subcontractors (LeBaron 2020).

SIDELINED AND ABSENT WORKERS

One of the most striking things about corporate leadership discourses pertaining to issues of "modern slavery" is that the experiences of workers and the conditions of their work are ancillary (Limoncelli 2024). Workers are both decentered and disempowered as corporate leaders design and implement solutions without involving them. It is a problem that a few INGOs noted. One explicitly addressed the absence of worker involvement on their website:

> Many companies believe that they can go-it-alone and create acceptable working conditions without allowing workers a stake in deciding what this looks like. We have found again and again, however, that where workers do not have a voice, abuses persist. In fact, we find that where workers have an active voice over their conditions, child labor and modern slavery are prevented as well.

An interviewee at another INGO also raised the issue while she was defending a labor approach for understanding and dealing with issues of "modern slavery." After first stating her dissatisfaction with other INGOs that see people who experience unfree labor as slaves, crime victims, or marginalized community members rather than workers, she went on to criticize the way private sector actors also overlook people as workers:

> You have companies like, even the private sector. . . that will engage in
> these issues [of "modern slavery" and] not even consult the workers who
> work for them about what would work. It's so paternalistic and I don't get it.

Her frustration with companies was palpable and so, too, was her criticism
of other "anti-slavery" INGOs. Some "anti-slavery" INGOs all too easily
join companies in paternalistic or top-down projects. One INGO in the
United States that sees people in unfree labor as slaves in need of protection and rescue provides an example. As the executive director told me in
his interview, the INGO had not done "a lot of bridge building" with labor
groups or unions, even though the communities the INGO worked in had
problems of debt bondage, forced labor, and child labor. Instead, the organization had been growing its connections to businesses because, the director
explained, "sophisticated businesses have learned to work constructively
with civil society."

The INGO had in fact worked in close collaboration with a global professional services firm on a project to make recommendations about
"anti-slavery" efforts. The ensuing report showed that, while NGOs,
funders, companies, survivor-activists, academics, and a few members of a
national government were interviewed for their expertise, no labor groups
were consulted nor were governmental agencies dealing with labor issues.
The report offers little that has not already been suggested in corporate
leadership discourses, just multistakeholder collaboration and, in its own
words, "incremental steps to improve the status quo."

IGOs have also sometimes sidelined workers in their partnerships with
businesses to address issues of "modern slavery." For example, IRIS, an ethical recruitment initiative created by the International Office for Migration
(IOM), hopes to safeguard migrant workers by providing a voluntary certification system for international recruitment agencies. According to one of
my interviewees, IOM reached out to trade unions when constructing the
program, but did not take all of their comments on board, including ones
that the unions deemed critical. IOM went ahead with the project in partnership with businesses, business associations, and nonprofit certification
groups. The trade unions, through the International Trade Union Confederation (ITUC), went on to start a separate platform with the ability for migrant workers to review recruitment agencies and learn about their rights.[17]

The UN Global Compact provides another example, one in which trade unions were not involved until after the MSI was launched. The unions raised ongoing concerns about companies talking with NGOs rather than unions, complained about Compact members violating workers' rights, and found that little action was taken (Ryder 2010). Few unions are involved today (Limoncelli 2024).[18]

When businesses are at the center of top-down "anti-slavery" responses and IGOs and INGOs fail to support the inclusion of workers, the workers become tools for the risk management of companies or components to be managed. As former International Labour Organization (ILO) Director-General and General Secretary of the International Trade Union Confederation Guy Ryder (2010) has written, workers, like natural resources in CSR, are treated as things to "take care of" rather than partners at the table. Companies are advised to gather information from workers as part of their risk assessment and for the purpose of protecting them from liability. Workers are seen as potential whistleblowers for Western brands to safeguard them from the actions of problematic suppliers.

It is not surprising, then, that worker-centered strategies, such as worker-driven social responsibility (WSR), which is meant to alter the relations of power between major companies, their contractors, and workers, are not very common (LeBaron 2020; Van Buren, III, Schrempf-Stirling, and Westermann-Behaylo 2019; Williams 2016). WSR involves workers being at the center of programs to protect their own rights.[19] They create, monitor, and enforce programs designed to improve their working conditions and wages, sign binding agreements with brands and retailers, and ensure that monitoring and enforcement mechanisms provide workers with an effective voice. WSR initiatives include worker education, rigorous inspections independent from brand and retailer influence, public disclosure of participating brands and suppliers, and complaint mechanisms that ensure action when workers identify abuses.

One example is the Fair Food Program, started by the worker-based nonprofit the Coalition of Immokalee Workers. It uses binding agreements with retailers to buy produce only from growers that follow the program's Code of Conduct, which covers a variety of worker protections (Asbed and Hitov 2017). A Fair Food Label helps consumers to identify food produced by growers in the program, and an independent body, the Fair Foods

Standards Council, monitors implementation and performs audits. Scholars have argued that the model is a success: it has raised compensation and reduced health and safety risks, forced labor, child labor, and gender-based violence for workers in retail, fast food, and food service companies (Anner and Fischer-Daly 2023, 56).[20]

CONCLUSION

Discourses promoting the use of "good" business to fix the "bad" business of unfree labor reframe it in ways that support business interests: turning businesses into victims, blaming suppliers, recasting the role of states as business supporters rather than regulators, contesting the legitimacy of INGOs as experts by claiming they are part of the problem, sidelining workers, and elevating other businesses that have little interest in upsetting the companies for which they are consulting and providing services. All of this perpetuates business as usual. The notion of efficient corporate leadership solving problems of "modern slavery" works to reassign responsibility to other actors while leaving systems of exploitation very much intact. Corporate outsourcing and purchasing practices escape scrutiny, as does the failure of states to ensure decent work and safe migration.

INGOs carry on their activities, but they have to navigate a field that has set the understanding of "modern slavery" according to these terms. In the next four chapters, we consider the ways the INGOs have been responding in their advocacy strategies and activities, their communications and representations of themselves in their branding and marketing, and in their own operations and structures.

Three

FRAUGHT COLLABORATIONS AND BUSINESS-FRIENDLY STRATEGIES

We always aim to define the approach that is right for your business.
We use our extensive experience and knowledge of all forms of modern
slavery and overlay this against the issues that you are facing. We do
not take a one-size-fits-all approach and we will work with you in the
right way for your company to tackle all aspects of modern slavery.
—"Anti-slavery" INGO offering bespoke services for companies

The strategies that "anti-slavery" INGOs pursue and the actions they
take matter for their constituencies and for the trends and directions of
the advocacy field. This chapter looks at actions being undertaken by
"anti-slavery" INGOs, the ways they see themselves relative to businesses,
the dilemmas they face, and the implications for addressing unfree labor.
Those working in "anti-slavery" INGOs are aware of power differentials between civil society organizations and companies, and they walk a fine line
whereby they seek to engage businesses but retain credibility as independent actors. Many INGOs, caught in this contradiction, have sought to move
toward market-based and business-friendly strategies for addressing issues
of "modern slavery" that seem to resolve the dilemma.

Such strategies, and the perception that INGOs "have to" partner with businesses, weaken their ability to hold them accountable, however, and help to shift the focus from workers to businesses; businesses in some sense become their constituents and business interests become INGO concerns. The result is an advocacy field that does little to press for changes that would upset the status quo. This also has implications for corporate accountability: with INGOs oriented toward being partners or providers of services to businesses, as the above epigraph demonstrates, their ability to act as corporate watchdogs is hampered. Regulation, which has been increasingly outsourced to nonprofits and civil society groups, is then shifted from INGOs to consumers via market-based "anti-slavery" strategies, in effect, ensuring that little regulation is happening at all.

"ANTI-SLAVERY" STRATEGIES

INGOs undertake a wide range of activities to address issues of "modern slavery," from research and advocacy to outreach, identification, and service provision for people who experience trafficking, and program development and support for partner organizations in other countries. The INGOs I interviewed were doing all of these things, and more, and they were also working toward ways to collaborate with the for-profit sector. The strategies that they were engaged in tended to group into the following categories:

Awareness Raising: Most of the INGOs had developed public awareness and education campaigns and outreach initiatives in conjunction with businesses. For example, one interviewee described a project generously funded by the foundation of a large technology company, the largest portion of which was going toward a campaign to educate vulnerable groups in a country of the global south and raise awareness in a country of the global north. Another had partnered with a technology company to help them target their public awareness campaign materials online more efficiently, while a third had jointly developed a project with a business association to raise awareness of forced labor and labor trafficking in the hospitality industry of the country in which the INGO was headquartered. Nonprofits have often cooperated with the private sector for awareness raising and continue to do so (Hoff and McGauran 2015, 138).

Trainings and workshops are also common strategies in "anti-slavery" work, just as they are in other advocacy areas. As Watkins et al. (2012, 298–301) explain using the example of development NGOs, the "talk" that organizations do via meetings, workshops, and trainings is seen as key for sustainability and allows organizations to be flexible in the face of changing donor preferences: whatever the problem, the solution is talk. In the "anti-slavery" field, companies and their employees have become an increasingly popular audience to target, branching out from prior trainings for public sector professionals such as law enforcement, teachers, and social workers.

For example, much like the INGO quoted at the beginning of the chapter, one UK-based "anti-slavery" INGO advertises its training packages, which are:

> . . . customised to match our partners' needs and can also be tailored to specific teams across the organisation. Our team develops relevant case studies to identify the ways in which staff may come across incidences, the risks each team might face, and the common red flags associated with trafficking. We work with a number of industries including financial services, healthcare, hospitality, and construction.

There are also general trainings for businesses, to help them understand "modern slavery," its manifestations in supply chains, and any requirements of "anti-slavery" legislation. There are even trainings to help local professionals move into a more entrepreneurial role in "anti-slavery" advocacy. For example, in the United States, one INGO initiated a project to train social work case managers to serve as business startup coaches so that they can provide clients who have experienced human trafficking with entrepreneurial skills training.

The sheer number of trainings that INGOs are engaged in prompted one INGO interviewee to complain:

> I'm getting cynical and jaded in my old age, but there are all of these training modules all over the place. How much money do you pour into that?

She wanted funding to support other strategies, particularly efforts to coordinate and collaborate INGO efforts in areas of the global south.

Market-Based Solutions: Codes and Certification Schemes: Aside from awareness and outreach, trainings and talk, INGOs were involved with codes of conduct or certification projects, either directly or as part of MSIs. These efforts boomed in the 1990s and have been growing since then; they have emerged, in part, because governments and IGOs have promoted them (Appelbaum 2016; Bartley 2007; Esbenshade 2004a). The initiatives are varied, but they commonly involve codes that companies voluntarily agree to follow and apply to suppliers. Many use nonprofits as the oversight organizations that provide model codes, trainings, auditing, and in some cases, certifications (Esbenshade 2012; Appelbaum 2016).[1] For example, the Fair Labor Association (FLA), an MSI that companies join, has a Code of Conduct addressing labor issues that they agree to follow; it was established in 1999 after media scandals exposing child and forced labor in apparel supply chains tied to brands such as Gap and Nike. Social Accountability International (SAI) is another example; its SA8000 Standard addresses child and forced labor, and companies that meet the standard are provided with a certification.

Among the INGOs I interviewed, one used a code as its central strategy for addressing labor exploitation, and another provided "principles" for companies to follow in working with suppliers and conducting third-party audits. The latter INGO advertised the principles as a simple, low-cost, and achievable way to improve exploitation in supply chains, appealing to businesses with the argument that a partnership can provide them with "a range of benefits including PR opportunities." A third INGO offered a certification system for products alongside its efforts to rescue and rehabilitate people who experienced child and forced labor. As the interviewee explained:

> We were trying to figure out a way to incentivize other companies to join [our certification program], at the same time providing really good-paying jobs for people who needed them so they wouldn't have to emigrate. It was a very multipronged approach to trying to stabilize local business and prevent exploitation all at once. So, we came up with this training program where [people] would be trained for free and then would go into [our] certified factories.

Codes and certifications were popular strategies; in addition to the examples above, eight other INGOs I interviewed were taking part in MSIs that involved codes and certifications, as either members or advisors.

At least one INGO interviewee in the United States, with long-term experience in the "anti-slavery" field, was concerned about the prevalence of both codes and certifications:

> . . . everybody's trying to do. . . . certifications and I really worry that some of these corporations are trying to fund certifications and you can't certify somebody's being—the term they use is slavery-free—you can't. . . . I often find myself in meetings going, "Codes of conduct are not going to work. Don't let the corporation talk you into getting X-NGO to endorse their code because it doesn't work and here's why. . ."

This interviewee also pointed out that most of the certification programs she knew about only looked at the first levels of a supply chain and therefore did little to change practices farther down.

In addition, this interviewee was concerned that the initiatives reinforced binary notions about labor exploitation, leading people to believe that "slavery-free" goods were free from exploitation of any kind:

> There's some group that's trying to put a freedom stamp on products that it will be certified by them as slavery free and my comment is, "Okay, so they might not have the worst form of forced labor in the first tier of their supply chain, but they still may be discriminating against workers, there still may be sexual harassment, they still may be firing workers for trying to organize, they still may not be paying wages on time, or underpaying people." It doesn't mean they're a good employer, and if I was a consumer who didn't do this work, I would see that and feel really good about buying it when you really should not feel very good about buying it.

As we learned in chapter 2, her concerns about certification strategies are well-founded and backed up by scholarly literature that shows little change for workers (see, e.g., Wells 2007; Bartley 2018; LeBaron 2020, 2021a; Seidman 2009; Seidman 2007). This is one reason why worker-driven MSIs such as the Fair Food Program have been cited by scholars as better alternatives to corporate-driven ones; centering workers can help to better ensure that their interests are addressed and tangible improvements occur (Braun and Gearhart 2005; Asbed and Hitov 2017; Fine and Bartley 2018; Mieres and McGrath 2021).

Market-Based Solutions: Transparency Laws and Ethical Consumption: Many of the INGOs I spoke with were very supportive of transparency laws that ask companies to voluntarily report what, if anything, they were doing to address issues of "modern slavery." They advocated for the laws and took credit for helping to shape their final versions. In its trustee's report, for example, one UK INGO lauded its "constant source of authority and influence on the direction of the UK Modern Slavery Bill." An interviewee with another UK INGO also highlighted her organization's role. She explained that they had exerted a lot of pressure to influence the legislation away from a criminal justice focus:

> The first version of this act appeared and there was absolutely no reference to labor exploitation, trafficking. . . . I mean, extraordinary. It was all about criminal justice. It was all about, "We need to find the traffickers, we need to lock them up, and we're going to lock them up for a long time. The bad guys. It's all going to be fine."

They lobbied for the transparency clause and, according the interviewee, put in a lot of work to bring a poor draft to a better place.

Across my interviews, many INGOs saw transparency laws as having the potential to "drive new conversations" and create a "race to the top" with businesses competing to show their leadership (Limoncelli 2017). I was told that the measures are "a big step forward" and a "crucial step" in reducing demand for products made with slavery. One interviewee at an anti-trafficking INGO in the United States explained: "There's been a push [by activists] for a long time to get a law in place so that corporations can have some obligations. It's an important move in the right direction" (Limoncelli 2017, 120).

The enthusiasm was not embraced by all of the INGOs, however. There were a few INGO interviewees who were critical of transparency laws. One interviewee in the United States said this about them:

> . . . they are quite toothless. . . it essentially is pushing companies to just have more inputs, like yes, we did trainings, yes we did audits, without giving any specific details. . . like we're part of another chain effort.

Two other INGOs saw them as potentially helpful but noted the poor compliance of companies in their reports. One, in the United States, called for a bill that would move beyond simple voluntary transparency approaches to a mandatory due diligence model that would legally require companies to assess and address human rights impacts associated with business practices and supply chains. The other, in the UK, suggested that the laws could be improved if there were more detailed requirements for what had to be included in transparency statements and if transparency legislation included criminal liability so that companies could be held responsible for violations of workers' rights.

In addition, one interviewee at an INGO in the United States suggested a trade-related strategy as an alternative. Declaring that she was not very enthusiastic about transparency laws, the interviewee went on to explain what she thought was better:

> The thing that's more exciting, I think, is the consumptive demand loophole that was closed in the Tariff Act. . . that [said a] product category is exempt from labor laws [when] there's no other way for us to get it. . . . Because if there is something that we don't produce here, then you can still import it and not face prosecution. . . . I think there is teeth to that.

The closure of the loophole allows United States Customs and Border Protection to detain, seize, and forfeit imported merchandise shown to be produced with forced labor. Since the interview, there has been an uptick in enforcement actions, but they address only a small fraction of the significant quantities of at-risk goods imported into the U.S.[2]

DILEMMAS OF COLLABORATION

With business-friendly strategies added to their repertoire of actions, and despite the concerns of some interviewees, many of the INGOs were actively working toward more collaborations with businesses. The hope, as governments, IGOs, and some "modern slavery" scholars have suggested, was that business-nonprofit collaborations would provide mutual benefits, visibility, and understanding for both organizations (Foot 2020; 2015, 65–66). Yet the potential difficulties are myriad. From the business side, as discussed in the last chapter, companies have many reasons for being reluctant to engage with INGOs, including seeing them as a threat to business interests due to self-interest or unreasonable demands (Arenas, Lozano, and Albareda 2009). Companies therefore engage with nonprofits when they see a strategic fit, and they select collaborators whose resources and objectives fit well with those of the firm (den Hond, de Bakker, and Doh 2015).

Companies prefer INGOs who engage in consensus building rather than radical action or conflict behavior involving action such as picketing, sit-ins, boycotts, or other forms of direct action; INGOs are expected to engage in "civil behavior" if they want to be considered legitimate partners (Baur and Palazzo 2011). This is why a study of the collaborative relationships of U.S. Fortune 500 companies found that they did not tend to include advocacy-based INGOs (O'Connor and Shumate 2011). Rather, businesses tended to partner with a small number of nonprofits that were child-focused, had big international or national federated structures with local offices, and were service-focused (O'Connor and Shumate 2011). These were more mainstream and presumably non-controversial organizations, following the pattern of leading INGOs in a field tending toward moderate and reformist positions (Stroup and Wong 2017; Yaziji and Doh 2013).[3]

From the INGO side, there can be concern that partnerships can lead civil society organizations to become more responsive to funders than their own constituencies; reluctant to adopt strategies that would hurt their relationships with business; or tie them together through personal relations and the recruitment of staff between them such that they risk their independence (cf. Baur and Schmitz 2011; Yaziji and Doh 2009). Corporations can dominate decision-making processes and lead to compromises around the lowest common denominator, for example, agreeing to voluntary standards for monitoring supply chains (Baumann-Pauly et al. 2016, 773). Moreover, the motivations of INGOs and businesses for collaboration have been different, with INGOs seeking to access funds and legitimacy in a particular field and businesses wanting social stability so that they can operate undisturbed (Lucea 2010).

The possibility of being caught in a conflict of interest that reduces their ability to effectively advocate for change was always a danger for the INGOs. This can lead to "vanilla" projects when nonprofits are reluctant to condemn the companies from which they receive funding (Stroup and Wong 2017; Hoff 2014; Hoff and McGauran 2015). Among other practical organizational considerations, INGOs have to decide how critical they want to be toward the private sector; whether they want to work with companies or against them; and reflect on what is motivating companies to work with them (Hoff and McGauran 2015, 118).

The INGOs that I interviewed were seeking collaborations and many already had them, but some did worry about the concerns listed above. As one INGO interviewee in Europe explained:

> NGOs are conflicted about partnerships [with for-profit companies]... more radical NGOs said you should not work with [the] private sector; you should work against them. Yet many other NGOs were quite eager to work with the private sector.

Despite the ambivalence, the interviewee confirmed, an increasing number of INGOs were pursuing opportunities for collaborations.

One major issue that many INGO interviewees brought up was the potential for collaborations to provide reputational cover for businesses to continue labor exploitation. An interviewee at an "anti-slavery" INGO in the UK explained that her organization had engaged in internal discussions about its collaboration with a multinational company:

> Kind of going, "Wait a second. If we're going to go working with an organization that we can tell you that we have a list of issues with, and they're addressing one or two of them at the start, is the use of our name going to be used as greed, whitewash or whatever, to give themselves some social credence, when we're not happy with a large scope of their practices?"

The director of an "anti-slavery" INGO in the United States had similar worries. In explaining his organization's recent shift toward a more open approach to business collaborations, he said:

> Frankly, we had not had much of a relationship with business because it's always been the concern about our not being used to mask... we don't want to be a "beard" for anybody. So, we've always been very cautious about that, but I think we're also evolving in that regard.

He went on to say that the organization is now "certainly open to good-faith, productive relationships with business, where our particular skillset can actually make a difference."

In addition to the potential problem of being used for reputational cover by businesses, some INGOs worried about conflicts of interest when they accept funding from companies. Most of the INGOs in this study were getting at least some funding from companies or, more often, corporate foundations, though this was typically only a small proportion of their overall budgets. More than one-quarter of the INGOs (28 percent) had budgets primarily based on donations, and another 28 percent relied most heavily on government and IGO funding. Just over a third (34 percent) received the majority of their funding from a combination of government and private grants, though half of these also relied to some extent on other sources, including donations, fees, and commercial revenue.[4]

The long-term head of the counter-trafficking program at an INGO based in the United States raised the issues of funding and conflicts of interest in her interview. From her vantage point, based on two decades of experience in the field, she said:

> Interviewee: You do see more corporations funding things, which scares me a little bit. Like Walmart funds anti-trafficking programs. . .
> Interviewer: Why does that scare you?
> Interviewee: Because it comes with strings. . . . The types of programs they support, who they're supporting. Some of the groups are really good, and I get why they take the money, but I just think you need to think about Walmart as one of the biggest abusers of labor around the world, and I'm sure there's trafficking in their supply chains. Especially since all they have is codes of conduct and that's not going to get you anywhere. That scares me.

Another staff member with two decades of experience working with an anti-trafficking INGO in Europe echoed the concern. She relayed the questions that her organization's nonprofit members asked each other:

> Should we accept this funding? Should we work with this company while knowing also that the bigger companies have always some kind of link with exploitation?

The concerns raised by interviewees are that the INGOs may lose credibility or suffer reputational harm working with a company that is contributing to the problems they are trying to solve; disapproval could come from the public or from other nonprofits. As one of the interviewees explained, when people in her organization began to work on increasing their business collaborations, they found some friction with other "more critical"

INGOs outside of the "anti-slavery" field who felt that they were "too nice to businesses."

Reflecting these tensions, one interviewee at an INGO in the United States proactively defended her organization's acceptance of corporate funding when I spoke with her. As she explained:

> [A major U.S. retailer] is funding our office [in another country]. And they're quite serious. And we're not promising them a clean supply chain; we can't possibly promise them that. But they recognize that you're just not going to get to the root of this problem unless there is a cost to be paid for using slaves.

She expressed confidence in the company's commitment to fighting "modern slavery."

Another "anti-slavery" INGO, also in the United States, defended its acceptance of corporate funding in a transparency statement available on their website:

> [The brand]. . . is a [INGO] donor. But once again, [the INGO], as a non-profit, does not singularly accept donations and distribute them to projects. [The brand] strives to be a slavery-free company and asked [the INGO] to assess their labor practices and offer best-practice solutions. This past year, we visited [the brand's] factories in several locations. . . . We are developing plans to continue this work. . .

This particular INGO does not engage in monitoring global supply chains despite its mention of visiting the brand's factories; rather, it provides services to people who experience issues of "modern slavery" and has added business collaborations and for-profit components as a means of revenue generation. Its transparency document provides little in the way of concrete mechanisms for ensuring that a conflict of interest does not occur. The company receives positive publicity and reassurance from the INGO to the public that they are a "good business," while the INGO receives resources and offers little publicly available evidence to support their claims about the company.

Despite the potential for conflicts of interest, a number of the INGOs I interviewed had either softened their stance on accepting corporate funding or were actively seeking it. One INGO in the United States, for example, had eschewed corporate funding for many years but was now receiving some funding from brands; this is notable because the INGO had in the past been strongly committed to corporate accountability and had a history of suing problematic companies. Others were so enthusiastic about reaching out to businesses that more seasoned leaders in the field felt the need to urge more caution. An interviewee at a European anti-trafficking INGO explained that she had ongoing conversations about this with other nonprofits in the field:

> . . . we had to balance it a bit, saying, "Okay, we understand you want this [to work with the private sector], but you also need to be critical."

The enthusiasm was not only due to a desire to potentially gain resources, she explained; it was also motivated by the hope of being able to influence some "good" companies:

> [Nonprofits think] we can work along with the businesses, preferably the best ones, and then try to see how can they change their businesses, maybe working with us and then motivate others.

In this view, INGOs can create change by helping one business at a time.

ENTICING COMPANIES, AVOIDING CONTESTATION

In seeking out companies as potential donors and collaborators, INGOs can reproduce rather than challenge corporate power; this is something that was brought out in the ways that INGO interviewees saw themselves in relation to companies and spoke about their interactions with them. While they hoped to develop and/or strengthen relationships with firms, they did not see INGOs as having much power or leverage to get businesses to collaborate. Instead, they often referenced large power differentials between INGOs and businesses. The CEO of an "anti-slavery" INGO in the United States recounted this experience:

> I distinctly remember nine years ago [speaking at a business conference]. And, I remember thinking, "These people know I'm a joke. [laughs] Because I'm here representing an ideal, but I'm not here representing any form of capital, I'm not here representing any type of brand. . ." and I even remember feeling a bit like the imagery of throwing rocks at a corporate window. Like, okay, change it because it's good. And, frankly, they don't care.

He later decided to put down the rocks and join the for-profit sector, starting social enterprise businesses (see chapter 6).

Rather than attempting direct confrontation themselves, many INGO interviewees commented that media pressure helped to equalize power differentials and convince companies to collaborate. As one interviewee in Europe explained about the businesses her INGO worked with:

> Quite often their responses are to media exposés. . . . In the case [I told you about], there were journalists sniffing around, and they discovered that there was all sorts of potentially very, very shady and problematic stuff going on [in the sector]. . . they [the businesses] said, "Actually, we want to contribute and can you help lead an analysis of what's going on?" And then we convened a series of meetings and guidance notes, and a whole range of things have been triggered from that. So, it's companies determining that they can't do this alone.

Another "anti-slavery" INGO in the UK explained that it was a newspaper exposé that initiated their collaboration with a multinational company, one that they had been unable to make much progress with before that:

> . . . the thing that changed that was the exposé in the [newspaper], which, going from long, drawn-out conversations with companies saying, "Is this business value for money?" going to "How quickly can you sign?"

The INGO had tried speaking with the company many times to no avail, but media pressure had finally worked to push the company into a formal relationship with the INGO as a consultant.

Media exposés were cited by interviewees as the most common reason that otherwise recalcitrant businesses take action on "modern slavery." There are many prominent examples that support this view. They include media coverage of child labor and forced labor in the production of Gap clothing in India; Nike soccer balls in Pakistan and shoes in Vietnam; cocoa beans in West African countries used by chocolate companies such as Nestle, Mars, and Hershey; and more recently, cobalt mining in the Democratic Republic of Congo for use by companies such as Apple, Google, Microsoft, and Tesla. A sentiment expressed by a UK INGO was common:

> No company wants to be 'named and shamed' in a media exposé linking their procurement to labour exploitation.

As one interviewee in the United States noted, though, a problem with relying on the media exposés is that most companies do not receive negative press coverage, so there is no incentive for them to partner with INGOs. In addition, some companies that receive negative press attention may actually be doing more to address labor exploitation than others that receive no bad press but are much worse in practice. Social movements tend to target certain companies (i.e., large, leading firms with good reputations and recognition for social responsibility) for their cultural vulnerabilities rather than their actual ties to labor exploitation (Bartley and Child 2014).

I note also that the examples of media exposés raised by the interviewees were not done in conjunction with INGO campaigns; they spoke of them as examples of external pressure that helped push the companies toward INGO collaborations. To work with media would be to join in confrontation, but most INGOs were seeking out ways to court rather than confront businesses that have issues of "modern slavery" in supply chains. Much like a potential dating relationship, INGOs would try to pique a company's interest and entice them into a collaboration. One interviewee at an anti-trafficking and "anti-slavery" program in a large faith-based INGO in the United States explained its strategy this way:

> So, we're focusing on two [food production] companies... that are already doing relatively well in terms of what's legally required.... But we're asking them, "Within that program, can you also talk about what you're doing to make sure that labor rights are being respected?" Whether it's talking about independent audits, we figured if we just slam a company, they're just going to ignore it. So, first we start by complimenting them, and saying, "How about taking it to the next step?" So, we'll see if that works.

The plan was to tread lightly and praise the company.

A UK-based INGO provides another example, seeking to attract businesses by promising to be an empathetic and nonintrusive partner:

> We don't consider that companies should feel compelled to reveal everything they know about the problems that exist or could exist... if companies can show us—with integrity, honesty, and courage—that they are doing the analysis, mapping their supply chains, understanding where the biggest risks lie, and engaging with workers, trade unions, and key stakeholders to

address and remediate the likelihood of modern slavery, then we believe
they should be rewarded, rather than exposed for their efforts.

This INGO's strategy was to oblige companies, something proponents of
"anti-slavery" INGO-business collaborations support. Foote (2015, 67–68),
for example, suggests that deferring to business can help INGOs to build
collaborative relationships.[5]

However well-intentioned, the process of courting companies carries
a high risk of rejection. One European anti-trafficking INGO that I spoke
with, for example, tried to develop a partnership with a banking and finance company as well as a chocolate company in the country where it
was headquartered, both of which proclaimed that they wanted to work on
issues of "modern slavery":

> [Members of the INGO] started to reach out to them, talk with them. But
> it requires a lot of work. You talk and have every meeting, and then the
> results are very skinny. . . you don't get much.

For this reason, at least one INGO in the United States was looking to improve their chances with prospective business suitors by showing up with
gifts. The organization was working on:

> . . . a campaign that would encourage the government to provide subsidies
> or other kinds of policy incentives to companies that can demonstrate that
> they are operating child-labor-free. So, tax incentives or some of the pro-
> cedural incentives, like you can have an expedited tax return or something
> like that. . .

In this case, the INGO was planning to pressure the government on behalf
of businesses. The hope was that incentives would attract businesses and
reassure them that INGOs are ready and willing partners rather than
threats.

INGOS: FROM WATCHDOGS TO CONSULTANTS

In courting rather than confronting businesses, the roles of INGOs risk
being reconfigured from potential corporate "watchdogs" to business consultants. Placing the onus on INGOs rather than states to monitor companies was already a problematic endeavor complicated by a host of factors,

not least a practical one: they lack the capacity and resources to do it. The co-founder of one INGO in the UK complained about that very issue in light of the passage of the UK Modern Slavery Act, which did not include a monitoring mechanism:

> . . . the government is always wanting to put all the onus on civil society to do all of the monitoring, all of the analysis, and all of the pressure, the enforcement stuff, which is quite a lot to ask.

In her view, civil society groups were not likely to press companies to comply with the law.

What INGOs *were* doing was seeking out ways to provide services to businesses. For example, after the UK Modern Slavery Act was passed, many of the INGOs I spoke with assumed the legislation would open up new opportunities for them to work with businesses. I spoke with a director of one INGO who looked forward to the possibility of increased consulting opportunities:

> [The law] has opened up a relatively new aspect of consultancy. . . we have always, up to a point, done some consultancy work, or depending on the context, worked with corporations in relation to supply chain management. At the moment, it's payment for consultancy, or payment for training. That's to meet the particular reporting requirements. If that was to bring up something that they looked and they saw, or maybe highlight an area that they thought maybe could do with a bit more attention, then I presume the expectation is then that they would say, "Right, well if you wanted to address this, or if you wanted to investigate and see what needed to be done, here." They would advise further on that, and [we would] work on a consultant basis.

The websites of this and other INGOs have reiterated the message that they are ready to partner:

> We recognise that slavery in the business context is a complex issue for which there are no simple solutions. By working in partnership with [us], you will access specialist guidance. . .

This UK-based INGO goes on to offer bespoke services that "provide viable and sustainable solutions to ensure not only compliance with the legal requirements, but also to strengthen your reputation."

> We invite your company to build a bespoke partnership with [us] that en-
> gages every part of your business—suppliers, staff, customers, and clients
> alike. Talk to our team today to start designing your perfect partnership.

The language emphasizes the needs of prospective business partners, as-
suring them that the INGO will be supportive and work to strengthen their
reputations.

One INGO even sought to differentiate itself from others in the nonprofit sector by explicitly promising businesses that it was a more knowl-
edgeable and supportive partner than others:

> . . . not all NGOs lack perception. . . . Sophisticated NGOs understand the
> complexity of modern supply chains and the difficult hidden nature of
> modern slavery. . . [we have] created an open, informal space for every-
> one. . . to build a spirit of collaboration in learning that can help to improve
> the impact of all our efforts.

All of these texts appear carefully worded to convince businesses that they
and the INGO are on the same side and to affirm to businesses that their interests are a shared concern.[6] It was common for INGOs offering a number
of tailored services, such as trainings, assessments, policy design and implementation review, supplier capacity building, and community engagement, to use the language of partnership and support.

In some cases, the message was even more direct. For example, one
U.S.-based "anti-slavery" INGO courts businesses in a video that explicitly tells companies, "This isn't a gotcha game" and assures them that "the
amount of product touched by slavery is so small, it shouldn't touch the
bottom line." The language in the video underscored the unity of INGOs
and businesses: ". . . we have to make sure that slavery doesn't reach into
our lives and touch us through the things that we buy and sell, that we produce, and that we use. . . we can fix the problem without blasting the bottom
line and we can make the consumers a lot happier when we do so." Note
the language emphasizing "we;" the INGO and businesses are together and
they want the same thing: for businesses to be safe from "modern slavery"
and profitable.

The director of an INGO in the United States also worked this angle, describing the way they sought to convince businesses that they would benefit
monetarily from addressing "modern slavery":

. . . over the years engaging with companies on supply chain practice around slavery. . . if you had an opportunity to engage with executive leadership and show how changing systems and practices could actually position them better in the marketplace, from a marketing perspective, and actually make them more money, à la a Ben & Jerry's type of model. You can prove it using their words and their language. Yes, you have a better chance.[7]

Other INGOs promised companies reputational benefits as a result of working with them, the concern about being a cover turned into a potential marketing tool: "A partnership with us can provide your business with a range of benefits, including PR opportunities and expert speakers at your events."

Several INGOs promise on their websites that they will be a "critical friend" and strategic partner. One calls themselves a "peer to business."

INGOs that were less articulate about how their activities would benefit companies struggled to market that message. An interviewee at an INGO in the United States that combines rescue, services, and a certification initiative explained:

We were trying to figure out some ways to have a third-party researcher work with us on the business case for our work because it is so hard to prove that what we're doing is better for business.

INGOs throughout the "anti-slavery" field were looking for ways to convince businesses to partner.

CENTERING BUSINESS CONSTITUENTS

As business services providers, "friends," and "peers," the INGOs courting consultancies understandably center business interests in their advertising, but to an outside audience, their entreaties sometimes seem to signal something more: that businesses were their main constituents, not people who experience or are at risk of unfree labor. INGO websites and pamphlets promise to help companies "stay ahead" of scandals, provide "updates that matter before the story breaks, as well as crisis communications support," help build trust with consumers, and help advertise brands working to be ethical: "Doing the right thing has never been better for your business."

One INGO that works on forced labor in seafood supply chains described their work with companies this way:

> . . . one of the things companies join us and value us for is being able to bring competitors in the same room to work on common issues. So, in a pre-competitive space, to get a bit of honesty and safety in being able to say, "What are we gonna do about this scandal that's just hit about this concern that we have in this country, in this sector, in this supply chain?"

This INGO acknowledged a host of political and economic processes at work in creating forced labor in the fishing industry, including efforts to suppress worker organization, but rather than partnering with workers as part of their efforts, they instead pivoted to businesses. They also suggested more transparency, more information for consumers, and the development of certification schemes as potential solutions.

Instead of seeking to empower workers at risk of labor exploitation, INGOs pitched themselves as "empowering businesses" by helping them to understand risks in their supply chains; they promised to "identify business sectors disproportionately vulnerable to trafficking" and "protect your brand." An evaluation of a UK-based INGO posted to their website highlights their success in appealing to businesses:

> What appears to have made [the INGO] so successful, and. . . seen as added value by its stakeholders, is [the] ability to engage with stakeholders and partners in a manner relevant to the partner's needs. It is rare for NGOs to be able to speak to businesses in a way that the businesses can understand and appreciate.

This has become a distinguishing feature of this particular INGO, which did not start with the intent of serving business constituents. It was originally aimed at education and awareness, advocacy, and community mobilization against human trafficking, but has moved steadily into partnerships with businesses and consulting for them.

In spite all of the above efforts that INGOs take to convince businesses they can be of service, the hope may be misplaced. They have to compete with business-led nonprofits as well as for-profit consulting companies mentioned in chapter 2. Those organizations also provide research, develop trainings, conduct audits, migrant worker assessments, and staff and supplier trainings, provide consultations on implementing human rights protections, give legal advice about transparency laws and disclosure requirements, and/or certify goods or services. As one INGO director remarked in his interview, for-profits had an advantage in the competition for consulting jobs because of the resources at their disposal, and also because they were able to quickly put up marketing materials, know what companies are looking for, do not press them as hard as the INGOs do, and give them what they want. Scholars concur (LeBaron et al. 2021; LeBaron 2020; LeBaron, Lister, and Dauvergne 2017; Anner 2012, 2017; Ford and Nolan 2020).

Competition extended to grants as well. One of the INGO interviewees in Europe explained:

> The EU puts out a call for an evaluation of, say, the national referral system, and while NGOs could do it, there are commercial firms that apply and win the project. Then they subcontract with the NGO, and so the NGO gets far less than if they had won the contract themselves.

There can also be competition in staffing. One INGO interviewee in the U.S. who explores labor rights violations in supply chains explained:

> Well, it hasn't always been easy. . . the work is really hard. It's increasingly dangerous for my colleagues around the world, and also there aren't that many people who know this issue really well and also may be willing to work for an NGO when they could be working for a company.

He went on to acknowledge that some workers prefer to be on the NGO side, but his experience speaks to the competition that INGOs face in relation to for-profits in the field. INGOs can find themselves outmatched by for-profits for any number of activities that they routinely engage in.

OUTSOURCING ACCOUNTABILITY TO CONSUMER MONITORS

If INGOs have become more focused on the interests and needs of businesses, and action to censure companies is not their responsibility, then whose responsibility is it? In the push for market-based "anti-slavery" strategies, INGOs increasingly reinforce the message that it is consumers that need to hold companies accountable for "modern slavery." Very much in keeping with the idea of individualized action, INGO websites are replete with links to "what you can do" to end "modern slavery," usually including items such as becoming more aware about the issue, educating others, engaging in ethical consumption, and providing donations. Consumers are depicted as "anti-slavery" heroes (O'Brien 2015, 2018).[8] A video by an INGO that combines rescue and service provision with a certification scheme provides an example. After explaining the problem of child labor, the narration tells viewers:

> Then a hero entered the picture: it was you. If you knew how the [products] were being made, you would no longer think they were so beautiful, and if you could choose a better [one], your buying power could end child slavery.

This was one of many INGO examples promoting ethical consumption as a solution to issues of "modern slavery." INGOs routinely ask consumers not to "buy into slavery" and assure them that their actions and agency are vitally important.

For example, a faith-based INGO in the United States, working on human trafficking, urged consumers to make ethical purchases:

> Together with the social responsibility of businesses, there is also the social responsibility of consumers. Every person ought to have awareness that purchasing is always a moral—and not simply an economic—act. . . . Through labeling, we as consumers can make educated purchasing choices that help eradicate human trafficking.

Another INGO in the UK laid out in a report some steps consumers needed to take with regard to seafood supply chains. They should:

> Demand proof. . . and require clear, specific assurance that products are caught or farmed legally, sustainably, and ethically. . . [and] use their individual and collective power to drive change wherever [the product] is sold.

Though the INGO referred to both individual and collective consumer power, it was not advising collective action or boycotts; rather, it was suggesting collective power as an aggregate of individual actions. If enough individuals ask restaurants where their food comes from, perhaps they will choose to change their buying practices.

Other INGOs also shied away from the idea of consumer boycotts. One in the United States, for example, suggested rewarding "good" companies with consumer purchases rather than punishing the "bad" ones. They highlighted what they deemed to be a "good" confectionary company in their newsletter:

> We often speak about using our consumer power to hold companies accountable for ensuring their supply chains are free of slave labor. Equally important is to uplift those businesses that are working hard to clean up their supply chains AND that disseminate their efforts to their consumers. Read about [this confectionary company] and if you are impressed, pick up some of their chocolate at a nearby store!

The appeals above are aimed at individual consumers and individual actions rather than couching them as part of coordinated consumer campaigns or tying them to social movements or collective action (Limoncelli 2020). Individual consumers are supposed to communicate expectations to businesses, demand that they trace their products, monitor their practices, pressure them for action, ensure their accountability, and reward them when they respond.

In this sense, consumption strategies function as a way for INGOs to eschew responsibility as corporate watchdogs. It is no longer civil society groups that have a clear mission to ensure that businesses act to address labor exploitation. Sociologists Appelbaum and Lichtenstein (2016) have argued that, with governments largely absent from the regulatory model overseeing global supply chains, oversight is left to brands, their contract factories, and nonprofits in Western countries. With the shift to consumption-based and market strategies, however, one may ask whether INGOs are still part of that triangle. INGOs seem increasingly oriented toward supporting businesses perpetuating unfree labor rather than challenging them.

CONCLUSION

In part due to funding potential, but also due to their embrace of the market-based "anti-slavery strategies," INGOs have been increasingly moving toward partnerships with businesses and away from "naming and

shaming" them. Yet these partnerships potentially compromise the autonomy of the nonprofits and limit their ability to challenge the business
practices of their partners in the commercial sector (Baur and Schmitz
2011). This has important implications for advocacy INGOs and for the
"anti-slavery" field. Consider the experiences of one interviewee who had
moved from being an activist to working for a business-led anti-trafficking
nonprofit to becoming an employee working on sustainability issues at a
multinational corporation:

> . . . when I was in college. . . I was protesting Nike, Gap, all the sweatshop,
> anti-sweatshop campaigns. I was part of the Worker Rights Consortium
> when that started, and I always thought that campaigners and activist
> organizations never really had much of an impact. Like, it sort of felt like
> you're just yelling and screaming at these companies, and maybe they're
> listening, maybe they're not, but at the end of the day, you're never really
> working on tangible issues. And so, I felt like with [business-led non-
> profits], it was a good step to get in there and actively start working with
> people in these companies, so they had a name and a face and they wanted
> to do good.

The interviewee, at that point, was convinced that he could work from the
inside to help companies address issues of "modern slavery" as part of their
CSR efforts. This he had proceeded to do, but his experiences as an insider
led him to change his mind:

> However, over the past eight years I have become much more aware of the
> impact that the outside activist organizations have, to the point where I
> don't think that any organizations like [the business-led nonprofit] or the
> [corporate CSR] job that I have right now, if Oxfam or Amnesty Interna-
> tional or Human Rights Watch or the Worker Rights Consortium, if they all
> disappeared, I would be out of a job in a day. They are putting an enormous
> amount of pressure on companies, [and] they don't always see the impact
> of what they're achieving. . . if I could do another iteration of my career,
> I'd probably want to go to one of those organizations and push companies
> harder. So, not work with them, but actually say, "We're not going to toler-
> ate anything less than you paying a living wage to all of your employees,
> and ensuring all the companies you work with are paying a living wage,
> full stop."

His story encapsulates the importance of advocacy INGOs and their "watchdog" roles as outsiders.

The shifting role of INGOs has them thinking about ways to be of benefit to their business constituents and has lead them to embrace business-friendly strategies that actually do little to challenge the existing practices of companies. As we will see in the next chapter, it has also led INGOs to partner with businesses in technological initiatives to address "modern slavery," with web-based platforms, apps, software programs, and other technological projects promoted as easy solutions to the complex problems of "modern slavery."

Four

TECHNOLOGICAL "FIXES" FOR COMPLEX PROBLEMS

Business engagement is essential in the global fight against modern slavery.... They bring a fantastic amount of technical expertise, in addition to huge clout. Technology offers transformational potential not just to disrupt and reduce modern slavery, but to support care and remedy mechanisms for survivors. We look forward to working together in partnership in the fight to end slavery for good.

—Testimonial from an INGO website in support of a business-led technology initiative to fight human trafficking

The business-friendly strategies that have been embraced in the "anti-slavery" movement have included an increasing focus on new technologies to fight exploitation, using what scholars Musto and boyd (2014) have called the "4As" of the trafficking-technology nexus: awareness of online sites assumed to promote human trafficking, amassment of data, augmentation of traditional surveillance techniques and tools, and automated or algorithmic techniques. Along with IGO and business proponents of technology-based strategies, newer INGOs in the "anti-slavery" field, especially, are embracing the technological turn. The words in the epigraph above, which were written to support a business-led initiative developed during the course of this study, shows the enthusiasm for technological approaches to "anti-slavery" efforts, much like what has been happening in other advocacy fields. Sociologists Dale and Kyle (2016), for example, call attention to "smart humanitarianism" relying on online technologies, apps, and expert systems management strategies, and there is an extensive amount of scholarship on technology in the field of international development (Fejerskov 2017; Iazzolino and Stremlau 2024; Cherlet 2014).

There are important social implications to consider about technological "fixes" in "anti-slavery" advocacy, including questions about the ways that they may be reinforcing or challenging power, as well as whether and how they actually work to ameliorate the problems they seek to address (Musto, Thakor, and Gerasimov 2020). This chapter critically analyzes technological initiatives touted by businesses and INGOs in "anti-slavery" advocacy. They are like other business-friendly strategies in that they are often based on criminal justice and market-friendly framings of labor exploitation. They tend to reinforce simplified notions of unfree labor that can create more problems than they solve, such as increasing surveillance of workers or the public, and they rarely include workers or labor groups as partners in their development.

Some may also be more adept at creating new products and marketing angles for companies and INGOs than actually addressing processes of labor exploitation, something that is especially problematic when they have little accountability for the harms that could come from their efforts. Even where technological innovation is leading to tools that could be used to fight issues of "modern slavery" in supply chains, the social conditions in which they are implemented and the possible misuse or unintended consequences of the tools have yet to be explored. When INGOs uncritically accept technology-based solutions, they again defer to companies' supposed expertise in "solving" complex problems and divert their efforts into initiatives that do little to hold businesses accountable for unfree labor or change the structures perpetuating it.

DOUBLE-EDGED DISCOURSES ABOUT TECHNOLOGY

In discourses about issues of "modern slavery," technology is often presented in a circular manner, as a tool that people use to perpetuate exploitation *and* the solution to fixing problems (Milivojevic, Moore, and Segrave

2020; Thakor and boyd 2013). Starting from the idea that issues of "modern slavery" are criminal matters, technology is said to enable perpetrators to commit crimes. For example, the Inter-Agency Coordination Group against Trafficking in Persons (ICAT), which is a policy forum that seeks to improve coordination among United Nations agencies fighting human trafficking, has released a statement and issue brief on technology. It points out that traffickers harness technology to hide identities and increase anonymity online; facilitate recruitment and exploitation of individuals; advertise people being trafficked online to attract customers and develop markets; and expand the means by which people may be controlled and exploited (Inter-Agency Coordination Group Against Trafficking in Persons 2019).

Traffickers are thought to use technology at every stage of the trafficking process, from recruitment and control of individuals to reaping the profits of their activities. They are said to use rapid technological changes as opportunities to adapt their methods, evade detection, and perpetuate crime in secret (Inter-Agency Coordination Group Against Trafficking in Persons 2022). Similarly, an IOM video on technology and human trafficking explains, "It's very clear that criminals are using technology, information technology, far more efficiently and more often than we are in responding." The video goes on to explain that "social media, the dark net, and mobile phones have given traffickers powerful tools to recruit, advertise, and organize. . ."[1]

Technology has at the same time been positioned as the solution to "modern slavery." ICAT, for example, highlights the opportunities that technology has to strengthen the response to trafficking in persons and improve intelligence collection, investigations, and awareness raising (Inter-Agency Coordination Group Against Trafficking in Persons 2022). It focuses on the "positive use" of technology, for example, for data analysis and easier monitoring of online activities; blockchain for tracing goods from source to destination; artificial intelligence (AI) and machine learning to target potential users of services provided by people who have been trafficked, identify exploited people and their locations, or find human trafficking networks; facial recognition for finding people in situations of exploitation; and technological tools for outreach, interviewing people who have been exploited, and teaching new job skills.[2] Likewise, the MSI Alliance 8.7 has sought to advance knowledge of computational science and

AI and machine learning to address issues of "modern slavery." It has held a conference exploring technological strategies such as using AI to find people in trafficking situations, assist in high-precision vulnerability mapping, and mine government data.[3]

A TECHNOLOGICAL TURN

IGOs and businesses have both been keen to explore and promote technological approaches to fighting issues of "modern slavery." For their part, IGOs have supported technology-focused business/IGO and business/civil society collaborations as well as specific initiatives. For example, the Organization for Security and Co-operation in Europe (OSCE) Office of the Special Representative and Co-ordinator for Combating Trafficking in Human Beings has worked with a coalition of companies, Tech Against Trafficking, to analyze technological tools for fighting trafficking. Now part of the Global Business Coalition Against Human Trafficking (GBCAT), Tech Against Trafficking was co-founded in 2018 by Microsoft, BT, and Nokia, and now includes members such as Amazon, Google, and Meta (OSCE Office of the Special Representative and Co-ordinator for Combating Trafficking in Human Beings and Tech Against Trafficking 2020).[4]

In addition, the IOM has partnered with Microsoft on a project to allow sharing of survivor data through a global portal to help with counter-trafficking interventions.[5] IOM has also helped to develop the online Interactive Map for Business of Anti-Human Trafficking Organizations in conjunction with GBCAT, the UN Global Compact, and other organizations.[6] It is a resource that lists initiatives and organizations partnering with the private sector to combat issues of "modern slavery."

Private sector companies are also leading the way in developing technological tools, both on their own and in partnership with IGOs or INGOs. Of the 305 technology tools analyzed in the OSCE and Tech Against Trafficking report, for example, 40 percent were developed by companies and 33 percent by nonprofits, charities, public interest organizations, or foundations with the support of companies (OSCE Office of the Special Representative and Co-ordinator for Combating Trafficking in Human Beings and Tech Against Trafficking 2020, 8).

States have also funded technology initiatives, though their involvement has been more limited (OSCE Office of the Special Representative and Co-ordinator for Combating Trafficking in Human Beings and Tech Against Trafficking 2020). That may be changing, at least in the United States, where the federal government has incorporated technology into its 2021 National Action Plan to Combat Human Trafficking, which calls for expanded partnerships with technology companies to investigate and prosecute human trafficking, data sharing with technology companies, and developing tools to address barriers to voluntary reporting of human trafficking and demand.[7] In the EU too, funding for technology projects has been increasing, and the majority of recipients, unlike for other EU "anti-slavery" funding, are broad partnerships of private companies, think tanks, public bodies, or universities rather than particular INGOs (Rossoni 2024, 112).

The annual United States *Trafficking in Persons* reports also show a recent focus on technology. The reports rarely mentioned technology prior to 2021, but that year discussed it as a factor in increased online sexual exploitation and trafficking during the pandemic. Technology was also said to be providing innovations for anti-trafficking efforts; the 2021 report mentioned online communication platforms as a means of continuing to support people who had been in trafficking situations and maintain communication between anti-trafficking stakeholders despite the restrictions on in-person contact during the pandemic (United States Department of State Office to Monitor and Combat Trafficking in Persons 2021). By 2023, the report was highlighting the OSCE and Tech Against Trafficking Initiative and discussing the need to leverage technology and promote partnerships to raise awareness, detect predatory behavior in online platforms, and identify and provide assistance to people in trafficking situations (United States Department of State Office to Monitor and Combat Trafficking in Persons 2023).

TYPES OF TECHNOLOGICAL APPROACHES TO ADDRESSING "MODERN SLAVERY"

The exponentially increasing array of technological initiatives purporting to address issues of "modern slavery" have catchy names like Traffic Jam; Be Free Text Line; Freedom! App; Safe App; End Slavery App; Slave Free Trade App; Stop App; Threat Nix; Traffick Cam; and Zero Abuse AI.

They range from those that take existing "anti-slavery" strategies and dig-
itize them to ones that purport to innovate entirely new approaches (OSCE
Office of the Special Representative and Co-ordinator for Combating Trafficking in Human Beings and Tech Against Trafficking 2020; Mendel and
Sharapov 2020).[8] Grouping technological initiatives by their intended use,
they most often fall into one of the following categories:

Awareness and Outreach: Many initiatives are for public awareness,
education, and outreach. Some INGOs use technology to advertise themselves and their work to the public, with apps functioning like a brochure
or pamphlet for the public to see. They may include information on issues
of "modern slavery," news items, promotional videos, or links to other
organizations, campaigns, and donation sites. Some apps are meant to
provide information about issues of "modern slavery" more broadly and
list resources, such as hotlines or helplines, information on migrant and
worker rights, and references to particular campaigns, organizations, or

Table 4.1: "Anti-Slavery" Technology Initiatives

Type	Examples
Awareness and Outreach	INGO and "modern slavery" information apps; interactive games, stories, and videos
Surveillance and Intelligence	Apps with hotlines; apps for first responders; apps for reporting suspected incidences of "modern slavery;" automated text messages; facial recognition software; camera forensics; AI crawlers; crowdsourced data projects; financial forensics; satellite data projects
Services and Protection	Apps to prove identity; centralized databases/registries of people receiving services; cloud-based case management systems
Ethical Consumption	Ethical consumption apps; chatbots; deterrence websites
CSR/Social Auditing/Global Supply Chains	Supply chain mapping software; risk assessment tools and resources; industry-wide platforms; blockchain initiatives
Worker Input and Exchange	Mobile phone surveys; migrant worker information apps; Yelp-like platforms for reviewing employers; hotlines; chat apps for migrant workers

documentaries. Other apps couch their information within games that can be downloaded to mobile phones and played. These are intended to reach specific audiences such as youth or migrants as a means of prevention and they have the goal of educating users while attempting to garner empathy for those who experience exploitation (O'Brien and Berents 2019; Dale and Kyle 2016).

A popular format for game-related apps involves interactive comic books or stories, with different characters, scenarios, and actions to choose from as the user goes through the storyline. In some, the user is positioned as a person vulnerable to exploitation, and if they pick an action incorrectly, their character experiences unfree labor; in others, the user is a witness and asked to identify red flags in the storyline as they go through it. For example, one app developed by an INGO with an IT services company, and funded by an IGO, allows users to pick from a list of six characters, taking them through an interactive journey. If you pick Kate, age twenty-two, a medical school graduate student looking for a job as a nurse, the storyline explains that you spoke with a woman who can link you to a job in another country. The hospital will provide language courses, but you have to decide right away. Your choice: accept or ask the woman for another day to decide. If you wait, the app responds "Good choice! You avoided ending up in a trafficking ring." If you accept, the storyline takes you to the airport and then to a family household where you are told you will stay until you get your work permit. If you then refuse to give the intermediary your passport, you wake up with a headache and find your documents missing. The app tells you "You become a victim of domestic servitude" and your character is shown scrubbing a floor. If you try to escape or ask a neighbor for help, the police treat you as a criminal and deport you even though you show them your bruises. You go back home disappointed because there is nothing you can do to get justice.

The interactive component of initiatives such as these is a central feature, with technology helping to place users in the center of the story and virtually simulate the experience of exploitation. For example, there has been an online immersive video developed with the collaboration of a major tech firm and "anti-slavery" INGOs; the video, which is about child sex trafficking, shows the viewer what is presumably a prison-like brothel room, filthy and dark, with a soiled mattress on a platform as the sole furnishing.

The words of those who have been exploited are read aloud in multiple languages describing their experiences. Viewers are asked to click the screen to move around within the space, before being transported into a bright, airy children's room with colorful bunk beds, desks, bookcases, toys, artwork, a sofa and table, curtains, rugs, and plants, which children are presumed to experience after being rescued. In this way, viewers are asked to project themselves into a scenario highly improbable in their real lives and engage in reflexive contemplation of a scene of suffering that at the same time distances them from the sufferers (Chouliaraki 2006, 174–175).

Surveillance and Intelligence: Some technology initiatives take the form of hotlines or apps that are intended to be used for reporting and collecting data on "modern slavery" incidences; such apps ask users to report suspicious activity to helplines, law enforcement, and/or civil society groups. Other apps are intended to be used by front-line responders, such as authorities or staff of nonprofits involved in investigations and rescue operations, to help them communicate with people being exploited. Front-line responders are supposed to give their phones to people in vulnerable situations, and using the app, bridge language divides, work with a common understanding of the indicators of human trafficking that are listed, and help them to self-identify and seek help.

Technology is also being used with the intent to target people vulnerable to "modern slavery" before they actually experience exploitation or to help rescue them by using targeted outreach to people involved in the sex trade, sending text messages to accounts where sexual services are being sold online. Some companies selling "smart jewelry" for women are also aimed at rescue; the wearers can press a button on the jewelry to alert emergency contacts that they need help. While the jewelry is mainly intended to help women in situations of stalking and sexual assault, at least one company has advertised it as a means of avoiding sex trafficking.

There are also a variety of initiatives using technology to support law enforcement investigations of sex trafficking. These include facial recognition software programs that scan people in social media and online sex industry ads to identify people in situations of exploitation; camera forensics that provide the ability to look for photos taken with the same camera; financial forensics to look for potential transactions that could indicate trafficking; software, search engines, and AI to look for images indicating exploitation on the dark web; application programming interfaces to allow data sharing among law enforcement groups at national and international levels; and crowdsourced data projects, such as an app allowing people to take photographs of their hotel rooms so that law enforcement can match them to online photos of people in situations of sex trafficking. There are also efforts to use satellite data to help map and track worksites, such as brick kilns and fishing camps, where forced labor is often found (Boyd et al. 2018).

Services and Protection: Technology initiatives to support service provision for people who have experienced issues of "modern slavery" include apps that have the goal of allowing people to prove their identity on their mobile phones; platforms to crawl websites to find images and videos of people who have been in sex trafficking situations and want host providers to remove the material; centralized databases/registries to keep track of people receiving services during rehabilitation and allow relevant stakeholders to see details about each case; and cloud-based case management systems that allow nonprofits to store, share, and analyze their case records, in the process providing data that can theoretically be used to identify trafficking trends.

Ethical Consumption: There are a number of initiatives that use technology to work on the demand side of issues of "modern slavery," educating consumers about ethical consumption (Page 2017). These often take the form of apps or websites that provide consumers with information about and/or ratings of major brands or their products with the hope that buyers will make conscientious purchases to reward "good" companies and avoid those that are benefiting from labor exploitation (Limoncelli 2020). Some include scanners for consumers to use, both to add individual products to the app's databases and to look up information on them. Technological initiatives have attempted to reach potential clients of the sex industry as well, with advertisements targeted to those searching online for sex; chatbots that simulate a person being trafficked for sexual exploitation via text messages; and deterrence websites that illustrate sex trafficking harms.

CSR/Social Auditing/Global Supply Chains: A variety of initiatives are aimed at helping businesses with their global supply chains. These include things such as software and other tools for mapping supply chains, assessing risks, and audit compliance; databases of anti-trafficking organizations and initiatives as a resource for companies; platforms to centralize and coordinate assessment when multiple buyers use one supplier; and websites or apps with resources such as guidelines, reports, case studies, and/or checklists to help companies comply with legal requirements. AI is a central feature of many initiatives, for example, some use it to gather information from online sources such as government, news, and social media webpages to purportedly identify risks to companies quickly. There are also initiatives to use blockchain for tracking products in global supply chains, using peer-to-peer networks of records that will allow materials (e.g., coffee, beef, fish, or minerals) to be followed from the site of extraction or production to purchase.

Worker Input and Exchange: Worker surveys and grievance tools available on mobile phones are popular initiatives, aiming to provide new mechanisms for worker voice and exchange in global supply chains (Rende Taylor and Shih 2019). One tool, for example, administers surveys about human trafficking, child labor, and forced labor to workers via SMS, interactive voice responses, and a mobile app, at no cost to them. There are also apps to help migrant workers share information in their own languages, setting up Yelp-like platforms for them to provide reviews and ratings of employers or recruitment agencies, and to access information about laws and migrant worker rights. There are also twenty-four-hour multilingual hotlines, social media channels, and chat apps for migrant worker communication. Finally, there are online platforms for centralizing and coordinating labor complaints and efforts to ensure that wifi is available to workers in isolated sites so that they can communicate when there are problems.

"ANTI-SLAVERY" INGOS AND TECHNOLOGY

The INGOs in this study were broaching technological initiatives in diverse ways, and their collaborations with companies were also varied. Sometimes companies provided staff or services to work with the INGO in an in-kind arrangement; other times, funders supported technology initiatives with the resources going to INGOs or MSIs. Some older, more established INGOs were using technology to support the INGO's existing activities, such as digitizing records or recording webinars or videos to reach more of the public. Some of the newer INGOs were embracing more extensive technological projects or even building an organizational brand around technological

innovation. Those INGOs were mainly working on surveillance or CSR/
supply chain strategies rather than technological tools for worker input or
empowerment.

Surveillance and Intelligence: In terms of surveillance, more than one
INGO was working on mobile phone apps for users to report suspected
trafficking cases. Invoking the idea of a *user-hero* by suggesting that "technology places the power to prevent into the hand of a person who holds a
mobile device," one INGO touted its app's potential benefit for intelligence
gathering. The interviewee from that organization explained:

> We've got such a large movement of people and such a massive connection
> on social media. If we can get those people to adopt the app and learn how
> to spot the signs in their communities and start telling other people how to
> use it, and they start putting bits of jigsaw puzzle pieces of information in,
> we can add it to all the different data sets that we've been given by other
> partner organizations.

The understanding was that the app's reporting information, along with
publicly available data collected by the INGO, would allow it to identify
trafficking trends more easily. The INGO's partnership with a multinational
technology company provided credibility for the project:

> We've been [a large tech company's] partner. They've given us database
> storage in their cloud. They've trained analysts for us. . . . We're in the pro-
> cess of gathering data now from lots of different places to then start analyz-
> ing it. The idea is to be able then to send back out to communities, "Did you
> know this is happening in this area? Let's have a conversation about what
> we can create together to prevent this from happening. . . ." [It's about] how
> do we use technology because that's the biggest growing tool, and traffick-
> ers are using it for their own purposes. How do we turn it on its head and
> use it for our purposes to stop trafficking?

The focus on surveillance was tied to both intelligence for fighting crime
and community engagement in the process.

For this INGO, trafficking was a technical problem, a data gap that could
be solved by sharing information to build a picture of the trends, hotspots,
routes, and networks of human traffickers on a global scale. Their website
explained:

Through innovative technology we are changing the environment to be high-risk and low-profit for traffickers and equipping people in communities to become more resilient. The future is predictive. Data sharing will determine more routes, trends, and hotspots. Technology will predict the next vulnerabilities before they happen.

The INGO claimed that its intelligence was helping to systemically disrupt and prevent human trafficking and "modern slavery" around the world.

An emphasis on surveillance apps and big data is very much in keeping with a criminalization perspective, positioning the INGO and their initiatives as intelligence "hubs" and "centers" that can act as information service providers to governments and businesses. The interviewee explained the origin of their technology focus:

This has come out of a partnership that we developed with a serious [national] crime agency back I think in 2009. . . .Through that, we've developed some really close links with people in levels of enforcement who work in human intelligence working in data and analytics.

Language on the INGO's website even mimics that of law enforcement: "Our intelligence specialists assess and corroborate intelligence from multiple sources and channels to produce actionable intelligence to degrade trafficking routes and hotspots."

Awareness and Outreach: Aside from technology-facilitated surveillance initiatives, some INGOs were applying technology to their outreach efforts. A number of them were engaged in targeted information campaigns for different at-risk groups. One INGO had a project to provide targeted spots on social media to youth in refugee situations. Another was sending mobile phone messages to people in a South Asian country's rural communities to inform them about bonded labor, relevant legislation, government rehabilitation programs, migration risks and tips, and information about the INGO's local partner. A third INGO had worked with a developer on a mobile phone app for migrants from sub-Saharan African countries. It provided information and advice in multiple languages about their legal rights in the recruitment process and in a dozen destination countries.

Those using technology for outreach saw it as an efficient and cost-saving tool. For example, one INGO interviewee explained that, instead of spending $20,000 on a billboard that may not be seen by the right people, his organization was working with a technology company partner to focus their efforts:

> With [the tech company] we can run all these ads at the same time. First [they] will optimize and say, "This is the ad that people want to look at more and they're clicking into more and we'll just put the money over there." They'll count the clicks, the impressions. . . . With the video ads, they can do that—how long people play the video, how many people engage at that volume on it, and things like that. They will, if we put all of them in the same ad budget, just shift the money towards the one that is the most engaging.

The technology company gauges how well the ads are being received and targets them accordingly.

This United States-based nonprofit, with a director who had previously worked in the technology sector, was also developing its outreach with a clear criminalization focus. It targeted three different groups: people vulnerable to sex trafficking, potential traffickers, and potential buyers of commercial sex services. First, it used software to search for phone numbers in paid sex ads and send text messages offering exit services to people in the commercial sex sector. As the director explained to me in our interview:

> Outreach to at-risk populations is extremely challenging and has a low response rate. Our efforts with text messages have produced over, I think it's now 130 positive interactions with twenty-four people leaving exploitative commercial sex situations, from getting text messages. . . . That's in less than a year. . . . That was really just connecting the dots of, "How do you reach people and what are the systems and how do business people reach out to people like that?". . . . That is us facilitating a technology need on behalf of a service provider to get people out of trafficking situations. That's incredibly powerful.

The organization was developing their projects with both a technology focus and a business mindset, assuming that the techniques and strategies used by marketing companies to advertise products and services would work just as well for outreach to those at risk of exploitation in the commercial sex trade. Here we see, again, the belief that issues of "modern slavery" can be efficiently addressed with technology.

Second, the nonprofit was seeking to address the demand side of the commercial sex sector by setting up a chatbot to conduct automated conversations with potential buyers who respond to fake ads. While the potential buyer is in unwitting "conversation" with the chatbot, it searches for information about them, such as their name and zip code, based on the phone number they are using. The potential buyer is then sent a deterrence message telling them that their information may be given to law enforcement and directing them to websites for survivors of the commercial sex industry and for sexual addiction therapists. While it is not clear that buyers' information was actually given to law enforcement, the deterrence messages *were* being sent at the time of the interview, and the nonprofit claimed that it had interacted with 1,000 people a year later.

Third, the nonprofit was piloting a project with two large technology companies to identify would-be traffickers and target information to them. The director explained:

> . . . it allows us to test out messaging to prevent exploitation for both labor and sex trafficking and target populations with an alarming level of accuracy within the trends of people there. We create look-a-like profiles based on people who we know are traffickers or know are sex buyers. We target advertising and sort of behavioral psychology nudges towards those people who are engaged in social media. . . . We're doing it with [a second tech company] as well, but the targeting is a little bit less accurate. [The first tech company] has a creepy amount of information about people and can really figure out not just what shoes you might want, but when you're going to want them and what color. . .

He went on to detail the process by providing an example:

> Let's say that we have a profile of people who would be exploiting people in restaurant work, so these are restaurant managers. We can get a set of data on who restaurant managers are, and just professional networks, [from professional social media sites], profiles, or things like that. We can put all of their information as a profile into [a social media platform] and say, "Hey [tech company #1], tell us. . . who are the people who are like these people? Like if you were going to generate a profile, give us an audience with 1 percent accuracy, of people who are most like these people who are in [the area]" and [tech company #1] will be like, "Okay. It's these 5,000 people." Then we can run whatever ad to them is influential.

Once the audience is identified, the technology company will run targeted ads. As he explained:

> We work with behavioral psychologists on what are the things that get people to exploit other people less and be less violent to them and to be more respectful and more compassionate to them. It costs about a penny every time we run the ad. So if we've got 5,000 people and we spend $5,000, we can run 100 ads to each one of those people, which is enough to make them think differently, and even if that's not one of the people who would be exploiting someone, they're going to be in the sphere of influence around the people who do because they interact with the other managers and they have the other business settings.

In its initiatives, this nonprofit was engaged in activities that raise numerous concerns about the ways technology may be used to impinge on people's freedom, allowing INGOs and technology companies to see, sort, analyze, and target people (Musto and boyd 2014). It raises questions about potentially expanding categories of criminality (e.g., is one guilty of a crime if they respond to a chatbot?) and the ways technology can be used to reinforce expectations about which individuals are most likely to offend. It also raises concerns about the racial and class-based aspects of these processes, since it is often people of lower socioeconomic status and people of color who are involved in migrant work and the commercial sex trade and so they are likely to be disproportionately targeted (Musto and boyd 2014).

CSR/Social Auditing/Global Supply Chains: Some of the INGOs I interviewed were using technology to help businesses assess and address risks in global supply chains, highlighting cloud-based platforms for data sharing, software, and websites with resources to support supply chain monitoring and assessment. Mapping technology was also popular, used to geo-spatially organize forced labor and human trafficking cases, "anti-slavery" organizations, suppliers, and auditing information. An interviewee at one INGO that conducts audits as part of its work, for example, said:

> We have a new project where we are actually digitizing our inspections data collection filing because it's all on paper. We have a lot of paper. We'll have a geo-tacking feature that we can use. Right now, our inspectors, it's mostly in their heads. A lot of these guys have been there almost twenty years as well. They just know the sector. They know who people are. They know who

is connected to whom. Now we are going to actually be able to lay it out on a map, the web of who is supplying whom and how it changes over time.

This INGO was using technology to help make the system more efficient. They were also taking a careful and stepwise approach with the hope of future data sharing:

> It would be great to be able to feed our information, whether it's the ILO or to the local government or the labor inspectorate, or whatever. Then also do some really good analytics, because I think we'll have a lot of raw data coming out of the system but it's still going to be a lot of work to get it to a point where we can then use it to be more strategic about our programming. We're trying to understand things like migration patterns and just where to invest, where do the worker communities have the highest risks and where could we better invest our program dollars.

In this case, technology was envisioned as a means of improving INGO operations and helping government and IGO partners.

Data sharing platforms were also being promoted, along with initiatives to recruit business members who will input data on suppliers so as to identify shared risks. As the CEO of one INGO explained in his interview:

> So obviously we do a great deal around labor recruitment issues, and basically the deal with [our project] is it's an opportunity to do a couple of things. One is essentially map[ping] the labor supply chain. . . what it's really all about is. . . how those farms and factories are doing with labor recruiters. A lot of that is still at the stage of mapping that is, literally, like doing their family tree. . . but also build on information that other companies are getting. Almost like the 23andMe databases, where companies can put in information. They don't know who else is putting in the information, so it's not an antitrust violation. They keep their privacy, but if they're digging up information on a particular recruiter and another company is digging up some additional, they can share that information.

He went on to explain the difference between the organization's platform compared to others:

> So there are other platforms out there that. . . enable companies to share audit data on facilities. This is essentially enabling companies to share information about risk on the labor recruiters. What's interesting about it,

is sharing audits, you're stuck within your sector because an electronics company wouldn't share an audit with a palm oil company, but they very likely do share the same recruiters. . . the same recruitment firm may be sending people from Bangladesh to an electronic factory and to palm oil facilities in Malaysia, for example. So this enables them to get that information but then also get a lot of information both about the recruitment agencies and how the suppliers are dealing or not effectively dealing with those recruiters. . .

Once companies have more information, they choose what to do with it:

They subscribe to [the platform] and then we work out with them which of their suppliers will go through the system, which is basically us gathering a lot of information about them and their neighbor recruiters, and that's put into the platform. The subscribers can then see [on their dashboard] how things are stacking up for their suppliers and the recruiters that are associated with those suppliers, including the data that's coming in on those recruiters from other companies. . . then they can say this one's really bad and other companies are also digging up bad information on them. . . . So, we now have to decide how to spend our budget on this and where we're going to do special investigations or extra work or tighten the screws on our suppliers.

Again, in this case, technology was being integrated into the ongoing activities of the INGO rather than being seen as a panacea. Yet it was not challenging existing practices of supply chains, either; rather, it was meant to help the INGO help companies to identify specific problematic suppliers.

Other INGOs had much higher ambitions, seeing new technologies as "game changers." One, for example, marketed its cloud-based platform this way:

. . . you will gain access to the largest global dataset of modern slavery and human trafficking data, regular intelligence publications authored by our team of intelligence analysts, and pioneering artificial intelligence and machine learning technologies. With all of this, your operations can be data-driven, highly effective, and more impactful—as well as making you a pioneer of change in your sector.

This INGO suggested that technology could solve human trafficking, claiming that it can "ensure that exploitation is denied access to your organization."

Only one INGO, based in the United States, expressed interest in the ways technology could be directly used for workers, to empower them to organize and press for labor rights. On its website, the INGO states:

> We see workers building and using technology to facilitate transnational communication and organizing, pushing back on technology purely as a tool of surveillance and control.

This INGO placed these developments within the context of "labor and social movements strategically prying open the cracks in neoliberal models of racialized capitalism." It had only been involved in one other technological initiative—an ethical consumption app developed by another INGO— but it had become interested in the use of technology initiatives to provide communication for workers on fishing boats at sea.

Unions and labor groups were not typically involved in the technology initiatives described above. Interviewing a representative of one tech-forward "anti-slavery" INGO with a reporting app, for example, I asked whether the staff or leadership had thought about reaching out to unions or other labor groups to collaborate on their technology initiatives or ask about sharing data. The interviewee went silent for a time, then repeated back to me, "Unions?" It was a good example of the way that technological approaches can overlook potential allies in "anti-slavery" efforts. The INGO, which is located in a large city, intends for its reporting app to be used by the public, other nonprofits, and people who are experiencing issues of "modern slavery," yet it had not considered labor groups or unions in hospitality, construction, manufacturing, or agriculture as relevant partners, even though these are common places where labor exploitation occurs and the INGO was already working with companies in these sectors.[9] Nor did the technology company the INGO partnered with on the project consider workers as partners; it has its own history of union busting and is dependent on global supply chains with unfree labor (Humphery and Jordan 2016; Limoncelli 2020).

There are, of course, examples of unions and labor groups involved in technology initiatives. For example, one union interviewee mentioned a website established, managed, and supported by trade unions in Europe. It includes information about the rights of migrant workers, referrals to job matching entities, recognition of qualifications, pre-departure information, trade union rights, rights of migrant family members, and contact information for trade union offices. It also has a search wizard in seven languages to help migrants get in touch with a trade union contact. Some corporate accountability groups are also exploring technology initiatives, such as creating a database of laws and cases as a helpful resource for activists or providing a free online data directory to facilitate connections among people working on the issue.

TECHNOLOGICAL LIMITS

Despite the enthusiasm of some INGOs for technology initiatives, others were more critically minded. An interviewee from a European INGO who had attended IGO meetings with technology companies said:

> So, now you get all the all the tech companies. . . who suddenly feel that they should do work, which on one hand is not bad. It's what we wanted. At the same time, they still don't look at their own exploitation practices. And it's a bit funny, [this technology company] saying that they have a perfect tool to reach out to victims, while you think, "Think about your own supply chain first and work on that."

This interviewee also corroborated the view that newer INGOs were more readily embracing technological strategies compared to established INGOs.

The director of an established INGO in the UK also critiqued technological approaches. He objected to the characterization of "modern slavery" issues as "technical" problems, pushing back on the claims of efficiency and quick fixes:

> I think another thing as well is the idea of a quick fix and saying, "Why hasn't this been fixed before?" Part of the reason it hasn't been fixed before is you don't need new quick fixes; what you need is the old stuff done properly. It's about unionization, it's about education, it's about better placing. It's about real flow in the capacity of courts, it's about holding people who indulge in racism and discrimination to their kind, it's about the whole variety of old stuff which simply hasn't been done adequately in sufficient parts of the world.

He was articulating the importance of existing strategies that have been currently overshadowed in the rush toward technology, especially in relation to international development, and he was lamenting the way historical experience and expertise in the field was being devalued.

His concerns have been echoed by scholars examining particular technology initiatives as well. For example, blockchain initiatives have been criticized for overstating the technology's abilities and separating it from its social context, allowing companies to claim that their supply chains are clean without that actually being the case (Boersma and Nolan 2020; Mehra and Dale 2020). While the records may be secure when they are created, there is no guarantee that they are not produced fraudulently or that workers are actually involved in validating blocks; the real-world political, social, and economic conditions under which blocks are created need to be considered and verified (Boersma and Nolan 2020; Mehra and Dale 2020). Technological approaches do not account for power structures or the mechanisms workers need for the improvement of working conditions and labor rights (Berg, Farbenblum, and Kintominas 2020; Mehra and Dale 2020).

It was not only interviewees at long-established advocacy INGOs who expressed reservations about technological approaches. Surprisingly, an interviewee at a business-led INGO shared his misgivings:

> I think that there's this... it's kind of elusive... that we want to be able to throw an app at one of the most difficult problems in the world and then just, poof, we can press a button and then people are out of trafficking, the same way that we can press a button and it shows us directions across the United States for a road trip, right? Which is also really complicated, but complicated in a different way. And so tech, I think, is struggling to kind of find itself in this space. There's all the goodwill in the world, but is this really a tech problem? Can we really just throw technology at this and expect to have any meaningful impact?

He was also concerned that most technological initiatives were doing little to help with prevention:

> ... when you actually map all this out, most of the technology applications are in trying to figure out how to provide support services to victims who have already become victims. So, linking them with other victims, or here's an app where you can report that trafficking, is happening. But is that really the best we can do?.... Just sort of provide them more services?

It's a start, but the real interesting action is at that front root causes, which are complicated.

An interviewee at an INGO in the United States working on child labor also expressed doubts:

> . . . everyone mobilizes around these things and it just seems like a lot of conferences and meetings and these slavery footprint calculators and this and that. Yeah, technology thrown at it. . . it [also] seems like a lot of factory level auditing happens but very few organizations are really going deep.

Both of these interviewees see technology as being applied to problems of labor exploitation without thoughtful integration into existing strategies, and they are both pushing back at the way technological initiatives claim to simplify and solve complex problems.

An interviewee at an INGO that provides consulting and audits of global supply chains called attention to an additional limitation: a disjuncture between the promise and reality of technological initiatives, including pragmatic problems related to data and methodology:

> . . . many of them [the initiatives] are rehashing a lot of the same information, just presenting it in a new way. . . and obviously, there are a lot of issues around the use of mobile phones as a source of getting information from workers and so on. They can sometimes have a lot of promise to them, but. . . there's always a desire from the companies to get more information in a cheaper way, which isn't necessarily bad, but [they] hope for that kind of a panacea that's something other than an audit, without knowing the limitations to it or really understanding how it looks from a worker's perspective.

Scholars have also noted these problems and underscored the need for developers to be cautious in building technology initiatives to combat unfree labor; this includes being clear about the target audiences for new apps; their goals, functionality, and usability; the feasibility of maintaining them over time; and an assessment of what happens when people use them (Mendel and Sharapov 2020).

An additional pragmatic problem is that the success of many technological initiatives depends on multiple users providing information, whether it is app users reporting cases of trafficking or businesses reporting supplier information. This often fails to happen. One of the INGOs I interviewed, for example, had partnered with a technology company to develop an app for ethical consumption that was not successful. The interviewee explained:

> [We] at one point had an app on the iPhone and Android. . . . So, you can walk into a store and scan a product and [see a message] pop up [that says], "This company does a lot of great work to mitigate its exposure to forced labor in the supply chain." Okay, cool. Well, now a lot of people need to use it. No one did.

The INGO stopped promoting the app and it is no longer available. Similarly, one of the INGOs with a surveillance app mentioned earlier in the chapter hoped to get 100,000 downloads in its first year, but eight years later had only somewhere between 10–50 percent of that goal on a major platform where the app is available. What happens with user generated information is also unclear. Over a nineteen-month period between January 2019 and August 2020, the INGO reported they received a thousand reports but shared them with authorities in only ninety-nine cases. They did not explain the criteria for such decisions nor report what, if anything, resulted from sharing the information with law enforcement.

A lack of users and a paucity of user data already pose formidable difficulties for technology initiatives, but there are others as well. The data that INGOs rely on for their intelligence and assessments can be misleading. For example, one initiative uses AI crawls of news reports to compile incidences of "modern slavery," but this is a highly flawed method that tells us little about the reality of cases. Not only could there be cases that are not identified, but those that do come to light may not be reported in the news or they could be reported on unevenly. Sex trafficking cases may be more consistently reported compared to labor trafficking cases, for example, or cases from one part of a city or country reported on more than others. In addition, when initiatives use methodologies that are based on proxies, they may be conflating different issues (e.g., looking at financial data that suggests money laundering may indicate organized crime operations but may or may not be related to "modern slavery" issues).

Data concerns are also an issue with worker input and exchange apps, websites, and platforms. Scholars and activists see potential when they are developed by, for, and with workers rather than by companies

(Fukushima 2020; Rende Taylor and Shih 2019; Milivojevic, Moore, and Segrave 2020, 30, 32). For example, they have favorably referenced Contratados.org, developed in 2015 by the nonprofit Centro De Los Derechos Del Migrante (CDM). It is a website for migrant workers to share information and employer reviews online, funded by the John D. and Catherine T. MacArthur Foundation and co-designed with Research Action Design, a community-led, worker-owned research, media organizing and technology collective.[10]

Scholars underscore challenges with the quality and quantity of data in many technology initiatives for worker input, however, which are due to the methodologies businesses use and their interest in uncovering risk rather than problematic working conditions and worker exploitation (Berg, Farbenblum, and Kintominas 2020; Rende Taylor and Shih 2019). For example, they may avoid certain topics or frame them in ways that allow only superficial responses, or they may employ tools that do not take into account workers' language needs, literacy levels, or ability to access them, leading to an underrepresentation of some groups of workers.

There are also serious privacy and data sharing concerns across initiatives, including questions about who owns the data, who has access to it, the conditions under which it can be shared, the procedures for safeguarding it, and whether and how it can be monetized. At least one INGO interviewee was unconcerned about these issues, bolstered by the belief that data protection was preventing law enforcement from doing their work:

> I think one of the biggest cultures that we've got to shed is this data protection. . . . It's risk adverse. "Oh, mustn't share data because somebody may get hurt if I share it in a wrong way." But what it already does is it ties people up and it allows exploitation to continue because nobody's sharing information and without that you can't get the picture.

Critical scholars, in contrast, call attention to concerning privacy issues and enhanced surveillance by nonstate actors (Musto and boyd 2014). Technology tools used for targeting, intelligence, and surveillance can end up eroding privacy for wide swathes of people—i.e., any person thought to be "at risk" of issues of "modern slavery." Moreover, it leaves both INGOs and companies free to regulate themselves when it comes to privacy; companies, especially, are able to wield power because consumers are loyal to platforms and trust companies to self-regulate more than they trust governments to regulate them (Culpepper and Thelen 2019).

Consider the example of the reporting app by the tech-forward INGO described earlier. Users report information on a suspected trafficking incident to the INGO and the organization promises not to share unless it has a court order and believes it to be safe and appropriate. The app's privacy policy states that "all exchanges of personal data will be specifically authorized by a competent officer" within the INGO, but there is no clarification about how the officer determines what is "appropriate" or "safe" nor what, if anything, happens if they are wrong or if a staff member abuses their access to the information.

These issues are also relevant for blockchain technology and tools for worker input and exchange. Using blockchain to create a digital and permanent identity for migrants or refugees raises privacy concerns and security risks for them (Mehra and Dale 2020; Walch 2018).[11] Worker input and exchange tools can also lead to harm for workers if they are used to supplant worker organizing or if they allow workers to be individually identified, leading to the risk of reprisals, further coercion, or worse (Berg, Farbenblum, and Kintominas 2020; Wilhelm et al. 2020). Similar concerns have arisen in the sex industry with technology companies' support for "anti-slavery" criminalization approaches. For example, META, Instagram, and X (formerly known as Twitter) have deplatformed and shadow banned people working in the sex industry, claiming that they were weeding out human trafficking, leading to a worsening of conditions for sex workers (Majic, Ditmore, and Li 2024; Musto, Thakor, and Gerasimov 2020; Barton, Brents, and Jones 2024).

One of the unions that I spoke with explained their concern, but also their optimism about technological tools:

> . . . with the development of tech and artificial intelligence and blockchain technology, we're also very wary about how it can be used against workers and unions. We're fully engaged. We're not dinosaurs like people like to call us, but we are also quite wary and skeptical of some of these initiatives. Having said that, we're also in the game in terms of developing apps, to help unions organize members, for example, right? Yeah, we're following all these trends and we do see the scope for, say blockchain technology, to really address some of these issues. For example, when it comes to

commodities or trading of commodities, tracking containers, tracking the transportation of goods, there is a major scope for technology to help.

He went on to stress the importance of labor being involved with tech initiatives and having a role in any context in which technology will affect workers and working conditions:

> We live in a very techno, deterministic world where Silicon Valley has an idea and it's like, oh, it's going to happen. It doesn't have to happen. It should be a policy decision.

He emphasized the importance of ensuring that technology initiatives and tools being worker-driven, just as many scholars working on labor issues, supply chains, and issues of "modern slavery" have suggested (Ford and Nolan 2020; Nolan and Boersma 2019; Berg, Farbenblum, and Kintominas 2020).

TECHNOLOGICAL COOPTATION?

The INGOs that were exceptionally enthusiastic about working with technology companies in some cases framed businesses as their constituents, seemingly operating as business service organizations rather than organizations pressing for the well-being of people at risk or experiencing issues of "modern slavery." Aiming to get businesses to join its cloud-based platform, for example, a video on one INGO website provided a rationale for joining the initiative: it would improve a major technology company's "advanced cognitive technology and ability to hone in and find trouble spots and actually uncover trafficking activity." In this example, the way businesses help to address issues of "modern slavery" is by helping a technology company to improve its AI.

It is clear that the technology company was getting public exposure from this particular initiative. Another video provided by the INGO features the technology company's Chief Marketing Officer saying that the company is involved in preventing human trafficking "because we can and because we must" and because the company "has sought to make the world work better and to change the way the world works." The CEO of the INGO also appears in the video, stating that the technology company gave the INGO the tools to take action and now "I wake up and I have hope." The video ends with a black screen and white letters spelling out #goodtech and the company's name. It is basically an extended commercial and public relations tool for the company.

There is also the issue of whether technology initiatives tend to benefit technology companies more than doing anything of substance to help workers. As one of the more critical INGO interviewees commented, technology companies have issues of "modern slavery" in their own supply chains, from the extraction sites where the raw materials are sourced to the factories where materials are processed and products manufactured to the logistics and transportation of products. Partnering with INGOs and law enforcement to look for potential criminals or help businesses further automate supply chain monitoring for compliance seems to sidestep those problems. The initiatives can also provide a sense that efficient action is taking place when little is actually occurring in practice.

The ownership of technology tools and the impetus for their development also deserve further scrutiny.[12] Some INGOs have sought to move beyond collaborations with technology companies to start their own for-profits selling technology products. One, based in the US, was attempting to develop a company specializing in the identification of child sex trafficking during the course of the research. One of their reports explained:

[The INGO] is incubating a new technology company. . . . The company's world-class engineers built a one-of-its-kind recognition technology to identify online child trafficking rings. These engineers asked us to help them scale their capacity to engage social media platforms. We are conducting due diligence, business development efforts, and recruitment of a U.S.-based leadership team. If successful, this company would have a massive impact on [our] mission to halt the exploitation of children. In addition, it would generate a healthy revenue share to [the INGO] to continue our direct impact work with survivors of trafficking.

The proposed ownership of the new company was not clarified in the document and there were no other mentions of it in the INGO documents, so it is unclear whether the project moved forward. However, at least one other "anti-slavery" nonprofit started by developing an ethical consumption website and app and later developed a for-profit software platform for companies to assess risks in supply chains. The nonprofit is now defunct, but the for-profit company has continued, suggesting that market won out over mission in that particular case.[13]

CONCLUSION

If voluntary market-based strategies are problematic for "anti-slavery" advocacy, so too are the typical technological "fixes" that have been pushed by states, IGOs, and businesses. INGOs have been mixed on technology initiatives, with some enthusiastically embracing them and others more skeptical and concerned that they may raise more problems than they solve. Still, a number of the INGOs have been working with tech companies and partipating in technology-based initiatives.

These efforts can have counterproductive consequences, including privacy concerns and increased surveillance and risks to those that the tools are intended to help (Musto, Thakor, and Gerasimov 2020; Musto and boyd 2014). Labor groups, unions, and people who have experienced or are at risk of "modern slavery" issues are rarely involved in the development of technology tools, which are often designed with the interests of businesses in mind. For the advocacy field, the push for tech solutions can take focus and resources away from other sorts of strategies and measures that involve more difficult and long-term work that has to be done to actually address exploitation.

Technology-based initiatives work in conjunction with criminalization and market-friendly approaches to "anti-slavery" advocacy, simplifying complex issues and replicating the problems repeatedly cited throughout the book. In addition, they raise questions about accountability for the businesses and INGOs that develop, use, and/or sell technology products and services; create the potential for for-profits to channel public resources into private gain; and fail to address the power relations that are leading to exploitation in the first place.

Five

COMMUNICATING LIKE A BUSINESS: BRANDING AND MARKETING "ANTI-SLAVERY" INGOS

Fund a Slavery Rescue Operation. $150+. . . . Help [our INGO] and partners
bring children and families trapped in modern slavery to safety and freedom
—INGO's online "Gift Catalog" aimed at potential donors

The growth of "anti-slavery" advocacy has led to an increasingly crowded field; as one INGO interviewee in Europe remarked, it seems that "suddenly everyone is an expert in human trafficking and human rights risk analysis." The INGOs were navigating this trend by finding niches within the field, specializing, branding, and marketing themselves. This chapter explores these processes by examing how the INGOs represent themselves in their communications to others via their websites, documents, and media content.

The INGOs emphasize their specializations, tout their efficiency with outcomes and statistics designed to show success, and expand their missions or rebrand themselves to pursue funding opportunities and appeal to donors. They provide media-friendly marketing narratives with INGO origin stories that elevate founders to celebrity status. They appeal to donors as heroes, and especially as consumers, as the quote above exemplifies. For some INGOs, people who have experienced unfree labor become marketing tools, as part of their advertising. Coupled with their support for voluntary and consumption-oriented strategies for addressing issues of "modern slavery," INGO communications contribute to the belief that consumers can buy their way to a less exploitative world and reinforce ideas about the efficacy of individual actions and market solutions in addressing issues of "modern slavery."

COMPETITION, COLLABORATION, AND NICHE

Many INGOs routinely collaborated with nonprofits in countries of the global south and/or were part of global or Western anti-trafficking or "modern slavery" networks at the behest of governments, IGOs, or funders, but collaborations between individual INGOs in the global north were more typically ad hoc. As one INGO interviewee in the United States explained:

> . . . one of my colleagues was just saying that it's odd that in the corporate culture, you're always looking for mergers and things. In the NGO culture, it's very territorial.

The co-founder of an INGO in Europe agreed:

> Many non-profits—and I'm not being mindlessly critical, I'm just stating a fact, if you like—I think many non-profits fall into the trap of thinking that activities that are exclusive to themselves and that are all-encompassing within their institutional mandate is the best way to do it. You find in the non-profit sectors there's very often little interest in collaboration as there is in the for-profit sector. Everyone is just [after], you know, the dollar, pound, or Euro, and as part of that function, there's a scramble for airtime and column inches. As part of that, there's an exclusivity that usually comes down from management, but not always.

For both interviewees, the idea that nonprofits seek collaboration for the public good did not match their experience of being in a competitive advocacy field.

Other interviewees, especially in the older, more established INGOs, were more likely to mention nonprofit collaborations positively, but they also had reservations about the growing "anti-slavery" field. For example, the director of a specialized "anti-slavery" INGO in Europe that has a long history said:

> I think part of the reason that we collaborate with each other is because there's an underlying understanding of the political nature of the problem. I think that's the philosophical unity there which makes us able to collaborate with each other more easily, because we're not seeing this as a technical problem. . . . We're saying this is several political issues, and work together with the philosophical piece that brings us together. There's a lot of the new entries that don't really see it like that.

His concern was about a more fragmented advocacy field, with multiple conceptualizations about issues of "modern slavery" in competition as newer INGOs entered. An interviewee at a large INGO in the United States reiterated a similar impression, referencing labor as well as sex trafficking:

> It's like every single day there are ten more trafficking organizations. . . . And what I see in the advocacy world. . . is a lot of it is just like coming down hard, criminalizing, making compelling prostitution a felony, in a way that [our INGO] has really limited stances on.

This interviewee, too, was concerned that divided conceptualizations were leading to divisions between INGOs in the field.

More established INGOs also pointed to several other concerns about the increasingly crowded field. First, they believed that newer INGOs could be ignorant about earlier efforts and likely to repeat past actions. One interviewee in the United States said:

> . . . a lot of US groups now who work on anti-trafficking are looking at supply chain work. For those of us. . . [that]. . . this is the meat of what [we do]. . . . I feel like sometimes it's reinventing the wheel. They're doing things that the anti-sweatshop movement did twenty years ago, thirty years ago. That's a little bit hard and that's where I wish we could have more cooperation. . .

Second, they raised the concern that newer entrants were lacking expertise that established INGOs had. Another interviewee in the United States explained:

I feel like all the sudden everyone and their brother is getting into this issue of slavery in supply chains. It's great that the issue is finally getting more attention, but we're also a little bit cautious sometimes about collaborations because it feels like there is a lot of false solutions all of the sudden out there, where people are claiming to work in the space and not necessarily working in a very deep way.

Another interviewee from a UK INGO put it more bluntly:

There's a lot more new entrants to [the field] and there's some very, very shoddy thinking going on still. . . there's just a lot of neophytes in this, if that's not too pejorative a term, and they are just not engaging in. . . a substantive enough way with people who have got previous experience on this. Consequently, the engagements that they are producing are not optimal.

From the vantage point of this interviewee, new entrants into the "modern slavery" field were lacking the experience, historical knowledge, and expertise necessary for fruitful collaborations.

Third, they worried that, while newer entries could bring innovation to "anti-slavery" advocacy, increased competition without increased funding would be harmful to the field:

I think very often small, new organizations will have a different perspective, and will have both the ambition and the energy to innovate and to think creatively. . . . You need those new players. You have a few colossally large institutional forces there in the non-profit sector, and one or two mid-sized, and a few small little organizations trying to punch their way through. I think it's suffocating. I don't think there's the oxygen for them. What it means is that you get campaigns that join the dots by numbers, you get a whole heap of received wisdom, and you get, going back to this whole thing of money. . . people jostling to get the glory. It's just not productive.

The perspective of this interviewee about competition over funding is supported by recent scholarship that shows increased competition over EU funding from 2014–2020 (Rossoni 2024, 103).

Most of the INGOs sought to distinguish themselves from their peers by specializing. Some INGOs claimed expertise in human trafficking prevention; others emphasized investigation of incidences, services and protection to people who had experienced issues of "modern slavery," rescue, capacity building and legal advocacy, and/or supply chain consulting. Some INGOs focused on specialization even within these categories. For example, one small INGO providing services for people who have experienced issues of "modern slavery" sought to work in geographic areas that were overlooked by larger INGOs, including those that might be considered difficult or dangerous due to their political situations and government regimes.

An interviewee at a large humanitarian INGO in the United States with a human trafficking program provided an example of the process by which they decided on their focus:

> We're a relatively small trafficking team. And so, there was kind of a decision that had to be made like we can't keep doing everything. And so then, when we reflected and were like, "Well, what are we really good at? Where do we have real expertise? What's not being done by others? And then. . . what are our extra kind of gifts or what sets us a little bit apart?" And really, it was the ability to get into immigrant communities because. . . we had that kind of brand recognition of being immigrant-friendly. And so we're like, "Well, let's use that, and take advantage of that, and not try to, in a way, work ourselves into something like the. . . [sex] trafficking arena, where that really isn't where our historic institutional expertise lies."

Some INGOs said that this way of working, with each organization filling a perceived gap in the field, allowed them to exist in a complementary manner.

Smaller organizations might occasionally seek out a partnership with other larger ones, emphasizing the different roles of each. For example, an interviewee from a small INGO in the United States that excelled in legal advocacy for exploited workers said that they were seeking to partner with another larger INGO that aids law enforcement in investigations:

> We are not really playing that role. We're not directly liaising with law enforcement, which is their specialty. So that means our work is complementary.

This supports what political scientists Stroup and Wong (2017) suggest about smaller nonprofits, which is that working with large INGOs can help to ensure survival in terms of ongoing projects, possible funding, and networks of propinquity.

INGOs looking to consult with businesses on supply chains were not just specializing but actively banking on their expertise providing them a niche in the field since transparency laws were being passed in multiple countries. One interviewee explained:

> . . . suddenly there's all these regulations, and companies are supposed to do things in their supply chains, and very few NGOs have the knowledge or insights or the wherewithal or the resources to go up against that challenge.

This particular INGO had expertise on these issues that set them apart from other INGOs.

Another INGO in the United States stressed its differences from others in the field in a way that precluded partnership. Its niche was its market-oriented strategies, including for-profit social enterprise business development. As the CEO explained in our interview:

> I don't think we find cross-collaboration working groups...to be very help-ful. They tend to be positioned from either a very traditional CSR perspec-tive or they're positioned from a strict NGO mindset. As you can tell, I just don't think in the traditional, legal subset silo, like, "I'm a 501(c)3, I'm a fund, I'm a business." I really don't operate that way, and so I don't find it to be really helpful.

This INGO saw itself in competition with for-profits rather than other non-profits, and the CEO did not see the need for collaborations between INGOs on issues of "modern slavery."

RESPONDING TO FUNDER INFLUENCE

Funding organizations influenced opportunities for and attitudes about INGO collaborations. For example, interviewees from a few different INGOs pointed out that when funding was tied to collaboration require-ments, INGOs may end up getting very little out of a contract, especially if there is a main awardee who receives the majority of the funds and then passes through only a small amount to their partner(s). There are also some INGOs that have reputations for being difficult to work with, creating prob-lems and unintended consequences when funders insist on collaboration as a condition of projects. In general, as scholars suggest about INGOs in the

UK and EU, they would like more funds for services, more flexibility in how funding is used, longer-term funding, and more direct funding that is not passed through lead organizations or intermediaries (Sharapov et al. 2024, 114; Rossoni 2024).

Funder influence in the field of "modern slavery" has come from big donors, such as foundations or governments, that can determine the projects that will go forward (Hoff 2014; Suhr 2016; Dottridge 2021). INGOs that rely primarily on donations have some leeway in deciding their activities, but most INGOs have little freedom to ignore big funders.[1] One interviewee from an INGO in the US lamented this:

> . . . especially now that I feel that there is this consolidation of funding too, like with the Freedom Fund and now even Omidyar starting to contribute to the Freedom Fund and seeing, like, The Global Fund to End Slavery. . . it seems like, increasingly, there is this consolidation and then if we're not within that you're really starting to be cut out. And the reasons for being included or not are not clear to me. It doesn't seem to be merit-based. I think that's the issue, and to me, it almost has to come down to connections and networks, and [it is] personal. I think that's the biggest challenge. On the horizon it's consolidation and in having just a few organizations, which ultimately comes down to a few individuals within, maybe a dozen in each organization, that are really calling the shots for a whole movement.

This interviewee is lamenting the outsized leverage that a few people have in "anti-slavery" advocacy as well as the way it undermines a sense of fair competition for resources and influence. Funders pick and choose INGOs to support based on personal connections or networks.

This can also mean that big funders ignore geographic areas that are in need of project support. One INGO interviewee, for example, described his frustration about big funders overlooking South American countries, and Brazil, in particular:

> You had a very proactive government dealing with the issues. . . . You've got a very healthy civil society there, very decent, but for some reason, people don't want to fund it. Talked to [a big funder] about. . . forced labor in bio-fuels in Brazil. We've been talking with [a local nonprofit] about doing a project; we just can't get anybody to fund it. No interest, no, to really grasp what's going on there. There's [also] considerable issues, trafficking

of people in the garment sector from other parts of South America, Argentina for example.

This interviewee also relayed an experience he had at a foundation-sponsored meeting in which the arbitrary nature of funding decisions was on display. The interviewee had encountered the head of another nonprofit attending the event and they had a conversation:

> He says to me, "We just had a meeting in the course of this from one funder who's at this hotel, and they're cutting their funding to us, but they say we really value you, it [the project] can't fall apart, it is very, very important. [He thought, well, then,] it would be nice if you funded us.

The nonprofit that had its funding cut was often mentioned, spontaneously and positively, across my interviews. It is seen by other INGOs as a leader in developing projects and strategies that identify and sanction companies that facilitate forced labor. In comparison to many INGOs dealing with issues of "modern slavery," it has been more strongly geared toward a corporate watchdog role and corporate accountability. In relaying this incident, the interviewee was implying that the INGO's funding was perhaps cut for this reason.

More than a few interviewees questioned the motivations of big funders in the field and expressed concern for INGOs. For example, one commented that:

> I think there's a sense of, "We'd like to displace this lot who've been there before, so we can be the new global forces." I think there's a bit of that going on, and there's not a recognition factor. There's value to some of the older organizations in this [field].

The interviewee later went on to say:

> I suspect, as well, there's a hidden agenda, but certain of them [the funders] just have complete contempt for the nonprofit sector.

This interviewee was referring to private foundations associated with business elites and his sense that nonprofits were under attack.[2]

Whether or not other INGOs agreed with this assessment, they absolutely factored in funder expectations and agendas in their daily work. For example, an interviewee in the UK said:

I think certainly when we started ten years ago there weren't very many organizations who really talked about trafficking. Ten years on, it's like it's saturated. I think there are lots of different organizations doing different things. I think again, [our organization] stands out because it was prevention, that is what we're focused on more than anything. Generally, I think in the UK it's quite difficult for funding anyway. It does make it hard. You've got to be able to show how what you're doing is different to what other people are doing. . . . It's much easier to be able to impact a measure when you're doing the advocacy side. It's quite difficult with prevention.

The pressure to specialize, prove their value in the marketplace of "anti-slavery" organizations, and please funders was first and foremost in many INGO agendas.

Some INGOs had shifted focus or rebranded their activities so as to better appeal to funders. At least one interviewee in the US admitted that her own organization had moved away from the issue of sex trafficking to focus on forced labor and labor trafficking in part because of funding:

. . . there's more money to be made in labor trafficking and it's a bigger problem. It's a larger problem. The criminalization focus means you look for. . . labor brokers that are actually enslaving and abusing workers.

Another described her INGO consciously rebranding their existing activities in order to get funding:

We decided more deliberately to start calling the work we were doing already on eliminating child labor, vulnerabilities to women workers in the informal economy, the migrant worker rights work, to put it under the trafficking umbrella. Part of that was it's been traditionally really hard for us to get funding to do migrant rights work or promotion of migrant rights. When we called it trafficking we got more funding, and that was just unfortunately the situation, but in some ways it was good. I say unfortunately because I think people should fund migrant worker programs directly, but at the same time it allowed us to do a lot of the advocacy and policy work and pushing both the. . . government and [IGOs] to see human trafficking is an issue of forced labor.

The first INGO was actually expanding its organizational focus to follow funding opportunities, while the second was repackaging its existing work to appeal to funders.

At least two of the INGOs were combining claims about organizational efficacy with rebranding efforts by purporting to have solved the problem of sex trafficking. In both cases, the interviewee stated that the INGO ended child sex trafficking in a country where it had been working and moved on to labor trafficking because the organization could not find any more children who needed help. The interviewee from the first organization said:

> . . . you shouldn't keep trying to raise money for things that don't exist anymore. Let's celebrate the victory and let's migrate our mission to where the real need is. And I think it sounds like labor trafficking is still a larger issue there.

The second organization claimed to have a replicable model that other non-profits can use to reduce child sex trafficking; they were marketing it and moving on to issues of labor trafficking and forced labor as well as prevention.

More than one INGO interviewee worried about changing funder priorities and INGOs chasing the "next big thing," jumping from one trend to another:

> . . . something gets a lot of attention and becomes the flavor of the month and everybody comes and jumps in that doesn't necessarily know what they're doing but will get a bunch of funding because it's new or exciting, or it's easier to fund trafficking than it is to fund a labor organization.

Another interviewee mentioned this as well, saying:

> It's a bit hysterical, let's say, or chaos. We always run for something new. We have a convention, we have legislation. And then without waiting for good implementation, we already tried to have new legislation.

Short-term and ad hoc projects and funding can make it difficult for INGOs to maintain a consistent focus on client, community, or social needs, instead leading them to chase new lines of funding. They can also coerce nonprofits into participating in projects that they do not actually support, because they are often called in at the latter stages of program development and asked to implement them. Nonprofits do not tend to say no when they are asked, because they cannot afford to burn bridges or turn down funding (Hoff 2014). At least one INGO CEO I interviewed was clearly pursuing any grant opportunities possible, and it was unclear the degree to which they coincided with their mission or strategic planning. The CEO was unsure what the projects were about, other than that they had to do with human trafficking.

The concern about big funders in the "modern slavery" field goes beyond the impact on INGO funding and survival. Some INGOs are concerned about the corruption of "anti-slavery" efforts and the damage that funders can do in countries of the global south. For example, the director of one INGO in the UK was quite direct about this:

> Bill Gates comes in and knows "fuck all" about development. Walk Free the same. It's fundamentally dangerous.

This is so, he went on to say, because funders move forward with misguided plans that are harmful:

> It's like we will engage with an area for five years and then we go. That is a license to assassinate the entire civil society within the area, because they become over-dependent. This becomes their source of funding. There's no institutional development coming as part of that.

Scholars in various fields and disciplines agree with the assessment of this INGO director, contending that donor-driven projects are particularly harmful to small nonprofits in the global south as well as the global north; they can also lead to a hierarchy of "elite" nonprofits in the global south closely tied to international funding and/or create divisions between organizations at the grassroots level (Roth 2007; Subramaniam 2007; Simpson 2006). Other scholars are more circumspect, suggesting that larger nonprofits within countries of the global south that are subject to donor preferences may be able to resist or negotiate and that they benefit from international support for survival. As one of my interviewees suggested, her global north "anti-slavery" INGO needed their main nonprofit partner in the global south way more than the other way around, since it was large, well-respected, and had multiple funders.[3]

COMMUNICATING EFFICIENCY

Representing themselves to funders, potential donors, and the general public, the INGOs commonly relied on websites as a means of communication. Through their websites, reports, and documents, the INGOs demonstrated their adoption of funder interests as well as business rhetoric and goals. The communications of all of the INGOs, including the smallest, reflect the isomorphism and rationalization that new institutionalist scholars suggest (Boli and Thomas 1999). Their websites emphasize their professionalism and efficiency, and they are standardized; typical subsections include: an introduction to issues of "modern slavery;" the mission and history of the organization; its structure, staffing, and board information; descriptions of its activities, programs, and services; recent news about the organization; and funding and donation information.

Most also had subsections dedicated to providing evidence of their impact or successes, with items such as financial reports, evaluations of their organization, or copies of annual reports showing their activities. The websites and reports are replete with statistics and graphics advertising the INGOs' successes in preventing or resisting issues of "modern slavery." They often quantify the INGO's achievements: the number of people rescued, sheltered, or otherwise provided services; the number of trainings done; the amount of people who were reached with public awareness campaigns; the laws passed; the local NGO partners supported; or the research projects conducted.

One INGO helped "strengthen over 17 anti-slavery movements across 19 projects in 14 countries" and empowered "77,388 people to understand, assert, and claim their rights." Another, stating that their model delivers results, cited "14,000+ people freed from slavery; 650,000+ people in trafficking hot spots reached through awareness raising and rights education to prevent their enslavement; and 300+ traffickers arrested." One INGO focusing on child labor reported:

> [We] have rescued over 6,700 children from labor, provided quality education to almost 26,000 rescued and vulnerable children, and deterred hundreds of thousands of children from entering labor. In 2018 alone, more than 75,000 workers are benefiting from [our] efforts.

In reporting such statistics, the INGOs are engaged in counting activities that are expected as part of monitoring and evaluation, and they are doing so in ways that seek to portray success to funders, donors, and the public (Watkins, Swidler, and Hannan 2012).

In keeping with the increasing move toward providing business services, some INGOs also included statistics related to INGOs' expertise in these areas. One INGO, for example, advertised to potential business clients that "We have risk-mapped over 40,000 suppliers, reached nearly 100,000 people with our bespoke training and workshops, and analysed the supply chains of circa 200 companies." Others emphasized similar metrics or added more: the number of tools developed for risk assessment or the number of audits completed.

Even with the ubiquitous advertisements of their impacts on their websites and in their documents, a number of INGOs mentioned how difficult it was trying to show outcomes and prove their efficacy. One INGO noted on its website that "Not-for-profits now are being held to a level of accountability even more severe than for-profits. And it's harder to demonstrate success." An interviewee at another INGO in the UK concurred with this sentiment, giving a concrete example of how the focus on outcomes can be problematic:

> . . . the impact of certain types of social advocacy is relatively difficult. . . . A lot of our projects use radio programs, and I'm always like, "Well that's wonderful, but how are we going to demonstrate it?" There's the part of your mind that knows that this is a society where radio is really, really important, [but] if you're doing something, say, outreach for domestic workers, how do you know that the radio was on in a given house?. . . [and] if it was on. . . was it being listened to? [And] if it was. . . being listened to, how do you know if it was the domestic worker that was listening to it?

The same interviewee was concerned about funder expectations: "You want us to show a change in a general population that we've funded for two years. It takes twenty! Twenty!" Likewise, an interviewee at an INGO in the United States complained about the difficulty of measuring success and the need to think more long-term:

> . . . so many times people are looking at the number of kids we rescue. We're like, that's not the point. If our model [is] working 100 percent, there would be no kids rescued. . . . We're trying to understand what's the larger change that's happened in the community because we were there. . . trying to engage the whole community around educating the child and raising awareness. All those things are so hard to measure.

Sociologists and other scholars studying nonprofits support these points. They argue that INGOs with broad, long-term, or otherwise difficult-to-measure goals and outcomes can be penalized for not being able to fit their work into simple indicators and quantitative measures; this is especially concerning with regard to advocacy INGOs and/or those working to address relations of power, since such measures do not easily capture all that they do (Walker and Oszkay Febres-Cordero 2020; Baur and Schmitz 2011; Watkins, Swidler, and Hannan 2012).[4]

The focus on demonstrating positive outcomes can also be counterproductive to progress in the field. As one INGO interviewee explained:

> . . . you read the impact and annual reports of all the organizations. . . [and] every single project has succeeded. That is one of the biggest collective lies in history.

The pressure to show success means that INGOs, their annual reports, and even their evaluations avoid discussion of failures that could be instructive in future efforts (Watkins, Swidler, and Hannan 2012; Harkins 2017).

The focus on outcomes can also affect the choice of INGO strategies and actions in ways that are not based on the needs of constituents but instead on the ability to show efficiency. For example, one INGO interviewee in the United States described how the organization has changed its partnerships with nonprofits in the global south:

> We are increasingly moving towards partners that can help us achieve impacts that scale. If you look at the array of partners that we've worked with historically, they've tended to be relatively modest-sized grassroots organizations. And, I want to be clear, I love them, we love them, they're doing God's work, they're great. Inherently, scale is an issue when you're working with [a] small, developing country, grassroots NGOs. . . so we've chosen to seek what we're calling high-impact partners, which are organizations that have a significant infrastructure reaching populations vulnerable to trafficking, but not doing trafficking work, but they may be doing health, schooling, community development, micro-finance or what have you. . . and integrate anti-slavery interventions into their portfolio.

In this case, there is a danger that smaller grassroots nonprofits in the global south are being disadvantaged, excluded from potential resources and collaborations in favor of larger organizations so that the INGO can demonstrate greater impact.

Even IGO interviewees at times complained about funder pressure to show outcomes. One IGO interviewee, for example, pointed out that it can take a long time for a country to pass a law, making it difficult for the organization to show success and to have all the work that they do acknowledged by funders. When the IGO reported on the steps that it was taking to create change, such as conducting workshops or trainings, it seemed "too trivial" and "funders do not understand the amount of work" that went into designing, organizing, and conducting training and all the paperwork and rules and processes that the IGO staff have to go through in order to be transparent.

In critically analyzing the implications of quantification and the emphasis on outcomes in addressing global social problems, scholars have echoed the concerns raised above and outlined others. At the broadest level of critique, they argue that quantification reinforces ideas of social problems as issues to be solved with technocratic expertise, as discussed in chapter 4 (Merry 2016). They also question the way quantification is used in the social construction of "modern slavery"—that is, who is counted or excluded and what that means for people experiencing exploitation. For example, categorizing people as trafficked or not using checklists of indicators has real implications for the types of services and protections that people are afforded (Yea and Chok 2018). For this reason, "anti-slavery" statistics and reports need to be read with attention to who and what is being included or excluded.

Relatedly, there is the problem of INGOs helping clients based on concerns about showing outcomes rather than need. For example, humanitarian relief INGOs may avoid the hardest to serve clients in favor of those who are easy to help, guaranteeing a successful project (Krause 2014). For "anti-slavery" INGOs, this could involve an avoidance of clients who, as we discussed in chapter 1, blur the lines between trafficker/trafficked or whose activities while in the situation of exploitation involved criminal actions. The potential for INGO evidence and reporting to be influenced by funders, political interests, or particular ideologies, means that audiences should carefully evaluate them (Yea 2017; Yea and Chok 2018).

INGO BRANDS AND FOUNDER-CELEBRITIES

In addition to emphasizing their efficiencies, INGOs were branding their organizations with unique logos and color schemes to bolster their public images, market themselves to the public, and assist in obtaining donations and funding. The color choices were often bold: red, yellow, or orange with black, for example, or a United Nations type of blue to signal an INGO's international focus. Logos centered on INGO names or incorporated symbols of freedom such as raised hands, broken chains, or birds; a few included slogans emphasizing these themes. These are meant to help the INGO stand out and promote awareness about them; they communicate to the public what the INGO does and why.

Another way that INGOs communicate their purpose to external audiences is through origin stories that are posted on their websites and communicated in their reports. A number of the INGOs have entrepreneurial origin stories in which a founder suddenly "discovers" issues of "modern slavery" and starts a nonprofit in response. This often happens when they travel to a country of the global south; founders also sometimes become aware of migrants being exploited within their own home countries in some of the origin stories.

One founder discovered labor trafficking at their local restaurant, for example, and another two founders learned about sex trafficking while they were abroad: one was volunteering and came across a teen girl involved in the sex trade, and the other while working as a human rights lawyer. Another INGO founder discovered "modern slavery" while investigating environmental issues in another country. One founder had already started one charity in another country and was running a school there when two of the students went missing and were believed to have been trafficked. There are other examples as well: a writer who met a slavery survivor in another country while on assignment for a news magazine; a journalist investigating the murder of a domestic worker that led him to discover "slavery-like" practices in European countries; two students who were shocked to learn about the conditions at a brothel located near their college apartment. These origin stories suggest that anyone can move into "anti-slavery" advocacy if they wish; you can be a college student, volunteer, or journalist one day and start a successful INGO the next.

In all of these examples, the founders are akin to celebrities who feature prominently on the INGO websites and are part of the brand. The *founder-celebrities* sell books based on their revelations, receive media attention, star in their own promotional videos, give prominent talks, and function as media influencers on topics of "modern slavery." Many INGOs work explicitly toward this. As one interviewee explained, "We did a lot of positioning of [the founder] as a thought leader in corporate social responsibility. And he has another book. . . so we were using that as a mechanism." Written or videotaped testimonials by other individuals who have converted to the cause are often provided on INGO websites to bolster the influence of the INGOs and their founder-celebrities, including ones by other celebrities and elites (Majic 2023; Haynes 2014; Mitchell 2016). The founder-celebrities, to some extent, become the INGO brand.

One can argue that this is just good marketing to make the issues better known and bring resources to the INGOs, but it can also lead to conflicts of interest in which founder-celebrities receive personal monetary or other benefits, and it can lead some to wield an inordinate amount of influence in the advocacy field. The entrepreneurial stories also reinforce the valor of individual awareness, courage, and action, rather than collective or coordinated responses, a parallel to the idea that the cause of "modern slavery" issues is an individual's calculus to exploit other people rather than the political, economic, and social structures that are intertwined to help create conditions for exploitation. It is also the case, as scholars have suggested for media celebrities who become involved in advocacy work, that western INGO founder-celebrities rarely acknowledge their own class, race, or national privilege in telling their stories (Haynes 2014). This feeds into what some scholars have termed a "politics of rescue" in "anti-slavery" advocacy with paternalistic, imperialist, and racist elements imbued; many of the founder-celebrities are well-off, white males (McGrath, Rogaly, and Waite 2022; McGrath and Watson 2018; Beutin 2017, 2023).

DONOR HEROES, SELLERS, AND BUYERS

INGO websites routinely appeal to the public for donations, with some of the more entrepreneurial organizations asking members of the public to be "freedom fighters" or "freedom partners" and to "stand with us against slavery," "give freedom," "join the freedom circle," "join our fight," "end slavery," "send rescue," or "fund a slavery rescue operation." One of the especially enterprising INGOs asks for donations throughout its website, from the running news header on its main page with a request to donate to the pop-up boxes with solicitations on each subsequent webpage that viewers explore.

Donor-heroes are portrayed in videos and written testimonials as fighting issues of "modern slavery" through their giving, sometimes along with other volunteer work. One INGO, for example, has a video series with donors explaining why they "free slaves" through their support, highlighting a teacher, psychologist, historian, musician, actress, and investor, among others. The beginning of each video assures viewers that "We don't free slaves; you do." Each profile centers the donor-hero as the main character, typically introducing them at the beginning, and proffering their personal connection to issues of "modern slavery."

As with INGO founder-celebrity origin stories, the testimonials of the donor-heroes often provide a narrative involving an individual's "discovery" of "modern slavery" followed by individual action such as meeting with the director of the INGO to offer services or donating money to the organization. To the extent that there is a reflection on the donor's social positioning, it is used to provide a reason for caring about "modern slavery," such as the photographer who had traveled globally and was constantly observing others in her work but who had missed that slavery existed, or the musician of faith who discovered "modern slavery" through his church and wanted to "contribute to somebody's freedom," or the investor who learned about "modern slavery" from a documentary and became an "abolitionist" in an hour, considering her donation to be an "excellent investment." The videos end with a request to donate today.

Media and sports celebrities are also sometimes highlighted as donors and supporters on the INGOs' websites as well, providing legitimacy for them and their brands.[5] Celebrities have helped with awareness campaigns, co-designed INGO merchandise, and invested in INGO social enterprise companies. Some have also branched out into their own advocacy endeavors or formed their own INGOs, something scholars have been exploring and critiquing. Celebrities can exert outsized power as norms entrepreneurs, helping to shape framings of "modern slavery" in ways that can be counterproductive (e.g., promoting retrograde gender norms) or helpful for those experiencing exploitation (Majic 2017; Majic 2023; Majic, O'Neill, and Bernhard 2020). They can bring attention to the issue of "modern slavery" and motivate people to act. They also, however, tend to reinforce ideas of ethical consumption as a solution to labor exploitation, ignore their own complicity in socioeconomic structures that perpetuate problems, and avoid broader discussions of political economy and cultural imperialism (Haynes 2014; Kapoor 2013; O'Manique and Rahman 2013; Budabin 2019). The feelings of celebrities, donor-heroes, and founder-celebrities about "modern slavery" can sometimes be highlighted more than the issues themselves, and the people whom they are seeking to help can be presented as ancillary characters in their own personal narratives (Nickel and Eikenberry 2009).

Along with appealing to donors as heroes who will end slavery through their contributions, INGOs were also working to engage them through fundraising activities such as dinners, celebrations, award ceremonies, and speaking events, some with celebrity attendance or performances. They also appealed to donors to organize fundraising events such as bake sales, luncheons, walks or marathons, raffles and silent auctions, film screenings, used clothing sales, and so on. One INGO tried to entice potential donors into becoming sellers for a partner company as a fundraising strategy:

> With the help of our partner, [a chocolate company], you can now offer 100% organic Fair Trade Certified chocolate to your friends and family! This chocolate comes from grower co-operatives that monitor their operations to ensure that forced labor was not used in the production of their chocolate. At a 40% profit margin, you earn $2.00 for every bar you sell for $5.00!

The appeal in this case was instrumental; the sellers could earn money for their own events while benefiting the INGO and the company. The offer is no longer listed on their website, however, and the company is no longer in business.

A few INGOs sought to entice potential donors by replicating the experience of shopping and buying items online. They had links to virtual shops or catalogs that "sell" INGO activities. *Donor-buyers* go to an online "store" that allows them to "purchase" blankets, coats, education, medical care, counseling, transportation services, or small business seed money for a person who experienced forced labor, child labor, or human trafficking or who is at risk. On one INGO site, donor-buyers can "purchase" a welcome kit for survivors of human trafficking with hygiene items, clothes, and bedding by adding it to a virtual shopping cart; they can also press a button to "continue shopping" if they want to add other items. On another INGO site, donor-buyers can "fund a slavery rescue operation," "fight sex trafficking," or "send an aftercare kit" to a rescued child by pressing a button to "give this gift." The item then goes into a "shopping cart" on the website, and the donor-buyer can press the button to "checkout" once they are ready to pay. The site even has the ability to shop the "catalog" by sorting it according to the most popular, price ascending, or price descending gifts, mimicking the way people can sort products to purchase from online retailers.

A third INGO took a similar approach, with donors able to gift "a rescue team that saves girls from the horror of exploitation," "trauma counseling," or "support skills training for women involving certification in medical services, tailoring, cosmetology, computer training, or primary teaching." Should viewers want to "rescue a young girl," they are taken to a webpage with four buttons that are labeled "$45 – Rescue 1 Girl;" "$90 – Rescue 2 Girls;" "$135 – Rescue 3 Girls;" and $180 – Rescue 4 Girls." These representations go beyond the "purchase" of tangible items, such as blankets or aftercare kits, for people who have experienced issues of "modern slavery." They actually present people as the "product" and let the consumer pick the quantity to "purchase" (Li 2016). Note, too, that they include "purchases" that support skills training to foster entrepreneurial intent on the part of women, reinforcing the idea that individual action and success in the marketplace are the keys to life after trafficking.[6]

In couching their fundraising appeals in these ways, the INGOs are building on consumer-oriented philanthropic campaigns that have become common fundraising tools among humanitarian organizations (Vestergaard 2013; Chouliaraki 2010). They celebrate donors-buyers as experts and emphasize their individual choices: should they rescue one girl or two? Is trauma counseling more important for people who have experienced issues of "modern slavery" or is clothing and bedding? Donors select their preferred option among basic human needs, translating the social relations of inequality and exploitation that create "modern slavery," as well as people who experience these issues, into "products" for consumption (Li 2016).

REPRESENTING "MODERN SLAVERY" AND THOSE WHO EXPERIENCE EXPLOITATION

People who have experienced issues of "modern slavery" are not only presented as objects for donor-buyers to purchase; they can also be used in marketing efforts that INGOs employ to garner public interest in their work. As with the visual representation and objectification of people who experience "modern slavery" in the media more broadly, the images they use have often been marked by paternalism, dehumanization, depersonalization, and sensationalism (Trodd 2013). Portrayals of sex trafficking, for example, often include voyeuristic images of young women bound, imprisoned, naked, wounded, or even dead, their suffering stylized and sexualized, meant to stand in for real people that could not be depicted (McGrath and Mieres 2021, 14; Andrijasevic 2007; Andrijasevic and Mai 2016). Representations also often present people in the global south as passive agents and reinforce ideas about the racial and cultural superiority of people in the global north (Fukushima and Hua 2015; McGrath, Rogaly, and Waite 2022; McGrath and Watson 2018; Trodd 2013; Beutin 2017, 2023).[7]

While many of these examples still abound in the media, the imagery used by most of the INGOs where I interviewed has been tempered, at least in their representations of women and suffering. One European anti-trafficking INGO even called attention to the issue of women's representation directly on its website, stating:

> With regard to the portrayal of trafficked women in the media, [the INGO] has noted the tendency of portraying women as helpless victims who have been forced to migrate and work in the sex industry. These depictions— including public awareness-raising campaigns by governments or NGOs— often include imagery of women's bodies in chains, battered, scantily dressed, or even processed like goods or packaged like animals. Although [the INGO] understands that the public and policy-makers needs to be informed about the extent of exploitation through trafficking, [the INGO] also firmly believes that this kind of imagery enhances the objectification of women by depicting them as commodities and disempowers them by portraying them as helpless victims without any agency. Anti-trafficking work should be based on the principle of empowerment, with the intention of increasing peoples' and/or communities' capacities to exert influence over their own lives.

One European INGO included in this study still needed to heed that call, since it included voyeuristic, sexualized images of naked, chained women of color in a video celebrating the organization's anniversary, but it was the exception.

Though they tended to avoid images of suffering women on their websites and in their documents, however, most of the INGOs did use images that convey vulnerability and innocence by highlighting children. They did also include adult men in their visual representations, as well as women, and they showed pictures of people in their communities, and in families, in action and working. Such positive images emphasizing dignity have also been criticized, however, as nonetheless emphasizing the "otherness" of people in the global south and concealing the complexities of social issues like poverty and development (see, e.g., Chouliaraki 2010).

CONCLUSION

In a crowded advocacy field subject to funder influences, INGOs have been looking for ways to communicate their specializations, foster their brands, and advertise themselves to funders, potential donors and the public. They are taking their cues from for-profit media and advertising based on entertainment and consumption and reinforcing neoliberalism in myriad ways. They emphasize efficiencies and outcomes, tout their successes, simplify and individualize issues of unfree labor, and make "anti-slavery" advocacy a consumable activity.

When INGOs showcase stories of entrepreneurial "anti-slavery" founder-celebrities, they reinforce the narratives of individual action and position the organizations and their leaders as the solution to unfree labor. The stories or narratives become the main focal point with founder-celebrities as the face of the INGO brand and the issues of unfree labor ancillary. Marketable narratives become prioritized over analysis of unfree labor.

These branding and marketing strategies also foster a superficial sense that action is happening through consumerism. Donor-heroes are not pressed to join in a collective movement or take part in pressing governments or companies for change. Rather, they "consume" the experience of being "slavery fighters" and "buying freedom" by supporting INGOs and entrepreneurial leaders who are poised as the efficient agents of change.

The public is reassured that markets will solve issues of "modern slavery," nevermind that disproportionate support may be going to INGOs with slick marketing on their websites, leaving others at a disadvantage, or that activities and projects that are publicly appealing may be privileged over those that might be long-term, policy-oriented, or complex.

The way that INGOs represent themselves and their constituents also adds weight to critical scholars' charges of paternalism in that narratives of vulnerability, rescue, and protection are often presented instead of collaborative efforts to work with and support people who experience or are at risk of unfree labor. Commodifying constituents' lived experiences and turning them into marketing tools further exploits people who have experienced labor exploitation and does little to ensure that their perspectives are being represented or their agency respected. Though many INGOs have moved away from spectacles of suffering, their representations of their constituencies, and their relations to them in practice, remain problematic issues. It is an observation that runs throughout this book.

Embracing corporate strategies of branding, marketing, and communication, and representing themselves and their constituents as objects of exchange for donors and funders, further ensconces INGOs, as well as the advocacy field, into market-based and consumption-oriented approaches. Having looked at these processes with regard to both INGO advocacy strategies and communications, the next chapter explores the organizations' operations and structures.

Six

MAKING INGO OPERATIONS AND
STRUCTURES MORE BUSINESS-LIKE

... in the NGO space, we look like all the other cats, we walk like all the
other cats, but we meow like dogs. When we open our mouths, people
are like, "What are you? I don't get it at all". . . because we're really a
hybrid model.
   —CEO of an "anti-slavery" INGO in the United States

In the short time that anti-trafficking advocacy has emerged, the nonprofit side of the movement has grown to include INGOs that are becoming more like their for-profit counterparts not only in their advocacy
strategies and communications but also in their operations and structures. This chapter explores the ways that INGOs incorporate business
practices and revenue generation in their organizations, leading them
to operate more like firms. This has happened along a continuum, from
changing leadership titles to adding corporate representatives on their
boards, hiring professionalized staff including business liaisons, and gen-
erating income from commercial revenue by selling INGO merchandise,
offering co-branding and cause-related marketing opportunities and
items produced by "survivor-entrepreneurs" as "proof" that the INGO's

strategies work and that people can innovate their way out of exploitive situations.

In a small number of cases, INGOs have developed for-profit social enterprise companies, leading to "hybrid" organizations that theoretically combine civil society and market goals, something exemplified by the quote from the CEO of an "anti-slavery" INGO above (Jager and Schroeder 2014).[1] These trends reflect and reinforce ideas about the superiority of business in solving social problems, and they introduce their own problems for INGOs and the people they are intended to help.

INGOS AND HYBRIDIZATION

A number of scholars see positives in nonprofits becoming more business-like: steady sources of revenue, better resource allocation, more effective use of philanthropic funds, the ability to respond quickly to market changes, increased accountability, and greater capacity (see, e.g., Dees and Battle Anderson 2003; Dees 1998). There are examples of nonprofits being competitive with for-profits and besting them in terms of quality and cost in certain areas, such as healthcare or education (Weisbrod 1997; Tuckman 1998b, 1998a). Some also see positives for democracy, arguing that marketization can free nonprofits from dependence on government resources and help to bolster civil society, for example, in post-socialist contexts (Yu and Chen 2018; Moeller and Valentinov 2011).[2]

Even when acknowledging potential problems such as mission drift, lower quality services, a decline in advocacy activities, or changes to the relationships between nonprofits and their beneficiaries, proponents argue that nonprofits can benefit if they move forward with marketization in a thoughtful and measured way (Chahine and Tannir 2010). They advise nonprofits to think through all potential sources of revenue generation, charge companies for cause-related marketing, plan for how much philanthropic support versus for-profit revenue they want, and train managers to be business people (Dees 1998). They suggest that, as long as managers with the right motivations are hired, the organizations will still run according to their missions (Ghatak 2020). The marketization of nonprofits will purportedly lead to better resource allocation, more effective use of philanthropic funds, and greater financial strength (Dees and Battle Anderson 2003).

These scholars suggest that there is nothing particularly problematic about nonprofits becoming more business-like; the business side can help the social side and nonprofits are able to negotiate the tension between mission and market just fine (Dart 2004; Sanders and McClellan 2012; Sanders 2013; Galaskiewicz and Barringer 2012). Staff can navigate entrepreneurship and managerialism with notions of benevolence, doing good and being effective, resist market cooptation, and still maintain rich relationships with beneficiaries and clients (Dey and Steyaert 2014; Dey and Steyaert 2010; Howorth, Parkinson, and MacDonald 2011). Worth noting here, also, are frequent underlying assumptions by economists and business scholars that the for-profit sector is more efficient, that nonprofits are needed only for aspects of markets that for-profits are unable to make a profit in, that charity is somehow "demeaning" while services that are paid for are more valued by recipients, and that professionalized for-profit staff are more qualified and skilled than nonprofit staff and therefore better suited to the private sector and/or social enterprises.

Concerns about hybridization have been raised by other scholars, including those in social welfare who study the field of human services. Like the fields of education and healthcare, the social welfare field has had a mix of nonprofit and for-profit organizations and a growing trend toward hybridization, at least in the United States. A major issue is that it can lead to clients' social rights becoming contingent on their participation in business enterprises; it also affects service provision when business logics override client needs (Hasenfeld and Garrow 2012; Garrow and Hasenfeld 2012; Gidron and Hasenfeld 2012). For example, one study of a large nonprofit social welfare organization in the United States that started retail stores and an industrial services business employing their low-income clients found that they tried to strictly separate the business and social services sides, but the market imperatives of the commercial side created tensions and placed demands on the social service side that conflicted with client needs (Cooney 2006).[3]

Aside from problems of commodifying clients and exploiting workers, there are issues with the competitiveness and longevity of the businesses. Take the example of nonprofits involved in work integration social enterprises, which provide job training and employment for disadvantaged workers in the United States. They have trouble breaking even, and most lose money; it is hard for them to maintain their commitments. They are also not successful in helping workers to obtain long-term employment or higher quality or skilled, better-paying work—the kind that would lift them out of poverty (Cooney 2011; Garrow and Hasenfeld 2012).

In becoming more business-like, social service nonprofits are subsuming process goals, such as advocating for a vulnerable group or helping to provide community cohesion or solve a social problem, with outcome goals related to professionalization, efficiency, and impact (Mosley 2020). This has led some scholars to call for further attention to the ways nonprofits may be negatively influenced by marketization, including questions about how nonprofit mission and identity may be affected (Mosley, Suárez, and Hwang 2022; Anheier, Lang, and Toepler 2020).[4]

The ability of nonprofits to challenge relations of power, including corporate power, is also of concern. The marketization of nonprofits has a de-radicalizing effect (Shamir 2004). More broadly, critics have repeatedly called attention to concerns that nonprofits becoming more business-like individualizes social problems, stabilizes capitalist relations and accumulation, affirms markets as the most appropriate solution to social problems, and fosters neoliberal subjectivities, such as reframing beneficiaries as consumers and activists as entrepreneurs (Maier, Meyer, and Steinbereithner 2016, 77; Eikenberry and Drapal Kluver 2004; Eikenberry 2009).

STRUCTURES AND OPERATIONS OF "ANTI-SLAVERY" INGOS

Nearly all of the "anti-slavery" INGOs I interviewed were operating as professionalized organizations, with hierarchical structures in business-like settings, with specialized staff and managers and rationalized operations (Hwang and Powell 2009). While a few of the smaller ones were in shared spaces, for example, with other nonprofits, in a faith-based organization, or a co-working space, most were located in commercial office spaces.

Leadership: Taking a cue from the for-profit world, 41 percent of the INGOs were using the term CEO rather than Executive Director to describe the head of the organization, with several of them changing the titles during the course of the study. This trend was not correlated to the size or growth of the INGOs; the title was used by both small and large INGOs, and though many of them increased their revenue over time, some switched to using the CEO title after years of revenue stability, while others started out with the title and grew larger afterward. Nor was the trend related to the actual duties of the leaders; both Executive Directors and CEOs were generally responsible for a broad range of responsibilities including operations, fundraising, staff oversight, planning, board relations, and external roles and representation. Rather, this seemed to be part of a broader cultural trend signifying the degree to which CEOs are seen as powerful cultural heroes, leaders, and winners who can solve societal problems (Bloom and Rhodes 2018).

Whether they were Executive Directors, CEOs, or the main "anti-slavery" or anti-trafficking program managers or staff in larger INGOs, nearly two-thirds of the interviewees working for the INGOs had made careers out of advocacy, often moving from other issue areas into the "modern slavery" field. Many (40 percent) had worked for large humanitarian, development, human rights, migrant, or environmental INGOs prior to working on issues of "modern slavery." More than a third (35 percent) had worked for governments, including international development agencies, or for United Nations organizations or other IGOs. Less than 10 percent had worked in the private sector, though the ones that did had come from technology, marketing, and design companies. They were also a highly educated group: 80 percent had post-graduate degrees; half of these were in areas such as international development, public administration, peace and justice studies, conflict resolution, sociology, or social work; 37 percent had law degrees; and 13 percent had a Ph.D. The INGOs were clearly professionalized in their leadership and "modern slavery" expertise.

More of the INGOs were led by men (60 percent) compared to women (40 percent), and women were more likely to be managing or staffing the "anti-slavery" or human trafficking programs of larger organizations. This is consistent with the nonprofit sector as a whole; in terms of leadership, men and women tend to found nonprofits in equal measure, but women are not promoted to top positions in larger organizations, at least in the United States (Camarena, Feeney, and Lecy 2021; Damman, Heyse, and Mills 2014). Consequently, there were more women (70 percent) than men (30 percent) among the people that I interviewed because they were in some cases leading "anti-slavery" programs in a larger organization headed by a man. This seems to reflect the broader gender composition of nonprofit employees in the United States, though the field is perhaps more "feminized" than others, such as humanitarianism or international development; more research is needed on gender and employment in INGOs in specific fields and in other countries (Holgersson and Hvenmark 2023; Camarena, Feeney, and Lecy 2021, 1171).

Most of the INGO interviewees were in their thirties or forties (62 percent), but 30 percent were in their fifties or sixties, indicative of the education and experience expected for their positions and the professionalization of the INGOs. They were also overwhelmingly white (94 percent), with the remaining 6 percent Asian. The dominance of white staffing and leadership is found in the nonprofit sector as a whole in the United States and in international development and humanitarianism, where racial hierarchies privileging whiteness are produced and reproduced in nonprofit organizations (LeRoux 2020; Kothari 2006, 14–17; Bian 2022).

Staffing: The INGOs ranged from having one full-time paid employee to many hundreds, with the vast majority between five and fifty. While the majority of the INGOs, even some of the smaller ones, had specialized staff for areas such as finance, development, research and evaluation, marketing and communications, and/or computer technology, some were just starting to add staff with expertise in the private sector. During the course of the research, for example, one added a business and human rights position, a second added a corporate partnerships manager, and a third added a business engagement and accountability position. Another had a director of business engagement since its inception, and a few of the INGOs already oriented to market strategies through business memberships, certifications, and/or codes had always had multiple business advisor and business development positions. In all, nearly 28 percent of the INGOs I interviewed had staff positions dedicated specifically to engagement with the private sector, a percentage more than double what was found in a 2013 survey of twenty-seven anti-trafficking nonprofits in Europe (Hoff and McGauran 2015, 11). That survey found that only 11 percent had such positions, suggesting a possible upward trend toward adding positions dedicated to business engagement among INGOs in the West.

In terms of career paths and movement between the public, private, and nonprofit sectors, the majority of interviewees (42 percent) remained in their positions and were still there as recently as 2024. Roughly 25 percent had moved to other INGOs, small domestic NGOs, foundations, IGOs, or government agencies. Nearly 20 percent moved into the private sector, almost doubling the percentage that had come from it before their time in the "anti-slavery" field. Several had become private for-profit consultants, including one that started their own for-profit consulting firm, and three had moved into private sector jobs in technology, investigation, and CSR for multinational companies.[5]

Boards: The boards of most organizations included a variety of business actors along with more typical representatives from other INGOs, politicians and/or political experts and advisors, academics, often from elite institutions, and religious leaders. There were social enterprise incubators and consultants as well as current or former representatives of global law firms and multinational corporations, including those focused on agriculture, banking and finance, business consulting, food and beverage, hospitality, marketing, media, retail, technology, and transportation. Several INGOs included foundation representatives on their boards and a few included celebrities and artists as well.[6]

The INGOs that did not have business representatives on their boards stood out for having a gender or labor focus. Two, for example, were particularly concerned with women in forced labor and/or human trafficking, and they both had female leadership and entirely female boards without corporate representation. Two of the more labor-focused INGOs had union and/or political, academic, religious, and community representatives rather than corporate actors. The faith-based "anti-slavery" INGOs were more mixed; some had boards comprised of religious leaders without private sector representation, while others had boards that contained a number of business representatives.

Unions and/or labor groups were on only three of the boards and a survivor was on only one. Those affected by unfree labor are not well represented in INGO structures or the advocacy field (Ewart-James and Fischer-Daly 2019). Some governments and INGOs have put into place formal mechanisms like alliances, councils, caucuses, or networks for getting survivor input on "anti-slavery" programs and policies to help address that gap.

Missions: The majority of INGOs had mission statements that placed issues of "modern slavery" and the people experiencing them at the center. They aimed to protect people; change the conditions that allow "modern slavery" to occur; eliminate slavery worldwide; prevent and address the exploitation of people; defend justice, dignity, and rights; promote a survivor-centered approach; help create a slave-free world; end "modern slavery" and human trafficking; fight human trafficking with advocacy and mobilization; work to prevent and address human trafficking for labor exploitation; and give people a chance to live a decent life.

Those INGOs that were market-oriented, such as combining codes or certifications with other advocacy strategies or adding for-profit components, had mission statements that centered businesses or highlighted them in relation to other stakeholders. One INGO stated that it sought to use the power of business to reduce "modern slavery," for example. Another included both businesses and workers in its mission statement, stating that they were working with companies to respect workers' rights. A third explained their mission as creating tools that engage businesses, government, and others by nurturing social enterprises to benefit enslaved and vulnerable communities; more succinctly, they explained, the enterprise *is* the mission. Another INGO was conspicuously missing a mission statement in its documents and website, alluding only to being a source of intelligence on human trafficking and exploitation that financial institutions, businesses, governments, and NGOs could trust and rely upon.

Most INGOs did not change their mission statements substantially over the course of the research, but they did revise them occasionally, making them more succinct, catchier, or accessible to the public by using plain language. This was sometimes done in conjunction with efforts to update branding and marketing. In a couple of cases, they also added language to reflect empowerment of their constituents or broaden their focus, for example, expanding from helping people who experience sex trafficking to also helping other groups. One INGO moved substantially from its original mission of ending trafficking through community transformation, campaigning, and sharing knowledge to its current one emphasizing prevention, technology strategies, and intelligence as part of a rebranding effort.

GENERATING REVENUE: SELLING INGO MERCHANDISE AND SERVICES

The examples of business-like INGO operations and structures highlighted above were accompanied, in some cases, with actions to develop mechanisms for commercial revenue generation. For 10 percent of the INGOs, fees were the majority of their funding. This was true of the more market-oriented INGOs that rely on business membership fees, consulting fees, or product sales, but sometimes even INGOs that provided services to people who experienced or were at risk of unfree labor also charged fees for things such as healthcare or education.

Some INGOs had branched out to sell merchandise, co-brand with companies, or partner with a social enterprise to make consumer goods for sale. Selling merchandise was common; INGOs set up their websites to allow people to shop for message T-shirts and sweatshirts, beanies, photography books, magnets, stationery, stickers, and jewelry with INGO logos. One INGO in the United States, for example, advertised a "Slavery Sucks" T-shirt, available for purchase through a link to an online internet retail company, along with other shirts sporting the INGO's logo. Similarly, an INGO in the UK had collaborated with fashion designers and celebrities to create a line of organic, fairly-traded T-shirts to support their campaigns, some including the organization's logo. There were also branded products intended for businesses rather than individuals. An INGO might trademark a technology tool like a software program or mapping tool for risk assessment, for example, and provide testimonials from companies on their websites lauding their knowledge, skills, and support when consulting on supply chain issues.

A few INGOs were seeking out co-branding opportunities. For example, one UK "anti-slavery" INGO had partnered with a company that provides co-branded corporate gifts, while an INGO in the United States had partnered with companies to produce INGO-branded products such as coffee or other food and beverage items, home goods, and toiletries. In its now-defunct online store, for example, it sold beer:

> [The INGO ale] is not just another beer! By channelling 100% of profits to
> fight human trafficking, it's unique in the world.

Information about the beer's nose and hops and a suggested food pairing was also included in the advertising.

The same INGO also signaled its interest in more co-branding initiatives. On its website, it urged companies to:

> Become a brand with a vision. Business[es] should not only make a profit,
> but also make the world a better place. Promote your business and mission
> together with [us].

The INGO provided testimonials on its website, not from donor-heroes but from businesses that the INGO worked with, such as one that assured the reader that "our supply chain is conflict-free, but many others around the world are not" and another that claimed that the employment opportunities they were providing to survivors of "modern slavery" to learn how to be baristas were "much more empowering to the people involved" because "this isn't charity."

Co-branding in these cases was used by companies as a marketing strategy, something the INGO advertised to them as a benefit: participation with the INGO would be useful for product messaging. They provided an example of the mutually beneficial partnership with a fashion designer, teaming up with the INGO to raise awareness about human trafficking through an INGO fashion line in stores and on social media. Celebrities picked the designs and helped spread the word.[7] They also described a project with a retailer in Europe in which each co-branded product carried a message about human trafficking and generated funds to support the INGO. They reported that, during the four-year campaign, over 200,000 co-branded soups, coffee capsules, and coffee beans were sold to consumers.

Scholars have critiqued cause-related marketing and consumption-based strategies for fundraising for a number of reasons. They have pointed out that they simplify causes and turn citizens into consumers, distancing them from more direct forms of participation in civil society (Richey and Ponte 2011). INGOs may be aiming to engage people through cause-related marketing campaigns, but they are instead helping them to remain disconnected from the end goal of addressing the problems and helping those in need (Eikenberry 2014). There are also risks involved for the INGOs. Some cause-related marketing campaigns can result in financial losses for nonprofits, placing them under pressure to promote products at the expense of direct donations, and the slogans and framings used can simplify issues, draw on stereotypical and racialized tropes of the people that are being helped, and contribute to the problem of some issues being favored over others because they are more appealing to corporations, noncontroversial (or can be framed as such), palatable to the public, and easier to market with slogans (Hawkins 2012; King 2004, 2008). In fundraising for "anti-slavery" advocacy, for example, a few INGOs highlighted the rescue of children exploited in sex trafficking rather than adult male migrant workers, even though they helped both; presumably this was because they deemed the rescue of children to be more "marketable" and able to garner public interest.

COMMERCIALIZING SURVIVOR-ENTREPRENEURS

Some of the INGOs market products made by people who have experienced issues of "modern slavery" or who are seen as vulnerable to them. In addition to the beer sold in the online INGO store mentioned above, for example, the INGO also sold:

> . . . adorable summer totes [that] are sewn by women rescued from a life of sex trafficking. . . . Each bag tells the story of one woman's journey to freedom—from a life of rampant poverty and forced prostitution, toward a life of dignity, a living wage with decent hours, and the opportunity to become literate.

As we saw in the last chapter, people who experience unfree labor are already used as marketing material for INGO appeals to donor-buyers, but having them produce goods for sale introduces a new mechanism by which they can appeal to consumers. In keeping with market-based strategies and ethical consumption, buyers are purchasing more than a product; they are purchasing the narratives of those exploited, their symbolic freedom, a claim to moral virtue, and a sense of action.

While only a few of the INGOs I interviewed were selling products made by people who experienced unfree labor, there are others in the advocacy field, especially among faith-based or domestic nonprofits and social enterprises. It is popular to have women who have experienced sex trafficking make jewelry or sew clothing, though one can also find them making soap, candles, spa kits, cards, wallets, and purses. As ethnographer Elena Shih (2023) notes in her study of two anti-trafficking INGOs based in the United States that have women in China and Thailand making jewelry for sale, the focus on these gendered products is tied to notions about restoring "appropriate" femininity. The projects she studied had cultural imperialist and racialized aspects as well; Shih points out the way white women from the United States lead the organizations, helping to ensure that the products are created to suit what they see as Western aesthetics; they also see themselves as imparting western values, and ultimately, she argues, imposing discipline and control under the guise of rehabilitating Asian women (Shih 2023).

Among the INGOs that I interviewed, there was an emphasis on skills training for service sector jobs such as administrative support, caregivers, cashiers, computer technicians, cooks, cosmetologists, customer service representatives in banks, loss prevention specialists, medical billing specialists, nursing assistants, and teachers. There was training in weaving and sewing as well, and support for agriculture and animal husbandry, but for many of the INGOs, these latter efforts were envisioned as a means of helping people to do more than simply try to survive: they would become *survivor-entrepreneurs* who would thrive. There were many examples of this in INGO materials. In one annual report, for example, the CEO of an INGO in the United States wrote:

> During the graduation of trainees from our new program. . . I was humbled to watch as one young woman stood up in front of her family and peers and declared "I didn't even know what a CEO was; now I want to be one." Moments like this are a testament to the power of our supporters, without whom [the INGO] could not exist and among whom I feel an ever-growing confidence that we will win the fight against modern-day slavery.

The same INGO also noted another program in which they provided seed funding to a farmer in a sub-Saharan country to help them become an "entrepreneur." They portrayed poverty as a "cycle" that the entrepreneurship was breaking, something an individual can innovate their way out of with the support of the organization.

Another INGO based in the United States, which provides shelter and services for people who experienced trafficking and had strong ties to local government and law enforcement, also dabbled in entrepreneurship. It collaborated with another nonprofit that provided training for case managers to become business startup coaches and provide shelter clients with entrepreneurial skills training and business startup funding. The success of the INGO's partner organization was touted on its website: they had conducted a pilot program that resulted in twenty-four new business startups turning profits of $200 to $3,000 monthly, and one-third of the clients moved into secure housing. The INGO supported the idea that small business creation and self-employment would help those in shelters to "create their own pathway to financial security and long-term stability." In the geographic area of the United States where the INGO works, however, monthly rents for a two-bedroom apartment were more than half of what the most successful survivor-entrepreneurs made, suggesting one possible reason why only a third managed to move into secure housing. On its website, the INGO nonetheless showcased a success story of one woman who completed training to become a stylist in an upscale salon and then launch her own style brand.

A third INGO assured readers on its website that "we're believers in innovation—and that community-inspired business approaches can offer sustainable economic opportunities." Their website also included the following:

> Market-based solutions to fight global poverty: We know that enterprises offering beneficial products and services can create a sustainable social impact for the poor. Even in the poorest places around the world, hardworking people struggle to improve the conditions of their families. While they are producing a good or product to sell, people may lack the knowledge or opportunity necessary to form a market or delivery system to benefit or grow their profit. That's why we work to lay the groundwork for healthy, private sector collaborations at the grassroots and global trading levels. We support the start-up of businesses that can help people out of poverty while providing a service that everyone needs—like growing food, producing power, and improving access to clean water.

The INGOs were in some cases following the cue of IGOs who are also funding projects for survivor-entrepreneurs. For example, though it funds different types of projects, the United Nations Voluntary Trust Fund for Victims of Trafficking in Persons has supported nonprofits providing training courses in entrepreneurship and business skills in Nepal, Uganda, and Ethiopia. It has also provided support to establish businesses based on crafts in Nigeria; livelihood support for goat rearing, small grocery shops, and tailoring businesses in Bangladesh; and vocational training and financial support to start small businesses in Albania (United Nations Voluntary Trust Fund for Victims of Human Trafficking 2022, 2021, 2015, 2019).

These efforts promote the idea of entrepreneurship as the catalyst for change, with individuals integrated into capitalist markets and innovating their way out of poverty. It reproduces the idea that markets are solutions to labor exploitation and minimizes the state's role in addressing the reasons why unfree labor is happening and seeking ways to prevent it. By encouraging what some scholars have called "adverse incorporation" into the global economy, survivor-entrepreneurs are purported to be "free" and unexploited despite ongoing conditions of precarity which have led them into exploitive labor in the first place (Phillips 2011).

ENTERPRISING INGOS: STARTING FOR-PROFIT COMPONENTS

They were a minority of the organizations in this study, but a few INGOs had gone on to start for-profit components. One INGO was adding a for-profit hospital, and the CEO explained in his interview why they were planning to charge for health services in the new project:

> It's a for-profit hospital, as opposed to a mission hospital. . . . Word will get out that the care is great. Everything works really well, and you can trust these people. People will come, and people that can pay will come. So the people that can pay will pay. . . . You can't give it away. If you give it away, it doesn't have any value.

His view exemplifies the market logic of reorienting nonprofit clients to consumers, though he does allude to a sliding scale fee for clients who might not have the means to pay.

It's worth examining in detail the case of another INGO that moved from a more "traditional" INGO model to a hybrid one. That INGO, quoted at the beginning of the chapter, has added for-profit companies and continues to do so. At the time of the interview, the CEO had just returned from traveling abroad, working hard to get some companies off the ground. As he proceeded to tell me about the evolution of the INGO, his infectious enthusiasm was such that I barely managed to get a word in edgewise for the next hour and a half. He explained:

> For the first three years, four years, we were a very traditional NGO model, fundraising by going to churches and universities and synagogues, anyone who would take us. We would beg people for money. I would say, "Look, there's some kids in [an Asian country] who need help, kids in [a Latin American country] who need help. Please open your heart and your wallet and help us out." And offers grew really quick—by four and a half, five

years in, we were close to five million annual revenue, which puts you in the top half of percent of all nonprofits. Which is okay, we do a lot of hard work to get there, but at the same time, realized that's pretty much a travesty if that's considered big. And if you look at the larger, broader issue, and are we even making a dent?

Despairing the traditional nonprofit business model, which he described as "not great" because it does not "grow our skills to the level of actually making a dent on crime like forced labor," they decided to start for-profit companies.

For their first company, which provides training and employment in the hospitality sector, they were able to raise funding from philanthropic capital, and the INGO owns it fully. It has been a success, and they have expanded the business to additional locations. They then moved on to help start another company that produces a consumable good; the INGO owned part of that company, had a board seat in perpetuity, and received a percentage of its income.

> The company itself has become really a project of [our INGO]. That's how I think about [it]. It is not a company looking for a cause; it was a cause that started a company. And I think we've seen the fruits of that. It's the fastest-growing [product] in the history of the United States. We raised $20 million last year, and we turned down at least twenty different suitors for that. How many NGOs have turned down $200 million? None. Zero. But, obviously, that wasn't money designated for [our INGO]. But, it was money to come into our platform and our ecosystem that does power [our INGO].

For this INGO, the for-profit components were, as proponents of hybridization suggest, allowing the INGO freedom in programming in a way that other funding sources did not:

> We used to only enter a new country through the direct service, and if we had a funding partner, a philanthropic funding partner who would come alongside [our INGO] and commit at least five years' funding to getting a program off the ground directly for survivors... I haven't had to ask anyone for a charitable contribution to [us] in two years. Again, what non-profit can tell you that? None. Zero... we can keep putting more impact brands into our ecosystem and as they are successful and they make money, they will waterfall additional money and revenue back to [the INGO], which will allow us to grow our work.

In the CEO's view, their success bolstered the idea that social enterprise was the superior approach:

> I think the traditional charitable model, and I'll speak from the cynical perspective, it is the bygone product of a rape and pillage capitalism that puts a veneer on top of capitalists that gives them this glow of positivity, and I hope it dies a vicious death.

He in fact saw social enterprise as no less than a way of transforming capitalism.

> . . . human trafficking is a driving and animating force; however, for me, I think we don't exist on this planet as human beings if we don't prove we can generate wealth while also doing good by planet and people. And so, ultimately, that's my ultimate animating force, I'd like my [child] to have a planet to live on. And I truly think that if we don't prove this, and evangelize this, we're dead. I really do. I think we're done.

His hope was to have one of the INGO's companies bought out by a big conglomerate with the stipulation that INGO representative(s) remain on the board, the idea being that they would "become a virus:"

> . . . it's a huge opportunity to go inside one of these brands, and again I mention, we built the poison toad from day one into the bylaws, the supply chain for the product. We built in the board seat in perpetuity. We built in percentage of revenue for [our INGO]. And so, if they want to eat us, that's fine. . . if we can become a voice of influence on the supply chain of [a big conglomerate]. . . . If at the end of my life, I know for a fact, that if we can help shift the supply chain practice of [a big conglomerate] a half a percent, that will be more impact in aggregate than I'll ever have through [the INGO]. Ever. And, what I would like to do is have a fleet of [companies] who will become viruses inside of global conglomerates and begin to shift the corporate mindset, but also prove financially that this is a better way of doing capitalism. . .

When I applauded the sentiment but expressed skepticism about the ability to influence the conglomerates, he was not deterred:

> I am now slightly positive about the future. Before, when I was stuck in the NGO mindset, I was like, "We're all fucked."

We encountered his allusion to being stuck in the NGO mindset in an earlier chapter, when he recalled the feeling of throwing rocks at a corporate window and not being taken seriously by business leaders. By starting for-profits, he saw himself as working within the system to change it. He had not worked with other INGOs in his geographic area, explaining that they do not understand his INGO nor does he have time. His reference point was squarely focused on other, larger businesses. He saw the INGO's companies as small fish among the big, for-profit whales in his city; for example, in the course of the interview, he mentioned the idea that he would be laughed at by big investors for the smaller amount of money (e.g., a few million) that he was seeking to raise for his "little" impact brands.

This positioning of the INGO as a scrappy social enterprise incubator separated from both other INGOs and from large companies was reinforced also in the organization's recounting of the origin story for their latest company:

> ... instead of doing research that turns into public policy or funding policy, what we did is we conducted research that turned into business development. . . we convened a group of leaders, entrepreneurs, so we were very adamant it was not NGO leaders, we wanted business people to be in the room. . . we start with thousands of ideas, brainstorming, and we have the groups compete against each other, and. . . the idea they came up with that day was a key company. . .

The company was doing well at the time of the interview, growing and being marketed in the INGOs reports.

However, having gone through the experience of starting a for-profit company and manufacturing a product from scratch, the INGO understood the risks and difficulties involved and decided to take a different approach for further business development. They were looking to find entrepreneurs to align with and have them "drive revenues back into [the INGO]:"

> And so, what we're exploring is coming at things from the business angle at the top and finding great entrepreneurs and wanting to be part of a global marketplace, who want to be part of a global network, who want their brand aligned with [us and the for-profit companies we started]. They want to be known as an impact brand as part of the [INGO] ecosystem. So, it elevates their standing in the world as well.

That is one way of handling the problem of INGO-related businesses having to compete with other for-profits that are not constrained by the costs of sustainable production, decent working conditions, and living wages. One of the INGOs that has a certification system explained part of the problem:

> There is also a whole market piece to it that [the INGO] is not a part of. That is critical, because how can you pay higher wages if you are not going to be able to get that [product] to a market who is actually willing to buy it? It's going to be probably double the cost.

This illustrates a dilemma for INGOs with for-profit components. They are expected to follow their missions, which means that their costs will be higher than other businesses and result in more expensive products and services.

PROBLEMS OF HYBRIDIZATION

For the more enterprising "anti-slavery" INGOs that added for-profit components, potential problems abound. In terms of charging fees for services, as we saw one INGO doing for healthcare in its for-profit component, the reorientation of clients into consumers can lead to inequalities of access; potentially undermine the goal of community and social support that INGOs are thought to foster; and run the risk of prioritizing profitability over client need. It also, as hybridization critics argue, justifies the commodification of social goods and constructs them as items to be purchased rather than rights that should be universally available.

Tensions between mission and market are not easily navigated. As one European INGO interviewee explained, she had seen a few nonprofits working on issues of "modern slavery" embrace business models, but in the cases she was familiar with, they could not adequately do both:

> The moment they started this business, let's say, a hotel, even though small scale, or barber shop or whatever, all that work and direction, they're addicted to that. And then all the work is focusing on that. If they were lucky, they could still have a shelter, but not that. In general, that's the problem. We sometimes see that a shelter manager is not called the shelter manager anymore, and he's not running the shelter. Now the shelter is funded because you do a project on CSR and then the CSR policy person is actually the shelter manager.

Her concerns echo those of hybridization critics; she is pointing to mission drift and a reduction in the INGO's other activities in relation to the for-profit component. One study of a nonprofit in the United States that sells commodities produced by women who experienced or were at risk of human trafficking provides an example supporting this view. It found that the organization spent most of its time creating consumer demand for its products (Henriksen 2018).

For the hybrid INGO quoted at the beginning of the chapter, one can certainly see the emphasis on fostering social enterprise businesses in its website text and organizational reports:

> We are looking to attract talented entrepreneurs, business people, and capital, for-profit capital to invest in companies that will assist those communities by making the best product possible. By blending these two worlds you are actually creating justice.

It remains a prominent theme in much of the INGO's organizational materials.

In terms of the way that the INGO marries market and mission, however, it seems that the market side is dominating. The CEO explained in his interview that ". . . research and business development. . . is really where [we] spend most of the time." Instead of starting with the issue of direct service and need, they look for business opportunities. Their approach is to find existing companies in other countries that are financially viable:

> And so, what we're exploring is coming at things from the business angle at the top and finding great entrepreneurs and wanting to be part of a global marketplace, we want to be part of a global network, who want their brand aligned with [our companies] and aligned with inside this impact conglomerate, they want to be known as an impact brand as part of [our INGO] ecosystem. So, it elevates their standing in the world as well. . . instead of starting from the bottom and working our way up, we will start at the top, which will automatically, which will almost instantaneously unlock not only a relationship with a great entrepreneur, but an opportunity on a quarterly basis to have a check written from them, from that company. . . into impact programming at the bottom."

The INGO has become so focused on business development that the CEO has to "trust that my project directors are living up to our expectations of efficacy and impact." This does suggest tension between the mission and market sides of the INGO, with its leaders being stretched in multiple directions and having to stay more distant from day-to-day operations of programs and the provision of services. The INGO documents also reinforce this perception:

> Beyond their fundraising and administrative roles in supporting [the INGO's] country operations, [its leaders] spend over 70 percent of their time conducting due diligence, social enterprise incubation, business development, and governance of social enterprises that generate impact through employment targets and supply chain and sourcing practices.

This shift is reflected in the history of the INGO. Early on in its history, their documents highlight the impact that they have with survivors, i.e., how many they helped and how. But they later began highlighting their work with companies, stating that they create:

> . . . business solutions to combat human trafficking through four key strategies: product collaborations; supply chain research & guidance; job training & employment; and incubating businesses.

The focus on business development and social enterprise has become a dominant feature of the INGO's purpose and activities.

There can be tensions of hybridization on the for-profit side of the organization as well. As the INGO representative on the board of the for-profit company selling a product with ingredients sourced from a country of the global south, the CEO has to press for ethical decision-making, not just short-term profit-oriented decision-making:

> "No, we can't buy cheaper products, because that means making a sacrifice on impact." Okay, well that means we're going to have to raise capital sooner rather than later, and that means less of a win for investors down the road. Well, they're impact investors; they just have to accept that. And we have to also trust that the market itself, that consumers and customers care about this, and that we know that this is where the bigger conglomerates, if they were to acquire a brand like [the one we started], that because these are impact brands, they're a premium, and this is where capitalism is going, and they should want to have companies where they might have to pay a premium, because the company itself is differentiated in the marketplace, and is aware of what people want to buy.

Social enterprises, when started by INGOs or otherwise, are subject to the same potential problems as other firms: they still need to make a profit, they need workers to be productive and have to find places to cut costs in order to be competitive, and if they are manufacturing a product, they need to sell it at a price point that consumers will accept.

Social enterprises are assumed to be better employers and ensure decent work, but having INGOs as employers and owners of businesses does not guarantee that workers will be exempt from exploitation, worker voices will be heard, producers will have more autonomy and/or be able to sell their products and goods at prices that will actually help them out of poverty, or that businesses in the global south will benefit. For example, while the for-profit company in this case does work with farmer coops to source ingredients for its product, it is owned by investors in the West. For all of the INGO's enthusiasm for what it sees as a new form of capitalism, it seems a very old form indeed. There is little to counter imbalances or injustices in supply chains whereby Western brands achieve extraordinary profits while producers in the global south receive a small fraction of the retail price, exacerbating inequalities between producing and consuming countries (Utting 2008, 962).

There are implications for democratic governance as well when INGOs become more business-like and move toward social enterprise and entre-preneurship. In reinforcing the neoliberal belief in markets and private approaches to social problems, such organizations help to redefine civil society as a space for parallel private institutions that circumvent the state and citizens' claims to rights and resources. People become customers and clients rather than citizens participating in democratic public institutions, and there is little to ensure that those institutions will reflect the will and needs of the people (Ganz, Kay, and Spicer 2018).

CONCLUSION

The "anti-slavery" INGOs in this study have adopted the language, cultures, and perspectives of business in their operations and structures to an increasing extent, even while continuing with their mission activities. However, there is also some movement toward hybrid INGOs with for-profit components, and they are indicative of some of the concerns critics have highlighted. Becoming more business-like exacerbates an already potentially problematic positioning for nonprofits in terms of power relations. They become sellers of services, employers of clients, and business entrepreneurs, further disconnected from, or even in a contradictory position to, the people they are intending to help. The entrepreneurial discourses belie the precarity of many of the jobs and business startups in which the survivors are involved, reinforcing the idea of markets as the basis for benevolent human relations and stabilizing the very processes that result in the exploitation it claims to want to end (Nickel and Eikenberry 2009, 976).

For INGOs that embark on for-profit components, there are questions about whether those companies are accountable to local communities (Banerjee 2008, 73), as well as whether they can offer long-term support, stability, or opportunities for people who experience issues of "modern slavery." Embracing capitalism in this way, encouraging ad hoc business development, is not going to challenge the structures perpetuating exploitation. In addition, just as there is concern about workers not having a voice or power in for-profit workspaces and organizations, so, too, can commercial components of INGOs and social enterprises replicate these problems.

CONCLUSION

In a booming "anti-slavery" field, where businesses now play a more central role, INGOs are responding to and navigating business influence. They work earnestly to help others and fight the worst forms of labor exploitation in the global economy even as they also focus on securing their places in the advocacy field. They reproduce framings about "modern slavery" being a criminal business that can be addressed with private sector action; engage in fraught collaborations with businesses; support business-friendly and market-based strategies; seek to be experts ready to compete in new markets for consultation and technological development; and they embrace, to varying degrees, business-like organizational communications, operations, and structures.

In highlighting these trends, I have argued that both INGOs and the advocacy movement are constrained by them; they help to perpetuate a status quo that does little to challenge issues of "modern slavery." INGOs and other organizations in the advocacy field reproduce understandings and framings of unfree labor shaped by and reinforcing neoliberalism, hampering their ability to press for structural changes or counter corporate power. INGOs are not passive agents of capital or funders, but they take up a complicated position in relation to businesses they are attempting to influence. As they center businesses as partners and become more business-like themselves, it minimizes what they can press companies to do and leads them to attend to businesses over workers, marginalizing those who are supposed to be the INGO's constituents and overlooking potential allies, including labor groups, unions, and activists working on corporate accountability.

"Anti-slavery" INGOs are not equal players in a pluralist arena of global governance, nor are they gradually, benevolently becoming like for-profits while companies become more nonprofit-like, as new institutionalist scholars suggest. Instead, INGOs are navigating a field with a great deal of business power and the broad changes in the field are strong: IGOs, states, and big funders have helped to incorporate unfree labor under CSR and MSIs, with voluntary codes, guidelines, technological "fixes," and ethical consumption as solutions. These do constitute a type of change in themselves, as new institutional scholars argue, but they are incremental at best. The lack of state regulation in many countries and continued business practices of subcontracting remain problematic, leaving room for labor exploitation to thrive (LeBaron 2020; Jaffee 2012).

This book shows that "anti-slavery" advocacy, like other movements, has been experiencing cooptation, with business ideas, activities, and practices saturating the field and curtailing possibilities for more extensive, broad, systemic change (Dauvergne and Lebaron 2014; Busa and King 2015; King and Busa 2017; Levy and Kaplan 2009). "Anti-slavery" INGOs have the authority to name and shame, even if their credibility has been called into question by companies, but they are not using it. They do not see themselves as the powerful actors that companies suggest when they call them out as threats to corporate reputations or when states expect that they will monitor the for-profit sector.

Furthermore, the push for collaborations between businesses and nonprofits leads to problematic power dynamics as "anti-slavery" INGOs work toward individualized relationships with businesses for self-survival. They address corporate accountability only obliquely through these relationships with business constituents, focusing instead on criminal actors and extending their efforts to address "bad" businesses to help the "good" ones they work with.[1] All of the above developments lend weight to those who question the ability of INGOs to press for social change, be accountable to those they are seeking to help, and act as stewards of the public good.

This book also corroborates critical scholarship that ties trends in advocacy fields to neoliberalism and the neutralization of dissent in contemporary global capitalism. INGOs are part of processes through which class relations are contested and reworked, resisted, or supported (Ismail and Kamat 2018, 573). Scholars of "anti-slavery" advocacy have often pointed out the way "anti-slavery" INGOs partner with states in ways that can erode rights and democratic governance, particularly the way that criminalization efforts in the "anti-slavery" field resonate with state surveillance and security measures that target and harm poor and working-class people, migrants, and people in informal work. This book adds a focus on the private sector and nonprofit/for-profit dynamics, pointing to the ways that INGOs may end up working to stabilize the neoliberal order through voluntary action, private-public partnerships, and consumption-based and technological "solutions" that reinforce deregulation, private governance, and corporate power.

In branding and marketing themselves and their constituents, adding mechanisms for commercial revenue, starting for-profit components, and pursuing strategies that help businesses, INGOs are working within a market-based system that has fostered the problems they are attempting to challenge. Western states, IGOs, and companies have been happy to support INGOs that are more "business-like;" they are not pressing states to deliver on economic and migration reforms, measures for wealth redistribution, social welfare programs to reduce vulnerabilities and social inequalities, increased corporate regulation, or improved labor rights, nor are they challenging corporate practices in a direct and substantial way.

A more radical approach might involve collective action with organizational actors in other advocacy fields and social movement actors that press for structural and systemic political, economic, and social changes. That would entail critiquing capitalism, attending to racial, ethnic, and class-based inequalities, challenging companies on their business practices, and questioning the parameters and implications of market strategies and technological "fixes" as solutions. It would also involve INGOs resisting marketing that emphasizes individual actions by founder-celebrities or appeals to donor-buyers that reinforce consumption as action, instead focusing on collaborative action with their constituents, and it could take the form of complicating simple narratives about unfree labor by making the case that matters are more complex than crime narratives suggest and are tied to political, economic, and social processes.

Finally, the book also bolsters the arguments of critical scholars who say that corporate influence is happening not only due to individual companies consciously intending to influence advocacy fields but also because of the broader cultural influence of business understandings, language, and framings in shaping them. Particular companies may have more or less power in relation to particular INGOs, but business influence is much broader than that. It is certainly tied to funding. Just as INGOs that receive a great deal of funding from states can be constrained from pressing those same states for change, so too can INGOs receiving funding from companies and elite private foundations, or seeking fees for business services, find themselves reluctant to challenge companies on unfree labor. However, corporate influence is not just coming from philanthrocapitalists and private foundations, but also IGOs, states, and some academics putting forward business framings and solutions to issues of unfree labor. Funding and funder expectations matter; individual corporate actions matter, but business discourses and paradigms matter, too, and they have permeated the advocacy field.

The stakes for vulnerable and marginalized people in the world are high, making it all the more important for scholars, INGOs, and others to question ideological assertions that purport to solve labor exploitation with private regulation, consumption-based strategies, and corporate-led approaches. In the West, and especially in the United States, elites continue to justify economic and social policy choices that make people economically vulnerable, remove safety nets and labor regulations, and perpetuate conditions that contribute to unfree labor; this affects poor and working class people and people of color disproportionately. For example, some states in the United States have been working to roll back restrictions and safety regulations for young workers, relaxing rules for things such as working overnight shifts and performing hazardous jobs, even as child labor violations have been increasing.[2] Migrant children from Latin America have been especially vulnerable, working in meat-packing plants, industrial cleaning services, construction, and factories, among other places (Milczarek-Desai 2024). The chief backers of laws working toward these rollbacks have been business groups (Cahn, Eichner, and Ziegler 2024, 274).

In addition, in the United States, the Trump administration has recently undertaken a whole host of efforts to weaken labor rights, create more vulnerabilities for workers, surveil and target migrants, and hinder efforts to assist people who experience issues of "modern slavery." At the time of this writing, the Trump administration's Department of Government Efficiency has fired staff and "paused" millions of dollars in federal grants administered by the United States Agency for International Development, the Department of Labor's Bureau of International Labor Affairs, the National Institutes of Health, the Department of Justice, and the Centers for Disease Control and Prevention, among others, including money going to anti-trafficking and "anti-slavery" work to support outreach, research, and services. This has directly impacted INGOs and programs addressing unfree labor both within and outside of the United States and some have had to lay off staff, cut services, or halt operations.[3]

The administration has also been working to undermine organized labor by hobbling the National Labor Relations Board (NLRB), which is an independent federal agency that enforces United States labor laws related to workers' rights, union representation, and collective bargaining.[4] Court battles are in process, but the agency cannot engage in formal actions in the meantime, affecting unionization efforts and unfair labor practice cases. All of these actions help to further dismantle the already flailing system of worker protections in the United States, leaving more people vulnerable to a continuum of labor exploitation, including issues of "modern slavery."

Further Research: Only a few INGOs included in the study addressed corporate power and this points to one avenue for future research. What makes some INGOs more willing than others to press for corporate accountability and systemic changes to current capitalist practices and structures? Part of the answer seems to lie with the missions and framings of INGOs, including whether they are drawing primarily from criminal justice, human rights, development, migration, and/or labor frameworks in understanding unfree labor.

My findings suggest that, at least among the INGOs I interviewed, the few that were operating with a labor framework were more attuned to the political economy of "modern slavery" and willing to suggest structural mechanisms for change beyond transparency laws and voluntary measures. This was true in comparison to INGOs with criminal justice, international development, or human rights approaches, which have dominated most international laws and program development related to unfree labor.[5] Still, at least one INGO with a labor focus had embraced voluntary, market-based solutions. Further research comparing framings of "modern slavery" in relation to INGO strategies and practices around corporate accountability would be useful, specifically: (a) whether or not INGOs coming from a labor perspective are more or less able and likely to press for corporate accountability on issues of unfree labor compared to INGOs using other frameworks; and (b) the reasons why some labor-focused INGOs oppose or resist market-based strategies while others embrace them.

Given that this book focuses on "anti-slavery" advocacy and INGOs in the West, another potential area of research could focus on the way business influence works in other geographic areas. For example, while some scholars suggest that business collaboration and support can help nonprofits garner independence from the state in China, others argue that the focus on state influence has obscured the way Chinese civil society and nonprofits are being coopted by business (cf. Lai and Spires 2020, 74; Yu and Chen 2018; Moeller and Valentinov 2011).

Similarly, one could explore these questions for countries of the global south. In conducting research for this project, for example, many interviewees referenced a nonprofit in a democratic country of the global south that has a history of strongly advocating for corporate accountability for forced labor. More recently, however, the nonprofit has been embracing business strategies and communications, including support for transparency laws and ethical consumption strategies, the development of an app, and a founder-celebrity model of marketing. How "anti-slavery" nonprofits headquartered in the global south navigate business influence and relationships would help to fill a gap in the literature that has often been focused on organizations in the West.

In addition, research that explores variations within the "anti-slavery" advocacy field in the West could be fruitful. While the general influence of businesses affects all of the Western INGOs included in this book, the ones in the United States and the UK were especially "enterprising" compared to others in Europe that were tied more closely to the state in terms of funding and service provision. Similar to Bair and Palpacuer's (2012) study of the national, political, cultural, and economic contexts shaping anti-sweatshop campaigns, for example, or Stroup's (2012) study of national factors leading to "varieties of activism" among INGOs, researchers could investigate the differences among "anti-slavery" INGOs in the West, with a focus on business and state influence.

INGO Strategies and Collaborations: A number of suggestions come out of this research and/or have been raised by scholars and activists to help to address the shortcomings of current efforts and strategies to combat issues of "modern slavery." First, contra the current dominance of private regulation in the West, and the rise of right-wing populist leaders who use state power to benefit business elites and merge state and corporate interests, states *could* do much to hold companies to account and support safe and fair migration, decent working conditions, and labor rights. By not doing so, they are contributing to unfree labor through a lack of labor market and business regulation and enforcement, and through migration regimes (LeBaron and Phillips 2018). INGOs can therefore press for states to invest or reinvest in labor inspection, work to ensure inspectorates have adequate authority and resources to inspect more workplaces, eliminate tied visas and recruitment fees, and safeguard freedom of association for all workers, including migrants. As one of the union interviewees said to me, issues of "modern slavery" would have difficulty continuing under such conditions.

INGOs can also take part in different models for enforcing labor standards in the face of the "fissured workplace" that has emerged as a result of large corporations outsourcing work through subcontracting, franchising, and temporary staffing instead of directly employing workers (Weil 2014, 2019).[6] Co-enforcement, involving government agencies partnering with unions, worker centers, and nonprofit organizations, is a model intended to help complement government enforcement and provide broader coverage of workplaces where state capacity is weak (Fine 2017a; Fine and Bartley 2018; Fine 2017b).

INGOs can enter into co-enforcement efforts by working on the ground in particular locations to support them, especially in areas without strong unions. They can conduct outreach and gather information from vulnerable constituents working in at-risk sectors; provide workers with access to information about their rights; refer cases; and help to mobilize support and pressure firms by publicizing problematic practices. For example, the Workers Defense Project in the United States is a nonprofit working on immigrant and worker justice that has partnered with law enforcement to address wage theft, and with the federal Occupational Safety and Health Administration and the City of Austin to improve health and safety and ensure livable wages in construction work (Fine 2017a).

INGOs can also advocate for states to actively work on prevention by focusing on the supply rather than demand side of unfree labor by supporting economic development, poverty alleviation, support to marginalized groups within countries, workforce development, and social protection programs. For example, supply-side responses such as cash transfers, vouchers, and food programs that are planned well and led by governments with stakeholders have been shown to produce long-term positive outcomes for child laborers, their families, and their communities (Okyere 2023, 85).

Second, "anti-slavery" INGOs can research and take positions on varied legal and policy responses intended to have more "teeth" than transparency laws. There has been a recent wave of mandatory due diligence laws passed in Europe, for example, that require companies to actively identify, prevent, mitigate, and remediate human rights, labor rights, and environmental risks in their operations and supply chains. The French Corporate Duty of Vigilance Law, enacted in 2017, allows any concerned party to file a complaint if a company fails to establish, implement, or publish a vigilance plan. If harm occurs, the company can be held liable and required to provide compensation.[7] Germany and Norway have also passed mandatory due diligence laws, though without reparations in the form of damages or compensation, and neither law provides for civil liability (Krajewski, Tonstad, and Wohltmann 2021).

These laws have been promoted as an important new legal mechanism, echoing some of the fanfare with which transparency laws were introduced, but concerns have already been raised by scholars that they do not adequately account for corporate power or do enough to promote access to remedy or corporate accountability (Deva 2023). "Anti-slavery" INGOs can weigh in on these laws as well as others that would help to compensate workers and hold corporate actors accountable for labor violations throughout supply chains, such as joint or several liability laws. The latter allows workers to seek justice and compensation from all parties involved in a supply chain. (Muskat-Gorska 2018; Muskat-Gorska and Kotiswaran 2017).

INGOs could also support other mechanisms to promote labor standards across supply chains. One approach involves voluntary agreements negotiated between unions, buyers, and contractors/suppliers; they place binding obligations on buyers to pay enough to ensure safe and decent work, guarantee payment to workers, and stabilize the subcontracting relationship (Anner, Bair, and Blasi 2016, 2013). Today, there are Global Framework Agreements (GFAs), which are negotiated at the global level between unions and multinational companies.

Scholars have viewed GFAs as progress that goes well beyond CSR in that they directly involve organized labor and usually place an emphasis on freedom of association and collective bargaining rights. One of the INGOs I interviewed strongly supported them as well. As they wrote about GFAs in an annual report:

> They differ from corporate codes of conduct in that they are the result of negotiations between organized labor and companies and they attempt to remedy the content and procedural deficiencies associated with unilaterally implemented corporate codes. . . . GFAs are qualitatively different from CSR initiatives that lack participation and oversight from trade unions.

The efficacy of GFAs has been tempered by limited enforcement mechanisms and the problem that forced labor in informal work falls outside the scope of such agreements (cf. Anner, Bair, and Blasi 2016; Ford 2015). Still, there are suggestions for how to make them more effective, including ensuring that they are tied to International Labour Organization standards, cover all levels of supply chains, include communications and educational activities with local unions and workers, and are enforceable, which entails transparent monitoring and binding arbitration or other forms of dispute resolution (Herrnstadt 2013). As with co-enforcement, INGOs can play a role in raising awareness of exploitive working conditions, advocating for the agreements, doing outreach and providing information to their at-risk constituents, and supporting unions and worker organizations.

INGOs can also press for trade-related mechanisms for addressing unfree labor in supply chains. We learned in chapter 3 about the closing of the United States Tariff Act loophole that one interviewee was excited about, for example, which allows Customs and Border Protection (CBP) to seize and forfeit goods produced with forced labor, but which has had only narrow enforcement. This could be expanded to cover broader quantities of goods, and regulations could be shifted to place the burden to prove that goods are not produced with forced labor and child labor onto importers, rather than leaving the burden with CBP to prove that they are (Higgens 2023). Scholars have also suggested the use of the "hot goods" provision of the Fair Labor Standards Act, which empowers the United States Department of Labor to seek a court order to prevent the interstate shipment of goods that were produced in violation of the Act (Anner, Bair, and Blasi 2013).[8] Finally, INGOs could advocate for bilateral and multilateral trade agreements to contain labor standards and protections as preventative measures, ensuring that they are applied to all workers, including migrants, and call for the elimination of countries' eligibility for trade preferences when they fail to address issues of "modern slavery."[9] Addressing core labor standards through international trade agreements is an area of common concern for INGOs and unions (Spooner 2005).

Third, "anti-slavery" INGOs could better work with other nonprofits, unions, labor groups, and migrant groups to advance areas of common interest, including the defense and organization of workers in sectors with low levels of union organization; support for workers in countries or regions with repression of labor organizing; campaigns for the inclusion of core labor standards in international trade agreements (per above); campaigns to ensure employers, including transnational corporations, adhere to core labor standards; and efforts to protect those in informal work (Spooner 2005, 14–15). They can, in short, work to help make "anti-slavery" advocacy:

> . . . more inclusive, focused on [the] protection of rights of all workers, irrespective of their residence status or sector of work, and fulfill their traditional capacities as service providers, whistle-blowers, and watchdogs (van Doorninck 2018).

INGO collaborations with unions and labor groups may seem a difficult recommendation to realize given long-noted divisions between nonprofits and unions exacerbated by a variety of factors (see, e.g., Eade and Leather 2005; Spooner 2005), but there are numerous examples of productive collaborations. I briefly discussed several in chapter 1, and there are others.

For example, nonprofits helping vulnerable migrant agricultural workers in Italy have provided them with services and information about their rights, and they have coordinated with unions to monitor their work situations (International Trade Union Confederation and Anti-Slavery International 2011). Thai workers who experienced human trafficking in Poland and wished to press for compensation in court provide another example. In that situation, the nonprofit La Strada International worked with both Thai and Polish trade unions to help build the case (International Trade Union Confederation and Anti-Slavery International 2011). These examples and others show that INGOs can partner with unions and labor groups to help with organizing and outreach to migrant workers, assistance to workers who experienced trafficking, advocacy campaigns, and training and education (Anner and Evans 2007; Ellis 2007; Yevgeniya 2007; International Trade Union Confederation and Anti-Slavery International 2011).

Fourth, INGOs can advocate for worker-centered solutions that support their agency in addressing unfree labor. Scholars have long argued that workers need to be centered in MSIs (Esbenshade 2004a; Braun and Gearhart 2005), and with the development of worker-driven social responsibility (WSR), some progress on that front has been made. The Fair Food Program (discussed in chapter 2), Milk with Dignity, and the International Accord for Health and Safety in the Textile and Garment Industry are examples that have been held up as models (Nolan and Boersma 2019; LeBaron et al. 2018, 64). Milk with Dignity is a WSR program created and implemented by the farmworker-led nonprofit Migrant Justice. Building on the Fair Food Program model, it seeks to improve working conditions for dairy workers in the United States via legally-binding commitments between the nonprofit and buyers. Participating buyers provide a premium to farms that agree to work toward the program's Code of Conduct, which sets conditions for wages, health and safety, housing, schedules, and rest, non-retaliation, and nondiscrimination.[10]

The 2023 International Accord, which came out of the earlier 2013 Accord for Fire and Building Safety in Bangladesh and its subsequent iterations, provides another example. The original Accord was a GFA that was signed by brands, retailers, and trade unions in the aftermath of the Rana Plaza building collapse in Bangladesh, which killed more than 1,100 people. It involved a five-year legally-binding agreement with an independent inspection component that was supported by brands and involved trade unions as well as the nonprofits Worker Rights Consortium (WRC) and Clean Clothes Campaign. It also included a commitment by brands to ensure funding to maintain sourcing relationships, democratically elected health and safety committees in all factories, and a worker complaints mechanism along with the right to refuse unsafe work. While it is limited to health and safety, it has been seen as a promising model that combines the agreement with WSR.

These efforts center workers and offer mechanisms for them to protect and enforce their own rights, but they are not without limitations. They work within existing systems to focus on the specific actions of individual corporate actors; they are dependent on negotiation and cooperation from companies; and they are limited to companies that agree to participate (Isaac 2001; Garwood 2011; Williams 2020). They offer just one of many strategies for INGOs to consider in the fight against unfree labor.

With neoliberal policies exacerbating conditions that contribute to issues of "modern slavery" and corporate-driven advocacy touted as the alternative to the purported shortcomings of state and civil society responses, INGOs have been embracing framings, actions, communications, and strategies that are inadequate for addressing labor exploitation in the global economy. Yet INGOs in the "anti-slavery" field have also been varied in their self-reflection, criticism, and responses. Some enthusiastically embrace business influence and market-based responses, a very few consciously resist, and most of the INGOs are somewhere in between. INGOs and the "anti-slavery" field can only benefit from reflexive and continuing critiques and analyses of these trends.

Appendix

In a dynamic advocacy field with a changing landscape of participating organizations, this project used a purposive sample to reflect some of the diversity of the field and its concentration in the West, where business influence, states, and INGOs have been dominant. Having worked as an academic studying "anti-slavery" advocacy for many years, and being based in the United States, I began this project with background knowledge of some organizations to contact and snowballed from those in the United States to eight additional countries, six of which I visited in person. I interviewed people at INGOs, IGOs, unions, and academic centers.

I started with organizations specifically dedicated to issues of "modern slavery;" I also reached out to INGOs that work on other issues but that have large dedicated "anti-slavery" programs, and I included some smaller "anti-slavery" INGOs as well. Given the expansion of "anti-slavery" efforts from sex trafficking to other forms of exploitation, I chose INGOs that focused on forced labor, human trafficking, and child labor (or a combination of these) in a variety of industries and supply chains. The resulting group of INGOs varied in terms of size, geographic reach, budget, business involvement, and primary activities, but all identified themselves as part of the advocacy field. They included both secular and faith-based INGOs, newer and long-established INGOs, and several that were market-oriented, with commercial components. I interviewed directors or CEOs of smaller organizations and the program managers of larger ones.

I conducted interviews between 2016 and 2019, traveling to meet the fifty interviewees and view the forty organizations (including twenty-nine INGOs) in person. In seven cases where scheduling issues precluded in-person meetings, I met with interviewees remotely. In all, only two INGOs I contacted declined to participate: one that was in the midst of a leadership change and experiencing some upheaval, and one that has since transitioned from a nonprofit to a for-profit organization.

I had guiding questions aimed at understanding the evolution of each organization, as well as its collaborations, partnerships, activities, operations, and strategies; the interviewee's responsibilities and experiences in the organization; and how the interviewee understood the organization's role and position in the advocacy field. I conducted the interviews in an open-ended manner, allowing each interviewee to raise issues as they saw fit. I was interested in how the interviewees perceived their organization, how they perceived businesses, how they thought about labor exploitation, who they partnered with, and how they understood their relation to their constituents.

The interviews were between one hour to ninety minutes long, and participants were given confidentiality so as to have the freedom to express views that might not be those of the organizations that they were representing and to minimize any potential concerns or harms that could result from being publicly quoted. For this reason, I have not used the names of the organizations in the text of the book, and I have sought to minimize details that could identify the interviewees and their organizations.

I also collected and analyzed the documents and materials of each organization at the time that I conducted an interview and again in 2020, after all of the interviews had been completed. This proved a useful strategy, since it allowed me to observe changes in the INGOs over time. The materials included reports, website text, and other print materials on the INGO websites, as well as transcripts of the videos and webinars they produced. From their documents, I also gathered information about their partners and networks, the amounts and sources of funding they received, and their organizational structures.

I uploaded all of the materials into NVivo, including 524 documents, 1,900 pages of organizational materials, and transcriptions of each interview. Drawing from all of the texts, I conducted an interpretive qualitative analysis, focusing on the framings of "modern slavery" and the solutions that extend from the ways the problems are understood and blame attributed (Benford and Snow 2000; Snow and Vliegenthart 2023; Snow, Vliegenthart, and Ketelaars 2019). I also coded the texts for themes related to understandings of INGO, business, and state roles in combating issues of "modern slavery" and understandings of the relationships between these groups.

I combined this analysis of framing with an explicit attention to power dynamics in the field (Bartley 2021), including what is being constructed, but also what is being left out, silenced, or obscured (Bacchi and Goodwin 2016; Bacchi 2012). The goal was to see how issues were characterized and what actions were taken, contextualize those findings within their broader political and economic contexts, and analyze whether and how they challenge, legitimate, or reproduce particular ideological perspectives and therefore power relations (LeBaron and Crane 2018; Caruana 2018).

Notes

Introduction

1. As of this writing, however, that company had been hit with a class action complaint claiming that it continues to perpetuate child labor while using deceptive labeling that misleads consumers into believing its products are procured with environmentally and socially responsible standards.

2. Child marriage, child soldiers, and the organ trade can be included as issues of "modern slavery" as well, but the main focus of the movement has been on human trafficking, forced labor, and child labor.

3. Scholars who have called for defunding "anti-slavery" work may see a silver lining in this trend. They have critiqued government-funded projects that bolster state surveillance and migration control rather than prevention or service provision (see, e.g., Sharapov et al. 2024; Sharapov, Mendel, and Schwartz 2024; Findlay 2024; Hebert 2024).

4. Hebert (2024) analyzed 1.2 billion dollars in funding that the United States spent to combat human trafficking from 2017–2021. She found that only 2.5 percent of 1,582 projects, comprising about 10 percent of the total funding, paid some attention to recruiters, global supply chains, or private sector employers. Of these, only one was focused entirely on altering private sector practices.

5. Another effort, the Global Fund to End Modern Slavery (GFEMS), was founded in 2016 and expected to secure the majority of its funding from the private sector, but governments remain its largest donors. See https://www.reuters.com/article/global-slavery-funding/official-correction-big-on-ideas-short-on-cash-modern-slavery-fund-seeks-to-transform-global-fight-idINL8N2KM5Fo?edition-redirect=uk [last accessed April 21, 2024].

6. Coordinated by the ILO, it includes partners in government, business, worker and employer organizations, nonprofits, academic institutions, and other UN entities and IGOs. It seeks voluntary action through "Pathfinder Countries" that commit to the creation of "Roadmaps" to address Target 8.7 and report annually. It also engages in research, awareness campaigns, sharing knowledge, and convening thematic groups on supply chains and migration.

7. This parallels the growth of NGOs more generally from 1991–2006 (Schofer and Longhofer 2020).

8. For counter evidence, see Meier and von Schnurbein's (2024) study of the mission statements of over 600,000 Swiss nonprofits and for-profits, which found that, to the extent that convergence was happening, it was due to nonprofits becoming marketized rather than for-profits becoming more nonprofit-like.

9. See Harvey (2007) on the historical development of neoliberalism.

10. It is interesting to compare this view with that of new institutionalist scholars who see these trends in power-neutral terms. For them, the business backgrounds of philanthropists lead them to benevolently diffuse business models and practices in the projects they support, while nonprofits "act like start-ups or incubators, prepared to scale and talk about ambitious plans for growth and impact" because they are adopting what has been successful for business (Horvath and Powell 2020, 121).

11. Businesses are not monolithic despite a tendency for scholars coming from both neoinstitutionalist and critical perspectives to paint them with a broad brush. Like INGOs, they may be more or less powerful in particular fields or in disagreement with each other, but common discourses do lead to similar understandings of problems and proposed solutions.

12. Political scientist and policy scholars see issues like "modern slavery" as "wicked problems" that are complex, intractable, and prone to framing disputes and contested solutions (Head and Alford 2013; Head 2022). There is debate about what counts as a "wicked" problem, however, and critiques of collaborative strategies for addressing them, which inadequately deal with power among stakeholders and seek to manage rather than solve the problems (Turnbull and Hoppe 2019).

13. The majority of INGOs working on issues of "modern slavery" have been disproportionately headquartered in the West, just like those working on other advocacy issues (Limoncelli 2016; Schofer and Longhofer 2020).

14. A few of the large INGOs with programs dedicated to issues of "modern slavery," particularly those that were faith-based, had much larger amounts of revenue for other activities, e.g., humanitarian aid, international development, poverty, and/or health programs. I am referring here only to the amounts for "anti-slavery" programs as I could best discern them.

Chapter 1

1. U.S. Department of Justice, https://www.justice.gov/usao-ri/human-trafficking [last accessed March 2, 2025].

2. See the UNICEF fact sheet entitled End Trafficking: Fast Facts, https://www
.unicefusa.org/sites/default/files/End%20Trafficking%20OnePager.pdf [last accessed March 2, 2025].

3. Leman and Janssens (2008), for example, document the growth of multi-
ethnic sex trafficking networks in Europe.

4. Here I return to the problematic use of the term "modern slavery," which can
evoke images of chattel slavery and overlook the historical specificity and racial op-
pression bound up in such systems—it can also promote the idea that contemporary
workers are being exploited only when they experience the most extreme forms of
physical coercion (Davidson 2010, Ollus 2015).

5. The large variations in estimates of human trafficking, as well as the profits it is
assumed to generate, demonstrates the ongoing difficulties of quantification. This has
been and remains a subject of much criticism (see, e.g., Feingold 2010; Merry 2016).

6. Howard (2017) elaborates on this point in his ethnography on Beninese ado-
lescent male labor migrants defined as trafficked.

7. Among these are differences in organizational structures, accountability to
workers, and organizational cultures.

8. For a counter view, see Michele Ford (2015), who is skeptical about the ability
of unions to address forced labor. While trade unions may advocate for legislative or
policy change, partner with non-governmental organizations to deal with particular
cases, or even engage directly with vulnerable populations, she argues, the integration of those populations into the day-to-day concerns of trade unions remains
elusive, especially in the global south, where forced labor is most prevalent.

9. See: https://corporatejusticecoalition.org/our-campaigns/modern-slavery
-act/ [last accessed March 3, 2025].

Chapter 2

1. https://www.prnewswire.com/news-releases/walk-free-calls-on-big-business
-to-end-slavery-worldwide-183689831.html [last accessed March 3, 2025].

2. See, e.g., https://www.youtube.com/watch?v=7gtaYuIFdR8 [last accessed
March 3, 2025].

3. See, for example, the MSI "The Code" intended to assist the travel and tourism industry to prevent the sex trafficking of children: https://thecode.org/ [last
accessed March 3, 2025]

4. See, e.g., https://hrbdf.org/dilemmas/forced-labour/ and https://hrbdf.org/
dilemmas/human-trafficking/ [last accessed March 3, 2025].

5. See https://www.walkfree.org/projects/business-and-investor-toolkit/
#understandingTheProblem [last accessed March 3, 2025].

6. Note, in this suggestion, that trafficking is seen as the fault of employees.

7. https://web.archive.org/web/20201019184746/https://www.babson.edu/about/
news-events/babson-announcements/babson-respect-initiative-against-human
-trafficking/ [last accessed March 3, 2025]

8. See https://themekongclub.org/ and https://themekongclub.org/kh-link/private-sector-heroes-fighting-modern-slavery-through-compliance [last accessed March 3, 2025]. I include the organization here, even though it is based in Hong Kong, because it lists businesses in both Europe and the United States as members.

9. https://www.trust.org/i/?id=b7fc7822-f256-4e7a-b21d-a5f6aa4c2871 [last accessed March 3, 2025].

10. The various strands of debate and suggestions for addressing shortcomings are too numerous to engage here. Some scholars argue that some combination of public and private regulation are needed (Posthuma and Bignami 2016; Locke 2013). Some argue for improvements in private regulation using transnational agreements between firms (Ashwin et al. 2020), more highly trained auditors and monitoring programs that are designed to facilitate knowledge transfer (Short, Toffel, and Hugill 2020), or more transparency (Robertson 2019). Some argue that worker voices/input will help while others offer examples of the limitations of worker input (Pike 2020) etc.

11. States can also be complicit. Kaplan and Lohmeyer (2021) provide a case study of Germany, in which businesses promoted CSR, civil society resisted, and the German government came in on the side of businesses, explicitly supporting the privatization of governance.

12. Data collected by the author for a related project (Limoncelli 2024).

13. This was an issue with at least one INGO I interviewed as well. Part of its strategy to combat forced labor is to certify goods that are being produced for export. The certification does not cover suppliers of raw materials or components, however, so even if forced labor is not occurring in the production of the goods, it may well be found at the base of the supply chain.

14. Esbenshade (2016) argues that codes are limited, so what is needed are contractual obligations that will impact the structure of sourcing. Monitoring of codes has not worked; neither has capacity building for suppliers, but contractual obligations can help.

15. See https://themekongclub.org/blog/we-spoke-to-ngos-about-the-private-sector-modern-slavery-this-is-what-they-said [last accessed March 3, 2025].

16. See https://www2.deloitte.com/us/en/pages/operations/solutions/anti-human-trafficking-social-impact.html [last accessed March 6, 2025].

17. Compare IOM's IRIS: https://iris.iom.int/ to ITUC's Recruitment Advisor: https://www.recruitmentadvisor.org/ [last accessed March 8, 2025].

18. The concern that NGOs may take over the role of unions is something that has been raised in the context of other MSIs as well. Connor (2007, 66) provides an example in the sweatshop movement, where ". . . U.S. NGOs involved in the Fair Labor Association finalized an agreement on factory monitoring with participating companies against the will and behind the back of UNITE, the U.S. clothing union. . ."

19. WSR entails six principles, including that the initiatives be worker-driven; obligations for companies must be binding and enforceable; buyers must afford suppliers the financial incentive and capacity to comply; consequences for non-compliant suppliers must be mandatory; gains for workers must be measurable and timely; and verification of workplace compliance must be rigorous and independent. See https://wsr-network.org/what-is-wsr/statement-of-principles/ [last accessed April 12, 2025].

20. They also suggest it can be extended, though its replicability depends on a strong civil society in which nonprofits are able to carry out the programs unhindered (Mieres and McGrath 2021; LeBaron 2020; Nolan and Boersma 2019, 193–195).

Chapter 3

1. Corporate codes have evolved over time, from those developed by IGOs in the 1970s, to ones promoted by individual governments and NGOs in the 1980s, to the development of individual company codes and broader industry codes in the 1990s (Esbenshade 2004a).

2. Some reasons for this include narrow enforcement actions targeting only a few businesses that account for only a small share of imports, and challenges identifying goods, among other issues (Higgens 2023).

3. I note here that INGOs can also exploit employees and become involved in scandals. While reports of human trafficking or forced labor by INGOs are not common, the recent case of Operation Underground Railroad in the United States provides an example of the founder of an INGO purportedly dedicated to rescuing children from sex trafficking being publicly accused of coercing employees into sexual acts and engaging in sexual assault. See https://www.nytimes.com/2024/09/09/us/tim-ballard-sound-of-freedom-sex-trafficking.html [last accessed April 23, 2025].

4. This mirrors the funding sources reported by anti-trafficking NGOs in the EU (Rossoni 2024, 114).

5. She cites the example of an anti-trafficking nonprofit dropping what a business association considered to be a sensitive topic from a training curriculum to show that they "respect the limits of the association's comfort zone." They were able to add it later.

6. The change in tactics from "naming and shaming" to quietly working with companies is highlighted and lauded in a Guardian article on the U.S.-based NGO Transparentum, which has specialized in investigating abuses in supply chains (Greenhouse 2019).

7. NGOs are sometimes advised to talk to businesses in "their own language," much as the interviewee does in this example (Hoff and McGauran 2015, 121).

8. Such depictions of consumer heroes can also reproduce "white savior of third world others" narratives (Page 2017).

Chapter 4

1. https://www.iom.int/video/leveraging-it-combat-trafficking-persons [last accessed April 25, 2025].

2. They reference ethical considerations and data protection issues as well and make recommendations to stakeholders about the use of technology. These are mainly to expand partnerships, identify gaps in legal systems to ensure effective investigation and prosecution of technology-facilitated trafficking, significantly expand data collection and research on the use of technology, build capacity amongst practitioners, and increase support for technology-based solutions.

3. https://cra.org/ccc/events/code-8-7-using-computation-science-and-ai-to-end -modern-slavery/#resources [last accessed April 25, 2025].

4. See https://www.gbcat.org/news/2023/7/27/gbcat-and-tech-against-trafficking -merge-to-scale-anti-trafficking-efforts [last accessed April 25, 2025].

5. https://www.microsoft.com/en-us/research/blog/iom-and-microsoft-release -first-ever-differentially-private-synthetic-dataset-to-counter-human-trafficking/ [last accessed April 25, 2025].

6. https://www.modernslaverymap.org/#section=welcome [last accessed July 9, 2025].

7. https://web.archive.org/web/20240807044131/https://www.whitehouse.gov/ wp-content/uploads/2021/12/National-Action-Plan-to-Combat-Human-Trafficking .pdf [last accessed July 6, 2025].

8. Almost half of the 305 technology tools found in the OSCE and Tech Against Trafficking report addressed labor trafficking. Businesses accounted for about 20 percent of the initiatives' target users, with civil society groups and law enforcement as the audience for about 25 percent, and people being exploited or at risk as another 25 percent of the intended users. (OSCE Office of the Special Representative and Co-ordinator for Combating Trafficking in Human Beings and Tech Against Trafficking 2020).

9. The INGO was in fact developing a separate membership network of businesses in some of these sectors for information sharing, allowing companies to have a "safe space" for reporting suspicions about exploitation and risks they may be facing, and promising that the INGO would not go to law enforcement as a first response.

10. See https://contratados.org/en/content/about [last accessed March 30, 2025].

11. At the time of this writing, for example, a government-issued app to track immigrants provided by Geo Group, a private prison firm in the United States, is being used by the Trump administration for deportations. See https://www.nytimes.com/ 2025/04/14/technology/trump-immigration-tech-geo-group.html [last accessed April 25, 2025].

12. Some ethical consumption apps are privately owned, and their methods for deriving income raise questions about their objectivity and motives for ranking companies and products. For example, they may receive a portion of sales through

affiliated marketing links or collect information about users that can be used for market research and targeted advertising and sold to interested third parties (Limoncelli 2020).

13. I contacted this company to ask for an interview but was refused.

Chapter 5

1. The effects of being tied to big funders are complicated. A steady source of income may allow a nonprofit to fulfill its mission instead of chasing other grant opportunities or it may be constraining due to the restrictions attached. Having multiple funders may provide nonprofits freedom from having to follow the ideological demands of a big funder but leave the nonprofit scrambling to secure resources (see, e.g., Pearce 2010; Stroup and Wong 2017).

2. Mike Dottridge (2021), former director of the INGO Anti-Slavery International, notes that some funders, such as the Oak Foundation and Porticus, have a record of supporting local activists.

3. In addition, funding from the global north can sometimes be used to help local organizations resist bureaucratic imperatives and support them in challenging existing power structures (Johansson et al. 2010; Richard 2009; Basu 2000; Pearce 2010).

4. This is one reason why the increasing salience of charity watchdogs has been critiqued by scholars who suggest that they may impede the autonomy of INGOs (Walker and Oszkay Febres-Cordero 2020; Baur and Schmitz 2011). Topics or problems that are too "hard" because they do not lead to easy indicators or the ability to show an upward trajectory may be penalized and receive less support.

5. Celebrities can also help to rehabilitate INGO reputations with the public after scandals (Scurlock, Dolsak, and Prakash 2019).

6. At least one scholar has found that people typically enter low-wage, insecure, and possibly exploitative work after experiencing trafficking in the United States (Brennan 2010, 2014).

7. See Beutin (2023, 2017), McGrath and Mieres (2021, 12–13), and Trodd (2013) on allusions to historical black slavery and abolitionism in the "modern slavery" field.

Chapter 6

1. A survey of 1,045 social enterprises in nine countries found that 50 percent were nonprofit, 26.7 percent for-profit, and 13 percent had combined legal forms. They financed much of their activity through selling products or services (57 percent on average), with some grant funding (26 percent on average). They saw for-profits as competitors and were most likely to be in development and housing, environment, or social services domains (Mair 2020).

2. For a counter position, see Lai and Spires (2020, 74) who provide the case of NGOs in China. They argue that they are "at risk of being co-opted by market forces

through business entrepreneurs' deep involvement in foundation funding practices, transforming groups initially formed with social change goals into social product providers and resource-chasing machines akin to commercial enterprises."

3. The conflicts were found in both commercial endeavors: the retail stores required workers to be available at specific times, but the clients, who were parents required to take welfare-to-work classes, had restricted schedules that did not match the needs of the stores. In the industrial services division, where clients with disabilities repackaged items, they were pressured to work fast so the business could obtain and retain contracts (Cooney 2006).

4. There are also concerns about the effects for democracy. Sociologist Theda Skocpol (2003) has argued that the professionalization and growth of advocacy groups in the United States has skewed civil society toward upper-class activities and concerns that diminish democracy; advocacy nonprofits are specialized, instrumental, and see themselves as "doing for" people rather than "doing with" them.

5. The remaining 13 percent went into academic positions, retired, or I was unable to track them.

6. On corporate elite involvement with civil society organizations, see Mills and Massoumi's (2025) study of the UK. They found that corporate elites tend to sit on the boards of high-status civil society groups and those that support traditional upper-class culture and class reproduction. They are also more likely to join civil society organizations that seek to shape politics and society rather than those involved in welfare and social service provision. This underscores a concern with shaping policy and supporting class institutions rather than supporting disadvantaged groups (Mills and Massoumi 2025).

7. Celebrities are often a key component of cause-related marketing and co-branded product lines (Richey and Ponte 2011; Eikenberry 2014).

Conclusion

1. As political scientists Stroup and Wong (2017) have noted, when lead INGOs in a field are collaborative, it does not typically lead to a division of labor in which some INGOs work to reform systems from within while other INGOs act as watchdogs and press for more radical change.

2. See https://perma.cc/WQC8-GNJF [last accessed May 4, 2025].

3. See https://apnews.com/article/trump-usaid-foreign-aid-cuts-6292f48f 8d4025bed0bf5c3e9d623c16 [last accessed March 1, 2025].

4. See https://www.nlrb.gov/about-nlrb/what-we-do [last accessed May 4, 2025].

5. This finding corroborates Shamir's (2012) call for a stronger labor approach to unfree labor, which supports workers as agents of change who can engage in collective action. While scholars have often advocated for either criminal justice, human rights, or development approaches while criticizing others (see, e.g., Aronowitz 2009; Kotiswaran 2019; Gallagher 2010), they have not typically done so from a labor perspective or with an emphasis on corporate accountability.

6. See Wolf et al. (forthcoming) for a discussion of enforcement regime approaches (e.g., complaint-based versus targeted, strategic enforcement, and generalized versus specialized regulatory bodies) and their ability to meet the challenges of regulation in neoliberal markets with fissured employment.

7. The burden of proof is on the claimant to establish the fault of the company for the harm, however, which is a barrier. The legislation also does not provide for criminal sanctions, disgorgement of profits made by the company through noncompliant subcontractors and suppliers, or punitive damages in the event of gross or willful violation or exclusion of access to the EU market (Clerc 2021).

8. https://www.dol.gov/agencies/whd/fact-sheets/80-flsa-hot-goods [last accessed April 28, 2025].

9. As one interviewee in the United States lamented, "I don't know how you give trade benefits to a country that is profiting from forced labor. . . . Why do we give them trade benefits? I can't understand that." See Ebert, Francavilla, and Guarcello (2023) for a discussion of trade policies to address forced labor.

10. See https://milkwithdignity.org/about [last accessed April 12, 2025].

References

Allin, Peggy-Jean M., and George M. Thomas. 2023. "Movements to Combat Sex-Trafficking: The Social Construction of a Global Problem and Its Solutions." *Millennium: Journal of International Studies* 52 (2): 304–30. https://doi.org/10.1177/03058298231212916.

Amengual, Matthew, Greg Distelhorst, and Danny Tobin. 2019. "Global Purchasing as Labor Regulation: The Missing Middle." *ILR Review* 73 (4): 817–840. https://doi.org/10.1177/0019793919894240.

Andrees, Beate. 2009. "Trafficking for Forced Labor in Europe." In *Forced Labor: Coercion and Exploitation in the Private Economy*, edited by Beate Andrees and Patrick Belser, 89–108. Boulder, Colorado: Lynne Rienner.

Andrijasevic, Rutvica. 2007. "Beautiful Dead Bodies: Gender, Migration and Representation in Anti-Trafficking Campaigns." *Feminist Review* 86: 24–44.

Andrijasevic, Rutvica, and Nicola Mai. 2016. "Editorial: Trafficking (in) Representations: Understanding the Recurring Appeal of Victimhood and Slavery in Neoliberal Times." *Anti-Trafficking Review* (7): 1–10. https://doi.org/10.14197/atr.20121771.

Anheier, Helmut K., Markus Lang, and Stefan Toepler. 2020. "Comparative Nonprofit Sector Research: A Critical Assessment." In *The Nonprofit Sector: A Research Handbook*, edited by Walter W. Powell and Patricia Bromley, 648–76. Stanford, CA: Stanford University Press.

Anner, Mark. 2012. "Corporate Social Responsibility and Freedom of Association Rights: The Precarious Quest for Legitimacy and Control in Global

Supply Chains." *Politics & Society* 40 (4): 609–644. https://doi.org/10.1177/0032329212460983.

———. 2017. "Monitoring Workers' Rights: The Limits of Voluntary Social Compliance Initiatives in Labor Repressive Regimes." *Global Policy* 8 (3): 56–65.

———. 2019a. "Predatory Purchasing Practices in Global Apparel Supply Chains and the Employment Relations Squeeze in the Indian Garment Export Industry." *International Labour Review* 158 (4): 705–727.

———. 2019b. "Squeezing Workers' Rights in Global Supply Chains: Purchasing Practices in the Bangladesh Garment Export Sector in Comparative Perspective." *Review of International Political Economy* 27 (2): 320–347. https://doi.org/10.1080/09692290.2019.1625426.

Anner, Mark, Jennifer Bair, and Jeremy Blasi. 2013. "Toward Joint Liability in Global Supply Chains: Addressing the Root Causes of Labor Violations in International Subcontracting Networks." *Comparative Labor Law and Policy Journal* 35: 1–44.

———. 2016. "Learning from the Past: The Relevance of Twentieth-Century New York Jobbers' Agreements for Twenty-First Century Global Supply Chains." In *Achieving Workers' Rights in the Global Economy*, edited by Richard P. Appelbaum and Nelson Lichtenstein, 239–258. Ithaca, NY: Cornell University Press.

Anner, Mark, and Peter Evans. 2007. "Building Bridges Across a Double Divide: Alliances Between US and Latin American Labour and NGOs." *Development in Practice* 14 (1–2): 34–47. https://doi.org/10.1080/0961452032000170613.

Anner, Mark, and Matthew Fischer-Daly. 2023. *Worker Voice: What It Is, What It Is Not, and Why It Matters.* Center for Global Workers' Rights, The Pennsylvania State University (University Park, PA).

Appelbaum, Richard P. 2016. "From Public Regulation to Private Enforcement: How CSR Became Managerial Orthodoxy." In *Achieving Workers' Rights in the Global Economy*, edited by Richard P. Appelbaum and Nelson Lichtenstein, 32–50. Ithaca, NY: Cornell University Press.

Appelbaum, Richard P., and Nelson Lichtenstein, eds. 2016. *Achieving Workers' Rights in the Global Economy.* Ithaca, NY: Cornell University Press.

Arenas, Daniel, Josep M. Lozano, and Laura Albareda. 2009. "The Role of NGOs in CSR: Mutual Perceptions Among Stakeholders." *Journal of Business Ethics* 88 (1): 175–197. https://doi.org/10.1007/s10551-009-0109-x.

Aronowitz, Alexis A. 2009. *Human Trafficking, Human Misery: The Global Trade in Human Beings.* Westport, CT: Greenwood Publishing Group.

Aronowitz, Alexis A., Gerda Theuermann, and Elena Tyurykanova. 2010. *Analysing the Business Model of Trafficking in Human Beings to Better Prevent the Crime.* OSCE Office of the Special Representative and Co-ordinator for Combating Trafficking in Human Beings (Austria).

Asbed, Greg, and Steve Hitov. 2017. "Preventing Forced Labor in Corporate Supply Chains: The Fair Food Program and Worker-Driven Social Responsibility." *Wake Forest Law Review* 52 (2): 497–532.

Ashwin, Sarah, Chikako Oka, Elke Schuessler, Rachel Alexander, and Nora Lohmeyer. 2020. "Spillover Effects Across Transnational Industrial Relations Agreements: The Potential and Limits of Collective Action in Global Supply Chains." *ILR Review* 73 (4): 995–1020. https://doi.org/10.1177/0019793919896570.

Bacchi, Carol. 2012. "Why Study Problematizations? Making Politics Visible." *Open Journal of Political Science* 2 (1): 1–8. https://doi.org/10.4236/ojps.2012.21001.

Bacchi, Carol, and Susan Goodwin. 2016. "Making Politics Visible: The WPR Approach." In *Poststructural Policy Analysis: A Guide to Practice*, edited by Carol Bacchi and Susan Goodwin, 13–26. New York: Palgrave.

Bain, Christina. 2017. "Entrepreneurship and Innovation in the Fight Against Human Trafficking." *Social Inclusion* 5 (2): 81–84. https://doi.org/http://dx.doi.org/10.17645/si.v5i2.924.

Bain, Christina, Effie-Michelle Metallidis, and Louise Shelley. 2014. *Hedging Risk by Combating Human Trafficking: Insights from the Private Sector.* World Economic Forum Network of Global Agenda Councils Task Force on Human Trafficking (Cologny/Geneva, Switzerland).

Bair, Jennifer, Mark Anner, and Jeremy Blasi. 2020. "The Political Economy of Private and Public Regulation in Post-Rana Plaza Bangladesh." *ILR Review* 73 (4): 969–994. https://doi.org/10.1177/0019793920925424.

Bair, Jennifer, and Florence Palpacuer. 2012. "From Varieties of Capitalism to Varieties of Activism: The Antisweatshop Movement in Comparative Perspective." *Social Problems* 59 (4): 522–543.

Bales, Kevin. 1999. *Disposable People: New Slavery in the Global Economy.* Berkeley: University of California Press.

———. 2000. "Expendable People: Slavery in the Age of Globalization." *Journal of International Affairs* 53 (2): 461–484.

———. 2007a. *Ending Slavery: How We Free Today's Slaves.* Berkeley: University of California Press.

———. 2007b. "What Predicts Human Trafficking?" *International Journal of Comparative and Applied Criminal Justice* 31 (2): 269–279.

———. 2016. *Blood and Earth: Modern Slavery, Ecocide, and the Secret to Saving the World.* New York: Spiegel & Grau.

Banerjee, Bobby. 2020. "Modern Slavery Is an Enabling Condition of Global Neoliberal Capitalism: Commentary on Modern Slavery in Business." *Business & Society* 60 (2): 415–419. https://doi.org/10.1177/0007650319898478.

Banerjee, Subhabrata Bobby. 2008. "Corporate Social Responsibility: The Good, the Bad and the Ugly." *Critical Sociology* 34 (1): 51–79.

Barrientos, Stephanie, Uma Kothari, and Nicola Phillips. 2013. "Dynamics of Unfree Labour in the Contemporary Global Economy." *Journal of Development Studies* 49 (8): 1037–1041. https://doi.org/10.1080/00220388.2013.780043.

Barrientos, Stephanie, and Sally Smith. 2007. "Do Workers Benefit from Ethical Trade? Assessing Codes of Labour Practice in Global Production Systems." *Third World Quarterly* 28 (4): 713–729. https://doi.org/10.1080/01436590701336580.

Bartley, Tim. 2007. "Institutional Emergence in an Era of Globalization: The Rise of Transnational Private Regulation of Labor and Environmental Conditions." *American Journal of Sociology* 113 (2): 297–351.

———. 2018. *Rules Without Rights: Land, Labor, and Private Authority in the Global Economy.* Oxford, UK: Oxford University Press.

———. 2021. "Power and the Practice of Transnational Private Regulation." *New Political Economy* 27 (2): 188–202. https://doi.org/10.1080/13563467.2021.1881471.

Bartley, Tim, and Curtis Child. 2014. "Shaming the Corporation: The Social Production of Targets and the Anti-Sweatshop Movement." *American Sociological Review* 79 (4): 653–679. https://doi.org/10.1177/0003122414540653.

Barton, Bernadette, Barbara G. Brents, and Angela Jones. 2024. "Introduction." In *Sex Work Today: Erotic Labor in the Twenty-First Century,* edited by Bernadette Barton, Barbara G. Brents, and Angela Jones, 1–13. New York: New York University Press.

Basu, Amrita. 2000. "Globalization of the Local/Localization of the Global: Mapping Transnational Women's Movements." *Meridians* 1 (1): 68–84.

Baumann-Pauly, Dorothée, Justine Nolan, Auret van Heerden, and Michael Samway. 2016. "Industry-Specific Multi-Stakeholder Initiatives That Govern Corporate Human Rights Standards: Legitimacy Assessments of the Fair Labor Association and the Global Network Initiative." *Journal of Business Ethics* 143 (4): 771–787. https://doi.org/10.1007/s10551-016-3076-z.

Baur, Dorothea. 2011. *NGOs as Legitimate Partners of Corporations: A Political Conceptualization.* Dordrecht, Heidelberg, London, New York: Springer.

Baur, Dorothea, and Guido Palazzo. 2011. "The Moral Legitimacy of NGOs as Partners of Corporations." *Business Ethics Quarterly* 21 (4): 579–604.

Baur, Dorothea, and Hans Peter Schmitz. 2011. "Corporations and NGOs: When Accountability Leads to Co-optation." *Journal of Business Ethics* 106 (1): 9–21. https://doi.org/10.1007/s10551-011-1057-9.

Belser, Patrick. 2005. *Forced Labour and Human Trafficking: Estimating the Profits.* International Labour Office (Geneva).

Bendell, Jem. 2004. *Barricades and Boardrooms: A Contemporary History of the Corporate Accountability Movement.* United Nations Research Institute for Social Development (UNRISD) (Geneva).

Benford, Robert D., and David A. Snow. 2000. "Framing Processes and Social Movements: An Overview and Assessment." *Annual Review of Sociology* 26: 611–639.

Berg, Laurie, Bassina Farbenblum, and Angela Kintominas. 2020. "Addressing Exploitation in Supply Chains: Is Technology a Game Changer for Worker Voice?" *Anti-Trafficking Review* 14 (2020): 47–66.

Bernal, Victoria, and Inderpal Grewal, eds. 2014. *Theorizing NGOs: States, Feminisms, and Neoliberalism.* Durham: Duke University Press.

Bernstein, Elizabeth. 2007. "The Sexual Politics of the 'New Abolitionism'." *Differences: A Journal of Feminist Cultural Studies* 18 (3): 128–151.

———. 2014. "Introduction: Sexual Economies and New Regimes of Governance." *Social Politics: International Studies in Gender, State and Society* 21 (3): 345–354.

———. 2016. "Redemptive Capitalism and Sexual Investability." *Political Power and Social Theory* 30: 45–80.

Berry, Jeffrey M., and David F. Arons. 2005. *A Voice for Nonprofits*. Washington, DC: Brookings Institution Press.

Beutin, Lyndsey P. 2017. "Black Suffering for/from Anti-Trafficking Advocacy." *Anti-Trafficking Review* (9): 14–30. https://doi.org/10.14197/atr.201220144.

———. 2023. *Trafficking in Antiblackness: Modern-Day Slavery, White Indemnity, and Racial Justice*. Duke University Press.

Bian, Junru. 2022. "The Racialization of Expertise and Professional Non-Equivalence in the Humanitarian Workplace." *Journal of International Humanitarian Action* 7 (1): 3. https://doi.org/10.1186/s41018-021-00112-9. https://www.ncbi.nlm.nih.gov/pubmed/37519833.

Birch, Kean, and Matti Siemiatycki. 2015. "Neoliberalism and the Geographies of Marketization: The Entangling of State and Markets." *Progress in Human Geography* 40 (2): 177–198. https://doi.org/10.1177/0309132515570512.

Birkey, Rachel N., Ronald P. Guidry, Mohammad Azizul Islam, and Dennis M. Patten. 2018. "Mandated Social Disclosure: An Analysis of the Response to the California Transparency in Supply Chains Act of 2010." *Journal of Business Ethics* 152 (3): 827–841. https://doi.org/10.1007/s10551-016-3364-7.

Bloom, Peter, and Carl Rhodes. 2018. *CEO Society: The Corporate Takeover of Everyday Life*. London: Zed Books.

Boersma, Martijn, and Justine Nolan. 2020. "Can Blockchain Help Resolve Modern Slavery in Supply Chains?" *AIB Insights* 20 (2). https://doi.org/10.46697/001c.13542.

———. 2022. "Modern Slavery and the Employment Relationship: Exploring the Continuum of Exploitation." *Journal of Industrial Relations* 64 (2): 165–176. https://doi.org/10.1177/00221856211069238.

Boli, John, and George M. Thomas, eds. 1999. *Constructing World Culture: International Nongovernmental Organizations Since 1875*. Stanford, CA: Stanford University Press.

Bourdieu, Pierre. 2005. *The Social Structures of the Economy*. Cambridge: Polity Press.

Boyd, Doreen S., Bethany Jackson, Jessica Wardlaw, Giles M. Foody, Stuart Marsh, and Kevin Bales. 2018. "Slavery from Space: Demonstrating the Role for Satellite Remote Sensing to Inform Evidence-Based Action Related to UN SDG Number 8." *ISPRS Journal of Photogrammetry and Remote Sensing* 142: 380–388. https://doi.org/10.1016/j.isprsjprs.2018.02.012.

Brace, Laura, and Julia O'Connell Davidson, eds. 2018. *Revisiting Slavery and Antislavery: Towards a Critical Analysis*. Cham, Switzerland: Palgrave Macmillan.

Brass, Tom. 2011. "Unfree Labour as Primitive Accumulation?" *Capital & Class* 35 (1): 23–38. https://doi.org/10.1177/0309816810392969.

Brass, Tom, and Marcel van der Linden, eds. 1997. *Free and Unfree Labour: The Debate Continues*. Bern, Switzerland: Peter Lang.

Braun, Ranier, and Judy Gearhart. 2005. "Who Should Code Your Conduct? Trade Union and NGO Differences in the Fight for Workers' Rights." In *Development NGOs and Labor Unions: Terms of Engagement*, edited by Deborah Eade and Alan Leather, 203–221. Bloomfield, CT: Kumarian Press, Inc.

Brennan, Denise. 2010. "Thoughts on Finding and Assisting Individuals in Forced Labor in the USA." *Sexualities* 13 (2): 139–152. https://doi.org/10.1177/1363460709359116.

———. 2014. *Life Interrupted: Trafficking into Forced Labor in the United States*. Durham: Duke University Press.

Bromley, Patricia, and John W. Meyer. 2014. "'They Are All Organizations': The Cultural Roots of Blurring Between the Nonprofit, Business, and Government Sectors." *Administration & Society* 49 (7): 939–966. https://doi.org/10.1177/0095399714548268.

Brown, David, Doreen S. Boyd, Katherine Brickell, Christopher D. Ives, Nithya Natarajan, and Laurie Parsons. 2019. "Modern Slavery, Environmental Degradation and Climate Change: Fisheries, Field, Forests and Factories." *Environment and Planning E: Nature and Space* 4 (2): 191–207. https://doi.org/10.1177/2514848619887156.

Brown, Wendy. 2015. *Undoing the Demos: Neoliberalism's Stealth Revolution*. New York: Zone Books.

Budabin, Alexandra Cosima. 2019. "Caffeinated Solutions as Neoliberal Politics: How Celebrities Create and Promote Partnerships for Peace and Development." *Perspectives on Politics* 18 (1): 60–75. https://doi.org/10.1017/s153759271900241x.

Busa, Julianne, and Leslie King. 2015. "Corporate Takeover? Ideological Heterogeneity, Individualization, and Materiality in the Corporatization of Three Environment-Related Movements." *Journal of Environmental Studies and Sciences* 5 (3): 251–261. https://doi.org/10.1007/s13412-015-0271-7.

Cahn, Naomi, Maxine Eichner, and Mary Ziegler. 2024. "Children at Work, Parental Rights—and Rhetoric." *Arkansas Law Review* 77 (2): 257–281.

Camarena, Leonor, Mary K. Feeney, and Jesse Lecy. 2021. "Nonprofit Entrepreneurship: Gender Differences in Strategy and Practice." *Nonprofit and Voluntary Sector Quarterly* 50 (6): 1170–1192. https://doi.org/10.1177/0899764021999436.

Caruana, Robert. 2018. "The Role of Discourse Analysis in Researching Severe Labour Exploitation." In *Researching Forced Labour in the Global Economy: Methodological Challenges and Advances*, edited by Genevieve LeBaron, 167–182. Oxford: Oxford University Press.

Caspersz, Donella, Holly Cullen, Matthew C. Davis, Deepti Jog, Fiona McGaughey, Divya Singhal, Mark Sumner, and Hinrich Voss. 2022. "Modern Slavery in

Global Value Chains: A Global Factory and Governance Perspective." *Journal of Industrial Relations* 64 (2): 177–199. https://doi.org/10.1177/00221856211054586.

Chahine, S., and L. Tannir. 2010. "On the Social and Financial Effects of the Transformation of Microfinance NGOs." *VOLUNTAS: International Journal of Voluntary and Nonprofit Organizations* 21 (3): 440–461. https://doi.org/10.1007/s11266-010-9136-6.

Chapkis, Wendy. 2005. "Soft Glove, Punishing Fist: The Trafficking Victims Protection Act of 2000." In *Regulating Sex: The Politics of Intimacy and Identity*, edited by Elizabeth Bernstein and Laurie Schaffner, 51–65. New York: Routledge.

Cherlet, Jan. 2014. "Epistemic and Technological Determinism in Development Aid." *Science, Technology, & Human Values* 39 (6): 773–794. https://doi.org/10.1177/0162243913516806.

Chilton, Adam S., and Galit Sarfaty. 2016. *The Limitations of Supply Chain Disclosure Regimes*. University of Chicago Law School (Chicago).

Choi-Fitzpatrick, Austin. 2017. *What Slaveholders Think: How Contemporary Perpetrators Rationalize What They Do*. New York: Columbia University Press.

Choudry, Aziz, and Dip Kapoor, eds. 2013. *NGOization: Complicity, Contradictions and Prospects*. London: Zed Books.

Chouliaraki, Lilie. 2006. *The Spectatorship of Suffering*. London; Thousand Oaks: Sage.

———. 2010. "Post-Humanitarianism: Humanitarian Communication Beyond a Politics of Pity." *International Journal of Cultural Studies* 13 (2): 107–126.

Chuang, Janie. 2015. "The Challenges and Perils of Reframing Trafficking as 'Modern-Day Slavery'." *Anti-Trafficking Review* 5 (2015): 146-149. https://doi.org/10.14197/atr.20121559.

Chuang, Janie, and Elena Shih, eds. 2021. *Philanthrocapitalism and Anti-Trafficking*. London: Beyond Trafficking and Slavery/openDemocracy.

Chuang, Julia. 2014. "Chains of Debt: Labor Trafficking as a Career in China's Construction Industry." In *Human Trafficking Reconsidered: Rethinking the Problem, Envisioning New Solutions*, edited by Kimberly Kay Hoang and Rhacel Salazar Parreñas, 58–68. New York, London & Amsterdam: International Debate Education Association.

Clerc, Christophe. 2021. *The French 'Duty of Vigilance' Law: Lessons for an EU Directive on Due Diligence in Multinational Supply Chains*. European Trade Union Institute (Brussels).

Cockbain, Ella. 2020. "From Conflict to Common Ground: Why Anti-Trafficking Can Be Compatible with Challenging the Systemic Drivers of Everyday Abuses." *Anti-Trafficking Review* (15): 155–161. https://doi.org/10.14197/atr.201220159.

Connor, Tim. 2007. "Time to Scale Up Cooperation? Trade Unions, NGOs, and the International Anti-Sweatshop Movement." *Development in Practice* 14 (1–2): 61–70. https://doi.org/10.1080/0961452032000170631.

Cooney, Kate. 2006. "The Institutional and Technical Structuring of Nonprofit Ventures: Case Study of a U.S. Hybrid Organization Caught Between Two Fields."

VOLUNTAS: International Journal of Voluntary and Nonprofit Organizations 17
(2): 137–155. https://doi.org/10.1007/s11266-006-9010-8.

———. 2011. "The Business of Job Creation: An Examination of the Social Enterprise Approach to Workforce Development." *Journal of Poverty* 15 (1): 88–107. https://doi.org/10.1080/10875549.2011.539505.

Crane, Andrew. 2013. "Modern Slavery as a Management Practice: Exploring the Conditions and Capabilities for Human Exploitation." *Academy of Management Review* 38 (1): 45–69.

———. 2017. "Modern Slavery from a Management Perspective: The Role of Industry Context and Organizational Capabilities." In *Contemporary Slavery: The Rhetoric of Global Human Rights Campaigns*, edited by Annie Bunting and Joel Quirk, 229–254. Vancouver, BC: UBC Press.

Crane, Andrew, Genevieve LeBaron, Kam Phung, Laya Behbahani, and Jean Allain. 2018. "Innovations in the Business Models of Modern Slavery: Exploring the Dark Side of Business Model Innovation." Academy of Management Annual Meeting.

———. 2021. "Confronting the Business Models of Modern Slavery." *Journal of Management Inquiry* 31 (3): 264–285. https://doi.org/10.1177/1056492621994904. https://www.ncbi.nlm.nih.gov/pubmed/35815001.

Crane, Andrew, Dirk Matten, Abagail McWilliams, Jeremy Moon, and Donald S. Siegel. 2008. *The Oxford Handbook of Corporate Social Responsibility*. Oxford: Oxford University Press.

Culpepper, Pepper D., and Kathleen Thelen. 2019. "Are We All Amazon Primed? Consumers and the Politics of Platform Power." *Comparative Political Studies* 53 (2): 288–318. https://doi.org/10.1177/0010414019852687.

Dale, John, and David Kyle. 2016. "Smart Humanitarianism: Re-imagining Human Rights in the Age of Enterprise." *Critical Sociology* 42 (6): 783–797.

Damman, Marleen, Liesbet Heyse, and Melinda Mills. 2014. "Gender, Occupation, and Promotion to Management in the Nonprofit Sector." *Nonprofit Management and Leadership* 25 (2): 97–111. https://doi.org/10.1002/nml.21114.

Dart, Raymond. 2004. "Being 'Business-Like' in a Nonprofit Organization: A Grounded and Inductive Typology." *Nonprofit and Voluntary Sector Quarterly* 33 (2): 290–310. https://doi.org/10.1177/0899764004263522.

Dauvergne, Peter, and Genevieve LeBaron. 2014. *Protest Inc. The Corporatization of Activism*. Cambridge: Polity Press.

Davidson, Julia O'Connell. 2006. "Will the Real Sex Slave Please Stand Up?" *Sexual Moralities* (83): 4–22.

———. 2010. "New Slavery, Old Binaries: Human Trafficking and the Borders of 'Freedom'." *Global Networks* 10 (2): 244–261.

———. 2015. *Modern Slavery: The Margins of Freedom*. London: Palgrave Macmillan.

Davies, Jon, and Natalia Ollus. 2019. "Labour Exploitation as Corporate Crime and Harm: Outsourcing Responsibility in Food Production and Cleaning Services

Supply Chains." *Crime, Law and Social Change* 72: 87–106. https://doi.org/10.1007/s10611-019-09841-w.

Davis, Gerald F., and Suntae Kim. 2017. "The Corporation in Sociology." In *The Corporation: A Critical, Multidisciplinary Handbook*, edited by Grietje Baars and Andre Spicer, 97–110. Cambridge: Cambridge University Press.

de Bakker, Frank G. A., Frank den Hond, Brayden King, and Klaus Weber. 2013. "Social Movements, Civil Society and Corporations: Taking Stock and Looking Ahead." *Organization Studies* 34 (5–6): 573–593. https://doi.org/10.1177/0170840613479222.

de Vries, Ieke. 2019. "Connected to Crime: An Exploration of the Nesting of Labour Trafficking and Exploitation in Legitimate Markets." *The British Journal of Criminology* 59 (1): 209–230. https://doi.org/10.1093/bjc/azy019.

de Vries, Ieke, Megan Amy Jose, and Amy Farrell. 2020. "It's Your Business: The Role of the Private Sector in Human Trafficking." In *The Palgrave International Handbook of Human Trafficking*, edited by John Winterdyk and Jackie Jones, 745–762.

Dees, J. Gregory. 1998. "Enterprising Nonprofits." *Harvard Business Review* (January–February): 55–67.

Dees, J. Gregory, and Beth Battle Anderson. 2003. "Sector-Bending: Blurring Lines Between Nonprofit and For-Profit." *Society* 40 (4): 16–27.

Demetriou, Daphne. 2015. "'Tied Visas' and Inadequate Labour Protections: A Formula for Abuse and Exploitation of Migrant Domestic Workers in the United Kingdom." *Anti-Trafficking Review* (5): 69–88. https://doi.org/10.14197/atr.20121555.

den Hond, Frank, Frank G. A. de Bakker, and Jonathan Doh. 2015. "What Prompts Companies to Collaboration with NGOs? Recent Evidence from the Netherlands." *Business & Society* 54 (2): 187–228. https://doi.org/10.1177/0007650312439549.

Deva, Surya. 2023. "Mandatory Human Rights Due Diligence Laws in Europe: A Mirage for Rightsholders?" *Leiden Journal of International Law* 36 (2): 389–414. https://doi.org/10.1017/s0922156522000802.

Dey, Pascal, and Chris Steyaert. 2010. "The Politics of Narrating Social Entrepreneurship." *Journal of Enterprising Communities: People and Places in the Global Economy* 4 (1): 85–108. https://doi.org/10.1108/17506201011029528.

———. 2014. "Rethinking the Space of Ethics in Social Entrepreneurship: Power, Subjectivity, and Practices of Freedom." *Journal of Business Ethics* 133 (4): 627–641. https://doi.org/10.1007/s10551-014-2450-y.

Ditmore, Melissa. 2023. *Unbroken Chains: The Hidden Role of Human Trafficking in the American Economy*. Boston: Beacon Press.

Dottridge, Mike. 2021. "Private Donors: The Pied Pipers of 'Modern Slavery'?" In *Philanthrocapitalism and Anti-Trafficking*, edited by Janie Chuang and Elena Shih, 20–23. London: Beyond Trafficking and Slavery/openDemocracy.

Downey, Liam, Elizabeth Lawrence, Micah Pyles, and Derek Lee. 2020. "Power, Hegemony, and World Society Theory: A Critical Evaluation." *Socius: Sociological Research for a Dynamic World* 6: 1–22. https://doi.org/10.1177/2378023120920059.

Eade, Deborah, and Alan Leather, eds. 2005. *Development NGOs and Labor Unions: Terms of Engagement.* Bloomfield, CT: Kumarian Press, Inc.

Ebert, Franz Christian, Francesca Francavilla, and Lorenzo Guarcello. 2023. "Tackling Forced Labour in Supply Chains: The Potential of Trade and Investment Governance." In *Integrating Trade and Decent Work Volume 2: The Potential of Trade and Investment Policies to Address Labour Market Issues in Supply Chains,* edited by Marva Corley-Coulibaly, Franz Christian Ebert, and Pelin Sekerler Richiardi, 103–138. Geneva: International Labour Office.

Eikenberry, Angela M. 2009. "Refusing the Market: A Democratic Discourse for Voluntary and Nonprofit Organizations." *Nonprofit and Voluntary Sector Quarterly* 38 (4): 582–596.

———. 2014. "A Critical Case Study of Cause-Related Marketing." *Administrative Theory & Praxis* 35 (2): 290–305. https://doi.org/10.2753/atp1084-1806350206.

Eikenberry, Angela M., and Jodie Drapal Kluver. 2004. "The Marketization of the Nonprofit Sector: Civil Society at Risk?" *Public Administration Review* 64 (2): 132–140.

Ellis, Jonathan. 2007. "More Than a Token Gesture: NGOs and Trade Unions Campaigning for a Common Cause." *Development in Practice* 14 (1–2): 248–253. https://doi.org/10.1080/0961452032000170811.

Esbenshade, Jill. 2004a. "Codes of Conduct: Challenges and Opportunities for Workers' Rights." *Social Justice for Workers in the Global Economy* 31 (3): 40–59.

———. 2004b. *Monitoring Sweatshops: Workers, Consumers, and the Global Apparel Industry.* Philadelphia, PA: Temple University Press.

———. 2012. "A Review of Private Regulation: Codes and Monitoring in the Apparel Industry." *Sociology Compass* 6 (7): 541–556. https://doi.org/10.1111/j.1751-9020.2012.00473.x.

———. 2016. "Corporate Social Responsibility: Moving from Checklist Monitoring to Contractual Obligation?" In *Achieving Workers' Rights in the Global Economy,* edited by Richard P. Appelbaum and Nelson Lichtenstein, 51–92. Ithaca, NY: Cornell University Press.

Ewart-James, Joanna, and Matthew Fischer-Daly. 2019. "Contemporary Social Movements to End Slavery – NGOs and beyond." In *The SAGE Handbook of Human Trafficking and Modern Day Slavery,* edited by Jennifer Bryson Clark and Sasha Poucki, 517–537. London: Sage.

Feingold, David A. 2010. "Trafficking in Numbers: The Social Construction of Human Trafficking Data." In *Sex, Drugs, and Body Counts: The Politics of Numbers in Global Crime and Conflict,* edited by Peter Andreas and K. M. Greenhill, 46–74. Ithaca and London: Cornell University Press.

Fejerskov, Adam Moe. 2017. "The New Technopolitics of Development and the Global South as a Laboratory of Technological Experimentation." *Science, Technology, & Human Values* 42 (5): 947–968. https://doi.org/10.1177/0162243917709934.

Ferguson, Michaele L. 2017. "Neoliberal Feminism as Political Ideology: Revitalizing the Study of Feminist Political Ideologies." *Journal of Political Ideologies* 22 (3): 221–235. https://doi.org/10.1080/13569317.2017.1348705.

Findlay, Joshua. 2024. "Anti-Trafficking and the Harm of Funding." *Anti-Trafficking Review* 23 (2024): 11–33. https://doi.org/https://doi.org/10.14197/atr.201224232.

Fine, Janice. 2017a. "Enforcing Labor Standards in Partnership with Civil Society: Can Co-enforcement Succeed Where the State Alone Has Failed?" *Politics & Society* 45 (3): 359–388. https://doi.org/10.1177/0032329217702603.

———. 2017b. "New Approaches to Enforcing Labor Standards: How Co-enforcement Partnerships Between Government and Civil Society Are Showing the Way Forward." *University of Chicago Legal Forum* 2017 (1): 143–176.

Fine, Janice, and Tim Bartley. 2018. "Raising the Floor: New Directions in Public and Private Enforcement of Labor Standards in the United States." *Journal of Industrial Relations* 61 (2): 252–276. https://doi.org/10.1177/0022185618784100.

Focus on Labour Exploitation. 2018. *Seeing Through Transparency: Making Corporate Accountability Work for Workers.* Focus on Labour Exploitation (London).

Foot, Kirsten. 2011. "Actors and Activities in the Anti-Human Trafficking Movement." In *The Dark Side of Globalization*, edited by Ramesh Thakur and Jorge Heine. United Nations Press.

———. 2015. *Collaborating Against Human Trafficking: Cross-Sector Challenges and Practices.* Lanham, MD: Rowman & Littlefield.

———. 2020. "Multisector Collaboration Against Human Trafficking." In *The Palgrave International Handbook of Human Trafficking*, 659–672. Cham, Switzerland: Palgrave Macmillan.

Foot, Kirsten, Helen Sworn, and AnnJanette Alejano-Stelle. 2019. "Structures and Practices of Cross-Sector Engagement in Counter-Human Trafficking Coalitions in the Global South." *Cosmopolitan Civil Societies: An Interdisciplinary Journal* 11 (1): 27–45. https://doi.org/10.5130/ccs.v11.i1.6259.

Ford, Jolyon, and Justine Nolan. 2020. "Regulating Transparency on Human Rights and Modern Slavery in Corporate Supply Chains: The Discrepancy Between Human Rights Due Diligence and the Social Audit." *Australian Journal of Human Rights* 26 (1): 27–45. https://doi.org/10.1080/1323238x.2020.1761633.

Ford, Michele. 2015. "Trade Unions, Forced Labour and Human Trafficking." *Anti-Trafficking Review* (5): 11–29. https://doi.org/10.14197/atr.20121552.

Freese, Barbara. 2020. *Industrial-Strength Denial: Eight Stories of Corporations Defending the Indefensible, from the Slave Trade to Climate Change.* Oakland: University of California Press.

Friedman, Matt. 2014. "Fighting Human Trafficking: The Role of the Private Sector." October 23, 2020. http://lastradainternational.org/lsidocs/3118-Fighting %20human%20trafficking%20-%20the%20role%20of%20the%20private%20sector _CSR%20Asia%20Weekly.pdf.

Fudge, Judy. 2015. "The Dangerous Appeal of the Modern Slavery Paradigm." openDemocracy: Beyond Slavery and Trafficking. https://www.opendemocracy .net/en/beyond-trafficking-and-slavery/dangerous-appeal-of-modern-slavery -paradigm/.

———. 2017. "Modern Slavery, Unfree Labour and the Labour Market: The Social Dynamics of Legal Characterization." *Social & Legal Studies* 27 (4): 414–434. https://doi.org/10.1177/0964663917746736.

———. 2022. "Bad for Business: The Construction of Modern Slavery and the Re-configuration of Sovereignty." *London Review of International Law* 10 (1): 3–31. https://doi.org/10.1093/lril/lrac001.

Fukushima, Annie Isabel. 2020. "Witnessing in a Time of Homeland Futurities." *Anti-Trafficking Review* 14 (2020): 67–81. https://doi.org/10.14197/atr.201220145.

Fukushima, Annie Isabel, and Julietta Hua. 2015. "Calling the Consumer Activist, Consuming the Trafficking Subject: Call + Response and the Terms of Legibil-ity." In *Documenting Gendered Violence: Representations, Collaborations, and Movements*, edited by Lisa M. Cuklanz and Heather McIntosh. New York and London: Bloomsbury.

Galaskiewicz, Joseph, and Sondra N. Barringer. 2012. "Social Enterprises and Social Categories." In *Social Enterprises: An Organizational Perspective*, edited by Benjamin Gidron and Yeheskel Hasenfeld, 47–70. Houndmills, Basingstroke, Hampshire; New York: Palgrave Macmillan.

Gallagher, Anne T. 2010. *The International Law of Human Trafficking*. Cambridge: Cambridge University Press.

———. 2021. "Private Giving Hides Government Inaction." In *Philanthrocapitalism and Anti-Trafficking*, edited by Janie Chuang and Elena Shih, 12–14. London: Beyond Trafficking and Slavery/openDemocracy.

Ganz, Marshall, Tamara Kay, and Jason Spicer. 2018. "Social Enterprise is Not Social Change." *Stanford Social Innovation Review* 16 (2): 59–60.

Garrow, Eve, and Yeheskel Hasenfeld. 2012. "Managing Conflicting Institutional Logics: Social Service versus Market." In *Social Enterprises: An Organiza-tional Perspective*, edited by Benjamin Gidron and Yeheskel Hasenfeld, 121–143. Houndmills, Basingstroke, Hampshire; New York: Palgrave Macmillan.

Garwood, Shae. 2011. *Advocacy Across Borders: NGOs, Anti-Sweatshop Activism, and the Global Garment Industry*. Sterling, VA: Kumarian Press.

Ghatak, Maitreesh. 2020. "Economic Theories of the Social Sector: From Nonprofits to Social Enterprise." In *The Nonprofit Sector: A Research Handbook*, edited by Walter W. Powell and Patricia Bromley, 319–332. Stanford, CA: Stanford Univer-sity Press.

Gidron, Benjamin, and Yeheskel Hasenfeld. 2012. "Introduction." In *Social Enter-prises: An Organizational Perspective*, edited by Benjamin Gidron and Yeheskel Hasenfeld, 1–15. Houndmills, Basingstroke, Hampshire; New York: Palgrave Macmillan.

Gordon, Jennifer. 2017. "Regulating the Human Supply Chain." *Iowa Law Review* 102: 445–504.

Greenhouse, Steven. 2019. "NGOs Softly-Softly Tactics Tackle Labor Abuses at Malaysia Factories." *Guardian*, 2019. https://www.theguardian.com/business/2019/jun/22/ngos-softly-softly-tactics-tackle-labor-abuses-at-malaysia-factories.

Grono, Nick. 2021. "The Catalysing Power of Philanthropy in Anti-Trafficking." In *Philanthrocapitalism and Anti-Trafficking*, edited by Janie Chuang and Elena Shih, 9–11. London: Beyond Trafficking and Slavery/openDemocracy.

Hanlon, Gerard. 2008. "Rethinking Corporate Social Responsibility and the Role of the Firm—On the Denial of Politics." In *The Oxford Handbook of Corporate Social Responsibility*, edited by Andrew Crane, Dirk Matten, Abagail McWilliams, Jeremy Moon, and Donald S. Siegel, 156–172. Oxford: Oxford University Press.

Hanlon, Gerard, and Peter Fleming. 2009. "Updating the Critical Perspective on Corporate Social Responsibility." *Sociology Compass* 2 (6): 1–12.

Harkins, Benjamin. 2017. "Constraints to a Robust Evidence Base for Anti-Trafficking Interventions." *Anti-Trafficking Review* 8 (2017): 113-130. https://doi.org/10.14197/atr.20121787.

Harvard University Ash Center's Government Innovators Network. 2012. "Best Practices to Combat Human Trafficking: Public/Private Partnership." Webinar available from: https://www.youtube.com/watch?v=Ry-MntU_QRw

Harvey, David. 2007. *A Brief History of Neoliberalism.* Oxford: Oxford University Press.

Hasenfeld, Yeheskel, and Eve E. Garrow. 2012. "Nonprofit Human-Service Organizations, Social Rights, and Advocacy in a Neoliberal Welfare State." *Social Service Review* 86 (2): 295–322.

Hawkins, Roberta. 2012. "A New Frontier in Development? The Use of Cause-Related Marketing by International Development Organisations." *Third World Quarterly* 33 (10): 1783–1801. https://doi.org/10.1080/01436597.2012.728315.

Haynes, Dina Francesca. 2014. "The Celebritization of Human Trafficking." *The ANNALS of the American Academy of Political and Social Science* 653 (1): 25–45. https://doi.org/http://dx.doi.org/10.1177/0002716213515837.

Head, Brian W. 2022. *Wicked Problems in Public Policy: Understanding and Responding to Complex Challenges.* Cham, Switzerland: Palgrave Macmillan.

Head, Brian W., and John Alford. 2013. "Wicked Problems: Implications for Public Policy and Management." *Administration & Society* 47 (6): 711–739. https://doi.org/10.1177/0095399713481601.

Hebert, Laura A. 2024. "US Anti-Trafficking Funding and the Discourse of 'Prevention'." *Anti-Trafficking Review* 23 (2024): 58–76. https://doi.org/https://doi.org/10.14197/atr.201224234.

Henriksen, Sofie. 2018. "Consuming Life After Anti-Trafficking." *Anti-Trafficking Review* 10 (2018): 14–33. https://doi.org/10.14197/atr.201218102.

Herrnstadt, Owen E. 2013. "Corporate Social Responsibility, International Framework Agreements and Changing Corporate Behavior in the Global Workplace." *Labor and Employment Law Forum* 3 (2): 263–277.

Hess, David. 2019. "The Transparency Trap: Non-Financial Disclosure and the Responsibility of Business to Respect Human Rights." *American Business Law Journal* 56 (1): 5–53.

Higgens, Matthew M. 2023. "Closed Loophole, Open Ports: Section 307 of the Tariff Act and the Ongoing Importation of Goods Made Using Forced Labor." *Stanford Law Review* 75 (April 2023): 917–977.

Hobbes, Michael. 2017. "The Myth of the Ethical Shopper." Huffington Post.

Hoff, Suzanne. 2014. "Where is the Funding for Anti-Trafficking Work? A Look at Donor Funds, Policies and Practices in Europe." *Anti-Trafficking Review* 3: 109–132. https://antitraffickingreview.org/index.php/atrjournal/article/view/67.

Hoff, Suzanne, and Katrin McGauran. 2015. *Engaging the Private Sector to End Human Trafficking: A Resource Guide for NGOs*. La Strada International (LSI) and Stichting Onderzoek Multinationale Ondernemingen (SOMO) (Amsterdam, NE).

Hofferberth, Matthias, Tanja Brühl, Eric Burkart, Marco Fey, and Anne Peltner. 2011. "Multinational Enterprises as 'Social Actors'—Constructivist Explanations for Corporate Social Responsibility." *Global Society* 25 (2): 205–226. https://doi.org/10.1080/13600826.2011.553533.

Holgersson, Charlotte, and Johan Hvenmark. 2023. "Gender in Nonprofit Organizations: A Critical Review and Research Agenda." *Nonprofit Management and Leadership* 34 (1): 195–209. https://doi.org/10.1002/nml.21560.

Horvath, Aaron, and Walter W. Powell. 2020. "Seeing Like a Philanthropist: From the Business of Benevolence to the Benevolence of Business." In *The Nonprofit Sector: A Research Handbook*, edited by Walter W. Powell and Patricia Bromley, 81–122. Stanford, CA: Stanford University Press.

Horwitz, Jill R. 2020. "Charitable Nonprofits and the Business of Health Care." In *The Nonprofit Sector: A Research Handbook*, edited by Walter W. Powell and Patricia Bromley, 413–444. Stanford, CA: Stanford University Press.

Howard, Neil. 2012. "Accountable to Whom? Accountable for What? Understanding Anti-Child Trafficking Discourse and Policy in Southern Benin." *Anti-Trafficking Review* 1: 43–59. https://doi.org/10.14197/atr.201213.

———. 2017. *Child Trafficking, Youth Labour Mobility and the Politics of Protection*. London: Palgrave MacMillan.

———. 2018. "Abolitionist Anti-Politics? Capitalism, Coercion and the Modern Anti-Slavery Movement." In *Revisiting Slavery and Antislavery: Towards a Critical Analysis*, edited by Laura Brace and Julia O'Connell Davidson, 263–279. Cham, Switzerland: Palgrave Macmillan.

Howorth, Carole, Caroline Parkinson, and Matthew MacDonald. 2011. "Discursive Chasms: An Examination of the Language and Promotion of Social Enterprise."

In *Enterprise, Deprivation and Social Exclusion: The Role of Small Business in Addressing Social and Economic Inequalities*, edited by Alan Southern, 249–260. New York: Routledge.

Humphery, Kim, and Tim Jordan. 2016. "Mobile Moralities: Ethical Consumption in the Digital Realm." *Journal of Consumer Culture* 18 (4): 520–538. https://doi.org/http://dx.doi.org/10.1177/1469540516684188.

Hunter, Philip, and Quinn Kepes. 2012. *Human Trafficking and Global Supply Chains: A Background Paper.* Verité (Amherst, MA).

Hwang, Hokyu, and Walter W. Powell. 2009. "The Rationalization of Charity: The Influences of Professionalism in the Nonprofit Sector." *Administrative Science Quarterly* 54 (2): 268–298.

Iazzolino, Gianluca, and Nicole Stremlau. 2024. "AI for Social Good and the Corporate Capture of Global Development." *Information Technology for Development* 30 (4): 1–18. https://doi.org/10.1080/02681102.2023.2299351.

Inter-Agency Coordination Group Against Trafficking in Persons. 2019. *Human Trafficking and Technology: Trends, Challenges and Opportunities.* United Nations (Vienna).

———. 2022. *Use and Abuse of Technology.* United Nations (Vienna).

International Corporate Accountability Roundtable, and Focus on Labour Exploitation. 2019. *Full Disclosure: Towards Better Modern Slavery Reporting.* International Corporate Accountability Roundtable and Focus on Labour Exploitation.

International Labour Organization. 2015. *Combating Forced Labour: A Handbook for Employers and Business.* International Labour Office Special Action Programme to Combat Forced Labour (Geneva).

International Trade Union Confederation, and Anti-Slavery International. 2011. *Never Work Alone: Trade Unions and NGOs Joining Forces to Combat Forced Labour and Trafficking in Europe.* ITUC (Brussels, Belgium).

Isaac, Jeffrey C. 2001. "Thinking About the Sweatshop Movement: A Proposal for Modesty." *Dissent* 48 (4): 100–112.

Ismail, Feyzi, and Sangeeta Kamat. 2018. "NGOs, Social Movements and the Neoliberal State: Incorporation, Reinvention, Critique." *Critical Sociology* 44 (4–5): 569–577. https://doi.org/10.1177/0896920517749804.

Jaffee, Daniel. 2012. "Weak Coffee: Certification and Co-Optation in the Fair Trade Movement." *Social Problems* 59 (1): 94–116. https://doi.org/10.1525/sp.2012.59.1.94.

Jager, Urs P., and Andreas Schroeder. 2014. "Integrated Organizational Identity: A Definition of Hybrid Organizations and a Research Agenda." *VOLUNTAS: International Journal of Voluntary and Nonprofit Organizations* 25 (5): 1281–1306.

Jägers, Nicola, and Conny Rijken. 2014. "Prevention of Human Trafficking for Labor Exploitation: The Role of Corporations." *Northwestern Journal of International Human Rights* 12 (1): 47–73.

Jenkins, Jean. forthcoming. "Unfree Labour: How Modern Is Modern Slavery?" In *Handbook on the Sociology of Work*, edited by Chris Rees, Ödül

Bozkurt, Stephanie Limoncelli, and Jonathan Preminger. Cheltenham, UK: Edward Elgar.

Joachim, Jutta, and Andrea Schneiker. 2018. "Humanitarian NGOs as Businesses and Managers: Theoretical Reflection on an Under-Explored Phenomenon." *International Studies Perspectives* 19 (2): 170–187. https://doi.org/10.1093/isp/ekx001.

Johansson, Karl-Erik, V. Johansson, Ole Engstrom, Ngolia Kimanzu, Jan-Erik Nylund, and Reidar Persson. 2010. "Trends in Development Aid, Negotiation Processes and NGO Policy Change." *VOLUNTAS: International Journal of Voluntary and Nonprofit Organizations* 21 (3): 371–392. https://doi.org/10.1007/s11266-010-9131-y.

Jordan, Ann. 2011. *Slavery, Forced Labor, Debt Bondage, and Human Trafficking: From Conceptual Confusion to Targeted Solutions.* American University Washington College of Law Center for Human Rights and Humanitarian Law (Washington, DC).

Kaplan, Rami. 2014. "Who Has Been Regulating Whom, Business or Society? The Mid-20th-Century Institutionalization of 'Corporate Responsibility' in the USA." *Socio-Economic Review* 13 (1): 125–155. https://doi.org/10.1093/ser/mwu031.

Kaplan, Rami, and Daniel Kinderman. 2017. "The Business-Led Globalization of CSR: Channels of Diffusion from the United States into Venezuela and Britain, 1962–1981." *Business & Society* 59 (3): 439–488. https://doi.org/10.1177/0007650317717958.

———. 2019. "The Business-Class Case for Corporate Social Responsibility: Mobilization, Diffusion, and Institutionally Transformative Strategy in Venezuela and Britain." *Theory and Society* 48 (1): 131–166. https://doi.org/10.1007/s11186-019-09340-w.

Kapoor, Ilan. 2013. "Humanitarian Heroes?" In *Age of Icons: Exploring Philanthrocapitalism in the Contemporary World,* edited by Gavin Fridell and Martijn Konings, 20–32. Toronto: University of Toronto Press.

Kara, Siddharth. 2010. *Sex Trafficking: Inside the Business of Modern Slavery.* New York: Columbia University Press.

Keck, Margaret, and Kathryn Sikkink. 1998. *Activists Beyond Borders: Advocacy Networks in International Politics.* Ithaca, NY: Cornell University Press.

Kempadoo, Kamala, Jyoti Sanghera, and Bandana Pattanaik, eds. 2005. *Trafficking and Prostitution Reconsidered: New Perspectives on Migration, Sex Work, and Human Rights.* Boulder, CO: Paradigm Publishers.

King, Leslie, and Julianne Busa. 2017. "When Corporate Actors Take Over the Game: The Corporatization of Organic, Recycling and Breast Cancer Activism." *Social Movement Studies* 16 (5): 549–563. https://doi.org/10.1080/14742837.2017.1345304.

King, Samantha. 2004. "Pink Ribbons Inc: Breast Cancer Activism and the Politics of Philanthropy." *International Journal of Qualitative Studies in Education* 17 (4): 473–492. https://doi.org/10.1080/0951839041000170955.

———. 2008. *Pink Ribbon, Inc.: Breast Cancer and the Politics of Philanthropy.* Minneapolis, MN: University of Minnesota Press.

Kothari, Uma. 2006. "An Agenda for Thinking About 'Race' in Development." *Progress in Development Studies* 6 (1): 9–23.

Kotiswaran, Prabha. 2019. "Trafficking: A Development Approach." *Current Legal Problems* 72 (1): 375–416. https://doi.org/10.1093/clp/cuz012.

Krajewski, Markus, Kristel Tonstad, and Franziska Wohltmann. 2021. "Mandatory Human Rights Due Diligence in Germany and Norway: Stepping, or Striding, in the Same Direction?" *Business and Human Rights Journal* 6 (3): 550–558. https://doi.org/10.1017/bhj.2021.43.

Krause, Monika. 2014. *The Good Project: Humanitarian Relief NGOs and the Fragmentation of Reason.* Chicago: University of Chicago Press.

Lai, Weijun, and Anthony J. Spires. 2020. "Marketization and Its Discontents: Unveiling the Impacts of Foundation-Led Venture Philanthropy on Grassroots NGOs in China." *The China Quarterly* 245: 72–93. https://doi.org/10.1017/S0305741020000193.

LeBaron, Genevieve. 2013. "Unfree Labour Beyond Binaries: Insecurity, Social Hierarchy and Labour Market Restructuring." *International Feminist Journal of Politics* 17 (1): 1–19. https://doi.org/10.1080/14616742.2013.813160.

———. 2018a. "Fighting Modern Slavery in Supply Chains from the Bottom Up." Delta 8.7, United Nations University Centre for Policy Research to Alliance 8.7. https://web.archive.org/web/20220125014234/https://delta87.org/2018/12/fighting-modern-slavery-supply-chains-from-bottom/.

———. 2018b. *The Global Business of Forced Labour: Report of Findings.* Sheffield Political Economy Research Institute (SPERI), University of Sheffield (Sheffield, UK).

———. 2020. *Combatting Modern Slavery: Why Labour Governance Is Failing and What We Can Do About It.* Cambridge: Polity Press.

———. 2021a. "A Market in Deception? Ethically Certifying Exploitative Supply Chains." In *Fighting Modern Slavery and Human Trafficking: History and Contemporary Policy*, edited by Genevieve LeBaron, Jessica R. Pliley, and David W. Blight, 156–178. Cambridge: Cambridge University Press.

———. 2021b. "The Role of Supply Chains in the Global Business of Forced Labour." *Journal of Supply Chain Management* 57 (2): 29–42.

LeBaron, Genevieve, and Andrew Crane. 2018. "Methodological Challenges in the Business of Forced Labour." In *Researching Forced Labour in the Global Economy: Methodological Challenges and Advances*, edited by Genevieve LeBaron, 25–43. Oxford: Oxford University Press.

LeBaron, Genevieve, Remi Edwards, Tom Hunt, Charline Sempéré, and Penelope Kyritsis. 2021. "The Ineffectiveness of CSR: Understanding Garment Company Commitments to Living Wages in Global Supply Chains." *New Political Economy* 27 (1): 99–115. https://doi.org/10.1080/13563467.2021.1926954.

LeBaron, Genevieve, Neil Howard, Cameron Thibos, and Penelope Kyritsis. 2018. *Confronting Root Causes: Forced Labour in Global Supply Chains.* openDemocracy and the Sheffield Political Economy Research Institute (SPERI), University of Sheffield (Sheffied, UK).

LeBaron, Genevieve, Jane Lister, and Peter Dauvergne. 2017. "Governing Global Supply Chain Sustainability Through the Ethical Audit Regime." *Globalizations* 14 (6): 958–975. https://doi.org/10.1080/14747731.2017.1304008.

LeBaron, Genevieve, and Nicola Phillips. 2018. "States and the Political Economy of Unfree Labour." *New Political Economy* 24 (1): 1–21. https://doi.org/10.1080/13563467.2017.1420642.

LeBaron, Genevieve, Jessica R. Pliley, and David W. Blight, eds. 2021. *Fighting Modern Slavery and Human Trafficking: History and Contemporary Policy.* Cambridge: Cambridge University Press.

LeBaron, Genevieve, and Andreas Rühmkorf. 2017. "Steering CSR Through Home State Regulation: A Comparison of the Impact of the UK Bribery Act and Modern Slavery Act on Global Supply Chain Governance." *Global Policy* 8: 15–28. https://doi.org/10.1111/1758-5899.12398.

———. 2019. "The Domestic Politics of Corporate Accountability Legislation: Struggles Over the 2015 UK Modern Slavery Act." *Socio-Economic Review* 17 (3): 709–743. https://doi.org/10.1093/ser/mwx047.

Leman, Johan, and Stef Janssens. 2008. "The Albanian and Post-Soviet Business of Trafficking Women for Prostitution: Structural Developments and Financial Modus Operandi." *European Journal of Criminology* 5 (4): 433–451. https://doi.org/http://dx.doi.org/10.1177/1477370808095125.

Lerche, Jens. 2007. "A Global Alliance Against Forced Labour? Unfree Labour, Neo-Liberal Globalization and the International Labour Organization." *Journal of Agrarian Change* 7 (4): 425–452.

LeRoux, Kelly. 2020. "Racial Diversity and Organizational Performance in the U.S. Nonprofit Sector." In *Race and Public Administration*, edited by Amanda Rutherford and Kenneth J. Meier, 119–139. New York: Routledge, Taylor and Francis Group.

Lerum, Kari, and Barbara G. Brents. 2016. "Sociological Perspectives on Sex Work and Human Trafficking." *Sociological Perspectives* 59 (1): 17–26. https://doi.org/10.1177/0731121416628550.

Levy, David L., and Daniel Egan. 2003. "A Neo-Gramscian Approach to Corporate Political Strategy: Conflict and Accommodation in the Climate Change Negotiations*." *Journal of Management Studies* 40 (4): 803–829. https://doi.org/10.1111/1467-6486.00361.

Levy, David L., and Rami Kaplan. 2009. "Corporate Social Responsibility and Theories of Global Governance: Strategic Contestation in Global Issue Areas." In *The Oxford Handbook of Corporate Social Responsibility*, edited by Andrew Crane, Dirk Matten, Abagail McWilliams, Jeremy Moon, and Donald S. Siegel, 433–451. Oxford: Oxford University Press.

Lewis, Hannah, and Louise Waite. 2015. "Asylum, Immigration Restrictions and Exploitation: Hyper-Precarity as a Lens for Understanding and Tackling Forced Labour." *Anti-Trafficking Review* (5): 50–68. https://doi.org/10.14197/atr.20121554.

Li, Vincci. 2016. "'Shopping for Change': World Vision Canada and Consumption-Oriented Philanthropy in the Age of Philanthrocapitalism." *VOLUNTAS: International Journal of Voluntary and Nonprofit Organizations* 28 (2): 455–471. https://doi.org/10.1007/s11266-016-9801-5.

Lim, Alwyn. 2017. "Global Corporate Responsibility in Domestic Context: Lateral Decoupling and Organizational Responses to Globalization." *Economy and Society* 46 (2): 229–254. https://doi.org/10.1080/03085147.2017.1359439.

Limoncelli, Stephanie A. 2010. *The Politics of Trafficking: The First International Movement to Combat the Sexual Exploitation of Women.* Stanford: Stanford University Press.

———. 2016. "What in the World Are Anti-Trafficking NGOs Doing? Findings from a Global Study." *Journal of Human Trafficking* 2 (4): 316–328. http://dx.doi.org/10.1080/23322705.2015.1135605.

———. 2017. "Legal Limits: Ending Human Trafficking in Supply Chains." *World Policy Journal* 34 (1): 119–123.

———. 2020. "There's an App for That? Ethical Consumption in the Fight Against Trafficking for Labour Exploitation." *Anti-Trafficking Review* 14: 33–46. https://doi.org/10.14197/atr.201220143.

———. 2024. "Business as Usual: Framing Labour Exploitation in the UN Global Compact." *Globalizations*: 1–19. https://doi.org/https://doi.org/10.1080/14747731.2024.2407207.

Lloyd, Danielle. 2020. "Human Trafficking in Supply Chains and the Way Forward." In *The Palgrave International Handbook of Human Trafficking*, 815–837. Cham, Switzerland: Palgrave Macmillan.

Locke, Richard M. 2013. *The Promise and Limits of Private Power: Promoting Labor Standards in a Global Economy.* Cambridge: Cambridge University Press.

Lucea, Rafael. 2010. "How We See Them Versus How They See Themselves: A Cognitive Perspective of Firm–NGO Relationships." *Business & Society* 49 (1): 116–139.

Ma, Yoon Jin, Hyun-Hwa Lee, and Kylie Goerlitz. 2015. "Transparency of Global Apparel Supply Chains: Quantitative Analysis of Corporate Disclosures." *Corporate Social Responsibility and Environmental Management* 23 (5): 308–318. https://doi.org/10.1002/csr.1378.

Mac Sheoin, Tomas. 2014. "Transnational Anti-Corporate Campaigns: Fail Often, Fail Better." *Social Justice* 41 (1/2): 198–226.

Maier, Florentine, Michael Meyer, and Martin Steinbereithner. 2016. "Nonprofit Organizations Becoming Business-Like: A Systematic Review." *Nonprofit and Voluntary Sector Quarterly* 45 (1): 64–86. https://doi.org/10.1177/0899764014561796.

Mair, Johanna. 2020. "Social Entrepreneurship: Research as Disciplined Exploration." In *The Nonprofit Sector: A Research Handbook*, edited by Walter W. Powell and Patricia Bromley, 333–357. Stanford, CA: Stanford University Press.

Majic, Samantha. 2014. *Sex Work Politics: From Protest to Service Provision.* Philadelphia: University of Pennsylvania Press.

———. 2023. *Lights, Camera, Feminism? Celebrities and Anti-Trafficking Politics.* Oakland: University of California Press.

Majic, Samantha A. 2017. "Real Men Set Norms? Anti-Trafficking Campaigns and the Limits of Celebrity Norm Entrepreneurship." *Crime, Media, Culture: An International Journal* 14 (2): 289–309. https://doi.org/10.1177/1741659017714518.

Majic, Samantha, Melissa Ditmore, and Jun Li. 2024. "440 Sex Workers Cannot Be Wrong: Engaging and Negotiating Online Platform Power." *Social Sciences* 13 (7): 337. https://doi.org/10.3390/socsci13070337.

Majic, Samantha, Daniel O'Neill, and Michael Bernhard. 2020. "Celebrity and Politics." *Perspectives on Politics* 18 (1): 1–8. https://doi.org/10.1017/s1537592719004602.

Malešević, Siniša. 2010. "Rational Choice Theory and the Sociology of Ethnic Relations: A Critique." *Ethnic and Racial Studies* 25 (2): 193–212. https://doi.org/10.1080/01419870120109458.

McGrath, Siobhán, and Fabiola Mieres. 2021. "The Business of Abolition: Marketizing 'Anti-Slavery'." *Development and Change* 53 (1): 3–30. https://doi.org/10.1111/dech.12701.

McGrath, Siobhán, Ben Rogaly, and Louise Waite. 2022. "Unfreedom in Labour Relations: From a Politics of Rescue to a Politics of Solidarity?" *Globalizations* 19 (6): 911–921. https://doi.org/10.1080/14747731.2022.2095119.

McGrath, Siobhán, and Samantha Watson. 2018. "Anti-Slavery as Development: A Global Politics of Rescue." *Geoforum* 93: 22–31. https://doi.org/10.1016/j.geoforum.2018.04.013.

Mehra, Ashley, and John G. Dale. 2020. "How Humanitarian Blockchain Can Deliver Fair Labor to Global Supply Chains." *Global Human Movement: A Transdisciplinary Forum on Movement, Mobility, and Migration* (blog), *University of Cambridge.* April 30, 2020.

Meier, Dominik S., and Georg von Schnurbein. 2024. "From Mission to Market: Assessing Sector Overlap Between Nonprofits and For-Profits." *Nonprofit and Voluntary Sector Quarterly* 54 (5): 1017-1042. https://doi.org/10.1177/08997640241300509.

Mekong Club. 2018. *Ending Modern Slavery: A Resource Guide for Businesses.* Mekong Club (Hong Kong).

Mende, Janne, and Julia Drubel. 2020. "At the Junction: Two Models of Business Responsibility for Modern Slavery." *Human Rights Review* 21 (3): 313–335. https://doi.org/10.1007/s12142-020-00596-9.

Mendel, Jonathan, and Kiril Sharapov. 2020. "'Stick Them to the Cross': Anti-Trafficking Apps and the Production of Ignorance." *Journal of Human Trafficking* 8 (3): 233–249. https://doi.org/10.1080/23322705.2020.1801284.

Merry, Sally Engle. 2016. *The Seduction of Quantification: Measuring Human Rights, Gender Violence, and Sex Trafficking.* Chicago: University of Chicago Press.

Meyer, John W., Shawn M. Pope, and Andrew Isaacson. 2015. "Legitimating the Transnational Corporation in a Stateless World Society." In *Corporate Social Responsibility in a Globalizing World*, edited by Kiyoteru Tsutsui and Alwyn Lim, 27–72. Cambridge: Cambridge University Press.

Mieres, Fabiola, and Siobhán McGrath. 2021. "Ripe to Be Heard: Worker Voice in the Fair Food Program." *International Labour Review* 160 (4): 631–647.

Milczarek-Desai, Shefali. 2024. "(Hidden) in Plain Sight: Migrant Child Labor and the New Economy of Exploitation." *Arkansas Law Review* 77 (2): 345–406.

Milivojevic, Sanja, Heather Moore, and Marie Segrave. 2020. "Freeing the Modern Slaves, One Click at a Time: Theorising Human Trafficking, Modern Slavery, and Technology." *Anti-Trafficking Review* 14 (2020): 16–32. https://doi.org/10.14197/atr.201220142.

Miller, Nick. 2014. "Andrew Forrest's Dream to Stop All Slavery." *The Sydney Morning Herald*, March 18, 2014. https://www.smh.com.au/national/andrew-forrests-dream-to-stop-all-slavery-20140317-34y2g.html.

Mills, Tom, and Narzanin Massoumi. 2025. "Elite Status-Seeking and Class Reproduction in Civil Society: An Analysis of Corporate Elite Appointments to Charity Boards." *The British Journal of Sociology* 76 (3): 605–621. https://doi.org/10.1111/1468-4446.13201. https://www.ncbi.nlm.nih.gov/pubmed/40016626.

Mitchell, Katharyne. 2016. "Celebrity Humanitarianism, Transnational Emotion and the Rise of Neoliberal Citizenship." *Global Networks* 16 (3): 288–306. https://doi.org/http://dx.doi.org/10.1111/glob.12114.

Moeller, Lioudmila, and Vladislav Valentinov. 2011. "The Commercialization of the Nonprofit Sector: A General Systems Theory Perspective." *Systemic Practice and Action Research* 25 (4): 365–370. https://doi.org/10.1007/s11213-011-9226-4.

Mosley, Jennifer E. 2020. "Social Service Nonprofits: Navigating Conflicting Demands." In *The Nonprofit Sector: A Research Handbook*, edited by Walter W. Powell and Patricia Bromley, 251–270. Stanford, CA: Stanford University Press.

Mosley, Jennifer E., David F. Suárez, and Hokyu Hwang. 2022. "Conceptualizing Organizational Advocacy Across the Nonprofit and Voluntary Sector: Goals, Tactics, and Motivation." *Nonprofit and Voluntary Sector Quarterly* 52 (1_suppl): 187S–211S. https://doi.org/10.1177/08997640221103247.

Muskat-Gorska, Zuzanna. 2018. "Can Labour Make an Effective Contribution to Legal Strategies Against Human Trafficking?" In *Routledge Handbook of Human Trafficking*, edited by Ryszard Piotrowicz, Conny Rijken, and Baerbel Heide Uhl, 459–469. London and New York: Routledge.

———. 2017. "Human Trafficking and Forced Labour: Mapping Corporate Liability." In *Revisiting the Law and Governance of Trafficking, Forced Labor and Modern Slavery*, edited by Prabha Kotiswaran, 443–468. Cambridge: Cambridge University Press.

Musto, Jennifer. 2016. *Control and Protect: Collaboration, Carceral Protection, and Domestic Sex Trafficking in the United States*. Oakland, CA: University of California Press.

Musto, Jennifer Lynne. 2010. "The NGO-ification of the Anti-Trafficking Movement in the United States: A Case Study of the Coalition to Abolish Slavery and Trafficking." In *Sex Trafficking, Human Rights and Social Justice*, edited by Tiantian Zheng, 23–36. New York: Routledge.

Musto, Jennifer Lynne, and danah boyd. 2014. "The Trafficking-Technology Nexus." *Social Politics: International Studies in Gender, State & Society* 21 (3): 461–483. https://doi.org/10.1093/sp/jxu018.

Musto, Jennifer, Mitali Thakor, and Borislav Gerasimov. 2020. "Editorial: Between Hope and Hype: Critical Evaluations of Technology's Role in Anti-Trafficking." *Anti-Trafficking Review* 14 (2020): 1–14. https://doi.org/https://doi.org/10.14197/atr.201220141.

Nadvi, Khalid. 2008. "Global Standards, Global Governance and the Organization of Global Value Chains." *Journal of Economic Geography* 8 (3): 323–343. https://doi.org/10.1093/jeg/lbn003.

New, Stephen John. 2015. "Modern Slavery and the Supply Chain: The Limits of Corporate Social Responsibility?" *Supply Chain Management: An International Journal* 20 (6): 697–707. https://doi.org/10.1108/scm-06-2015-0201.

Nickel, Patricia Mooney, and Angela M. Eikenberry. 2010. "Philanthropy in an Era of Global Governance." In *Third Sector Research*, edited by Rupert Taylor, 269–279. New York: Springer.

———. 2009. "A Critique of the Discourse of Marketized Philanthropy." *American Behavioral Scientist* 52 (7): 974–989.

Nolan, Justine, and Martijn Boersma. 2019. *Addressing Modern Slavery*. Sydney: NewSouth Publishing.

NORC. 2020. *NORC Final Report: Assessing Progress in Reducing Child Labor in Cocoa Production in Cocoa Growing Areas of Côte d'Ivoire and Ghana*. NORC at the University of Chicago (Chicago, IL).

Nova, Scott, and Chris Wegemer. 2016. "Outsourcing Horror: Why Apparel Workers Are Still Dying, One Hundred Years After Triangle Shirtwaist." In *Achieving Workers' Rights in the Global Economy*, edited by Richard P. Appelbaum and Nelson Lichtenstein, 17–31. Ithaca, NY: Cornell University Press.

O'Brien, Erin. 2015. "Human Trafficking Heroes and Villains: Representing the Problem in Anti-Trafficking Awareness Campaigns." *Social & Legal Studies* 25 (2): 205–224. https://doi.org/10.1177/0964663915593410.

———. 2018. "Human Trafficking and Heroic Consumerism." *International Journal for Crime, Justice and Social Democracy* 7 (2): 51–66. https://doi.org/10.5204/ijcjsd.v7i4.430.

O'Brien, Erin, and Helen Berents. 2019. "Virtual Saviours: Digital Games and Anti-Trafficking Awareness-Raising." *Anti-Trafficking Review* (13): 82–99. https://doi.org/10.14197/atr.201219136.

O'Brien, Erin, and Alissa Macoun. 2021. "Responsible Citizens, Political Consumers and the State." *Acta Politica* 57 (2): 377–395. https://doi.org/10.1057/s41269-021-00194-8.

O'Connor, Amy, and Michelle Shumate. 2011. "Differences Among NGOs in the Business–NGO Cooperative Network." *Business & Society* 53 (1): 105–133. https://doi.org/10.1177/0007650311418195.

O'Manique, Colleen, and Momin Rahman. 2013. "(Product) RED: Glam Aid, Consumer Citizens, and the Colonization of Governance." In *Age of Icons: Exploring Philanthrocapitalism in the Contemporary World*, edited by Gavin Fridell and Martijn Konings, 114–131. Toronto: University of Toronto Press.

Okyere, Samuel. 2023. "Worker Voice and Organizing in Efforts to Eliminate Child Labor." In *Worker Voice: What It Is, What It Is Not, and Why It Matters*, edited by Mark Anner and Matthew Fischer-Daly, 82–95. University Park, PA: Center for Global Workers' Rights, The Pennsylvania State University.

Ollus, Natalia. 2015. "Regulating Forced Labour and Combating Human Trafficking: The Relevance of Historical Definitions in a Contemporary Perspective." *Crime, Law and Social Change* 63 (5): 221–246. https://doi.org/10.1007/s10611-015-9566-6.

OSCE Office of the Special Representative and Coordinator for Combating Trafficking in Human Beings, and Tech Against Trafficking. 2020. *Leveraging Innovation to Fight Trafficking in Human Beings: A Comprehensive Analysis of Technology Tools*. The Organization for Security and Co-operation in Europe (Vienna).

Page, Allison. 2017. "'How Many Slaves Work for You?' Race, New Media, and Neoliberal Consumer Activism." *Journal of Consumer Culture* 17 (1): 46–61.

Palumbo, Letizia, and Alessandra Sciurba. 2015. "Vulnerability to Forced Labour and Trafficking: The Case of Romanian Women in the Agricultural Sector in Sicily." *Anti-Trafficking Review* (5): 89–110. https://doi.org/10.14197/atr.20121556.

Parreñas, Rhacel Salazar. 2021. *Unfree: Migrant Domestic Work in Arab States*. Stanford, CA: Stanford University Press.

Patterson, Orlando. 2012. "Trafficking, Gender and Slavery: Past and Present." In *The Legal Understanding of Slavery: From the Historical to the Contemporary*, edited by Jean Allain, 322–359. Oxford: Oxford University Press.

Patterson, Orlando, and Xiaolin Zhuo. 2018. "Modern Trafficking, Slavery, and Other Forms of Servitude." *Annual Review of Sociology* 44: 407–439.

Pearce, Jenny. 2010. "Is Social Change Fundable? NGOs and Theories and Practices of Social Change." *Development in Practice* 20 (6): 621–635.

Peksen, Dursun, Shannon Lindsey Blanton, and Robert G. Blanton. 2017. "Neoliberal Policies and Human Trafficking for Labor: Free Markets, Unfree Workers?" *Political Research Quarterly* 70 (3): 673–686. https://doi.org/10.1177/1065912917710339.

Phillips, Nicola. 2011. *Unfree Labour and Adverse Incorporation in Global Production Networks: Comparative Perspectives on Brazil and India*. Chronic Poverty Research Centre.

———. 2015. "Private Governance and the Problem of Trafficking and Slavery in Global Supply Chains." In *Vulnerability, Exploitation and Migrants*, edited by Louise Waite, Gary Craig, Hannah Lewis, and Klara Skrivankova, 15–27. Basingstoke, Hampshire UK: Palgrave Macmillan.

Phillips, Nicola, and Fabiola Mieres. 2014. "The Governance of Forced Labour in the Global Economy." *Globalizations* 12 (2): 244–260. https://doi.org/10.1080/14747731.2014.932507.

Pike, Kelly. 2020. "Voice in Supply Chains: Does the Better Work Program Lead to Improvements in Labor Standards Compliance?" *ILR Review* 73 (4): 913–938. https://doi.org/10.1177/0019793920911905.

Plant, Roger. 2015. "Debate: Forced Labour, Slavery and Human Trafficking: When Do Definitions Matter?" *Anti-Trafficking Review* (5): 153–157. https://doi.org/10.14197/atr.201215511.

Pope, Shawn, Patricia Bromley, Alwyn Lim, and John W. Meyer. 2018. "The Pyramid of Nonprofit Responsibility: The Institutionalization of Organizational Responsibility Across Sectors." *VOLUNTAS: International Journal of Voluntary and Nonprofit Organizations* 29 (6): 1300–1314. https://doi.org/10.1007/s11266-018-0038-3.

Posthuma, Anne Caroline, and Renato Bignami. 2016. "Deepening Compliance? Potential for Multistakeholder Interaction in Monitoring Labor Standards in the Value Chains of Brazil's Apparel Industry." In *Achieving Workers' Rights in the Global Economy*, edited by Richard P. Appelbaum and Nelson Lichtenstein, 112–136. Ithaca, NY: Cornell University Press.

Powell, Walter W. 2020. "What is the Nonprofit Sector?" In *The Nonprofit Sector: A Research Handbook*, edited by Walter W. Powell and Patricia Bromley, 3–22. Stanford, CA: Stanford University Press.

Powell, Walter W., and Patricia Bromley, eds. 2020. *The Nonprofit Sector: A Research Handbook*. Stanford, CA: Stanford University Press.

Prasad, Kiran Kamal. 2015. "Use of the Term 'Bonded Labour' is a Must in the Context of India." *Anti-Trafficking Review* (5): 162-167. https://doi.org/10.14197/atr.201215513.

Prasad, Monica. 2006. *The Politics of Free Markets: The Rise of Neoliberal Economic Policies in Britain, France, Germany, and the United States*. Chicago and London: University of Chicago Press.

Preminger, Jonathan, Stephanie Limoncelli, Ödül Bozkurt, and Chris Rees. forthcoming. "Introduction." In *Handbook on the Sociology of Work*, edited by Chris Rees, Ödül Bozkurt, Stephanie Limoncelli, and Jonathan Preminger. Cheltenham, UK: Edward Elgar.

Quirk, Joel, Caroline Robinson, and Cameron Thibos. 2020. "Editorial: From Exceptional Cases to Everyday Abuses: Labour Exploitation in the Global Economy." *Anti-Trafficking Review* (15): 1–19. https://doi.org/10.14197/atr.201220151.

Reed, Judy Hale. 2013. "Addressing the Problem: Community-Based Responses and Coordination." In *Human Trafficking: Interdisciplinary Perspectives*, edited by Mary C. Burke, 256–277. New York: Routledge.

Rende Taylor, Lisa, and Elena Shih. 2019. "Worker Feedback Technologies and Combatting Modern Slavery in Global Supply Chains: Examining the Effectiveness of Remediation-Oriented and Due-Diligence-Oriented Technologies in

Identifying and Addressing Forced Labour and Human Trafficking." *Journal of the British Academy* 7 (s1): 131–165. https://doi.org/10.5871/jba/007s1.131.

Ricard-Guay, Alexandra, and Thanos Maroukis. 2017. "Human Trafficking in Domestic Work in the EU: A Special Case or a Learning Ground for the Anti-Trafficking Field?" *Journal of Immigrant & Refugee Studies* 15 (2): 109–121. https://doi.org/10.1080/15562948.2017.1310340.

Richard, Analiese M. 2009. "Mediating Dilemmas: Local NGOs and Rural Development in Neoliberal Mexico." *Political and Legal Anthropology Review* 32 (2): 166–194.

Richey, Lisa Ann, and Stefano Ponte. 2011. *Brand Aid: Shopping Well to Save the World*. Minneapolis: University of Minnesota Press.

Robertson, Raymond. 2019. "Lights On: How Transparency Increases Compliance in Cambodian Global Value Chains." *ILR Review* 73 (4): 939–968. https://doi.org/10.1177/0019793919893333.

Rossoni, Isotta. 2024. "Understanding EU Funding of Anti-Trafficking Initiatives: Where Is the Money (Not) Going?" *Anti-Trafficking Review* 23 (2024): 98–118. https://doi.org/https://doi.org/10.14197/atr.201224236.

Roth, Silke. 2007. "Sisterhood and Solidarity? Women's Organizations in the Expanded European Union." *Social Politics: International Studies in Gender, State & Society* 14 (4): 460–487. https://doi.org/10.1093/sp/jxm019.

Ryder, Guy. 2010. "The Promise of the United Nations Global Compact: A Trade Union Perspective on the Labour Principles." In *The United Nations Global Compact: Achievements, Trends and Challenges*, edited by Andreas Rasche and Georg Kell, 44–58. Cambridge: Cambridge University Press.

Sanders, Matthew L. 2013. "Being Nonprofit-Like in a Market Economy: Understanding the Mission-Market Tension in Nonprofit Organizing." *Nonprofit and Voluntary Sector Quarterly* 44 (2): 205–222. https://doi.org/10.1177/0899764013508606.

Sanders, Matthew L., and John G. McClellan. 2012. "Being Business-Like While Pursuing a Social Mission: Acknowledging the Inherent Tensions in US Nonprofit Organizing." *Organization* 21 (1): 68–89. https://doi.org/10.1177/1350508412464894.

Sarfaty, Galit. 2020. "Translating Modern Slavery into Management Practice." *Law and Social Inquiry* 45 (4): 1027–1051.

Scherer, Andreas Georg, and Guido Palazzo. 2007. "Toward a Political Conception of Corporate Responsibility: Business and Society Seen from a Habermasian Perspective." *The Academy of Management Review* 32 (4): 1096–1120.

———. 2011. "The New Political Role of Business in a Globalized World: A Review of a New Perspective on CSR and Its Implications for the Firm, Governance, and Democracy." *Journal of Management Studies* 48 (4): 899–931. https://doi.org/10.1111/j.1467-6486.2010.00950.x.

Schnable, Allison. 2015. "New American Relief and Development Organizations: Voluntarizing Global Aid." *Social Problems* 62 (1): 309–329. https://doi.org/http://dx.doi.org/10.1093/socpro/spv005.

Schofer, Evan, and Wesley Longhofer. 2020. "The Global Rise of Nongovernmental Organizations." In *The Nonprofit Sector: A Research Handbook*, edited by Walter W. Powell and Patricia Bromley, 603–617. Stanford, CA: Stanford University Press.

Schuller, Mark. 2009. "Gluing Globalization: NGOs as Intermediaries in Haiti." *PoLAR: Political and Legal Anthropology Review* 32 (1): 84–104.

Schumann, Stefan. 2020. "Corporate Criminal Liability on Human Trafficking." In *The Palgrave International Handbook of Human Trafficking*, edited by John Winterdyk and Jackie Jones, 1651–1669. Cham, Switzerland: Palgrave Macmillan.

Scurlock, Rebecca, Nives Dolsak, and Aseem Prakash. 2019. "Recovering from Scandals: Twitter Coverage of Oxfam and Save the Children Scandals." *VOLUNTAS: International Journal of Voluntary and Nonprofit Organizations* 31 (1): 94–110. https://doi.org/10.1007/s11266-019-00148-x.

Seidman, Gay. 2007. *Beyond the Boycott: Labor Rights, Human Rights, and Transnational Activism*. New York: Russell Sage Foundation.

———. 2008. "Transnational Labour Campaigns: Can the Logic of the Market be Turned Against Itself?" *Development and Change* 39 (6): 991–1003.

Seidman, Gay W. 2009. "Labouring Under an Illusion? Lesotho's 'Sweat-Free' Label." *Third World Quarterly* 30 (3): 581–598.

Sexsmith, Kathleen, and Rebecca Tarlau. forthcoming. "Agricultural Work: Unfreedom and Resistance." In *Handbook on the Sociology of Work*, edited by Chris Rees, Ödül Bozkurt, Stephanie Limoncelli, and Jonathan Preminger. Cheltenham, UK: Edward Elgar.

Shamir, Hila. 2012. "A Labor Paradigm for Human Trafficking." *UCLA Law Review* 60 (1): 76–136.

Shamir, Ronen. 2004. "The De-Radicalization of Corporate Social Responsibility." *Critical Sociology* 30 (3): 669–689.

Sharapov, Kiril, Suzanne Hoff, Jonathan Mendel, and Borislav Gerasimov. 2024. "Editorial: Rethinking Anti-Trafficking Funding: Following the Money, Again." *Anti-Trafficking Review* 23 (2024): 1–9. https://doi.org/https://doi.org/10.14197/atr .201224231.

Sharapov, Kiril, Jonathan Mendel, and Kyle Schwartz. 2024. "Expansion, Fracturing, and Depoliticisation: UK Government Anti-Trafficking Funding from 2011 to 2023." *Anti-Trafficking Review* 23 (2024): 34–57. https://doi.org/https://doi.org/ 10.14197/atr.201224233.

Shelley, Louise. 2003. "Trafficking in Women: The Business Model Approach." *The Brown Journal of World Affairs* 10 (1): 119–131.

Shelley, Louise, and Christina Bain. 2015. "Human Trafficking: Fighting the Illicit Economy with the Legitimate Economy." In *Social Inclusion Special Issue: Perspectives on Human Trafficking and Modern Forms of Slavery* 3 (1): 140–144.

Shih, Elena. 2016. "Not in My 'Backyard Abolitionism': Vigilante Rescue Against American Sex Trafficking." *Sociological Perspectives* 59 (1): 66–90. https://doi .org/10.1177/0731121416628551.

———. 2023. *Manufacturing Freedom: Sex Work, Anti-Trafficking Rehab, and the Racial Wages of Rescue.* Oakland, CA: University of California Press.

Shih, Elena, Jennifer Rosenbaum, and Penelope Kyritsis. 2021. "Undermining Labor Power: The False Promise of the Industry-Led Antislavery Initiatives." In *Fighting Modern Slavery and Human Trafficking: History and Contemporary Policy,* edited by Genevieve LeBaron, Jessica R. Pliley, and David W. Blight, 141–155. Cambridge: Cambridge University Press.

Short, Jodi L., Michael W. Toffel, and Andrea R. Hugill. 2020. "Improving Working Conditions in Global Supply Chains: The Role of Institutional Environments and Monitoring Program Design." *ILR Review* 73 (4): 873–912. https://doi.org/10.1177/0019793920916181.

Showden, Carisa, and Samantha Majic, eds. 2014. *Negotiating Sex Work: Unintended Consequences of Policy and Activism.* Minneapolis, MN: University of Minnesota Press.

Showden, Carisa R., and Samantha Majic. 2018. *Youth Who Trade Sex in the U.S.: Intersectionality, Agency, and Vulnerability.* Philadelphia: Temple University Press.

Siegel, Dina, and Sylvia de Blank. 2010. "Women Who Traffic Women: The Role of Women in Human Trafficking Networks – Dutch Cases." *Global Crime* 11 (4): 436–447. https://doi.org/http://dx.doi.org/10.1080/17440572.2010.519528.

Simpson, Meghan. 2006. "Local Strategies in Globalizing Gender Politics: Women's Organizing in Kyrgyzstan and Tajikistan." *Journal of Muslim Minority Affairs* 26 (1): 9–31.

Skocpol, Theda. 2003. *Diminished Democracy: From Membership to Management in American Civic Life.* Norman, OK: University of Oklahoma Press.

Smith, Steven Rathgeb. 2014. "Hybridity and Nonprofit Organizations: The Research Agenda." *American Behavioral Scientist* 58 (11): 1494–1508. https://doi .org/10.1177/0002764214534675.

Snow, David A., and Rens Vliegenthart. 2023. "An Imperious, Closed Sandbox? A Rejoinder to Van Dijk's Critique of the Framing Perspective on Social Movement Mobilization." *Discourse Studies* 25 (2): 297–308. https://doi.org/10.1177/14614456231155079.

Snow, David A., Rens Vliegenthart, and Pauline Ketelaars. 2019. "The Framing Perspective on Social Movements: Its Conceptual Roots and Architecture." In *The Wiley Blackwell Companion to Social Movements, Second Edition,* edited by David A. Snow, Sarah A. Soule, Hanspeter Kriesi, and Holly J. McCammon, 392–410. John Wiley & Sons Ltd.

Soederberg, Susanne. 2007. "Taming Corporations or Buttressing Market-Led Development? A Critical Assessment of the Global Compact." *Globalizations* 4 (4): 500–513. https://doi.org/10.1080/14747730701695760.

Soskis, Benjamin. 2020. "A History of Associational Life and the Nonprofit Sector in the United States." In *The Nonprofit Sector: A Research Handbook*, edited by Walter W. Powell and Patricia Bromley, 23–80. Stanford, CA: Stanford University Press.

Soule, Sarah A. 2009. *Contention and Corporate Social Responsibility*. Cambridge: Cambridge University Press.

Spapens, Toine. 2018. "The Business of Trafficking in Human Beings." In *Routledge Handbook of Human Trafficking*, edited by Ryszard Piotrowicz, Conny Rijken, and Baerbel Heide Uhl, 535–545.

Spooner, Dave. 2005. "Labor Unions and NGOs: The Need for Cooperation." In *Development NGOs and Labor Unions: Terms of Engagement*, edited by Deborah Eade and Alan Leather, 11–31. Bloomfield, CT: Kumarian Press, Inc.

Stroup, Sarah S. 2012. *Borders Among Activists: International NGOs in the United States, Britain, and France*. Ithaca, NY: Cornell University Press.

Stroup, Sarah S., and Wendy H. Wong. 2017. *The Authority Trap: Strategic Choices of International INGOs*. Ithaca: Cornell University Press.

Subramaniam, Mangala. 2007. "NGOs and Resources in the Construction of Intellectual Realms: Cases from India." *Critical Sociology* 33 (3): 551–573. https://doi.org/10.1163/156916307x189022.

Suhr, Brigitte. 2016. *Funding the Fight Against Modern Slavery: Mapping Private Funds in the Anti-Slavery and Anti-Trafficking Sector: 2012–2014*. The Freedom Fund and Humanity United.

Tandon, Shraysi. 2018. Invisible Hands. First Run Features.

Taylor, Lisa Rende. 2020. "Letting Go of the Dream of Traffickers Behind Bars: We Can Do Better for Exploited Workers." *Anti-Trafficking Review* (15): 176–181. https://doi.org/10.14197/atr.2012201513.

Thakor, Mitali, and danah boyd. 2013. "Networked Trafficking: Reflections on Technology and the Anti-Trafficking Movement." *Dialectical Anthropology* 37 (2): 277–290. https://doi.org/10.1007/s10624-012-9286-6.

Theron, Colleen. 2019. "Modern Slavery and Transparency in Supply Chains: The Role of Business." In *The Modern Slavery Agenda: Policy, Politics and Practice in the UK*, edited by Gary Craig, Alex Balch, Hannah Lewis, and Louise Waite, 187–218. Bristol: Bristol University Press and Policy Press.

Thompson, Carol. 2017. "Philanthrocapitalism: Rendering the Public Domain Obsolete?" *Third World Quarterly* 39 (1): 51–67. https://doi.org/10.1080/01436597.2017.1357112.

Tilly, Chris. forthcoming. "Informal Work: Definitions, Drivers, Agency." In *Handbook on the Sociology of Work*, edited by Chris Rees, Ödül Bozkurt, Stephanie Limoncelli, and Jonathan Preminger. Cheltenham, UK: Edward Elgar.

Trodd, Zoe. 2013. "Am I Still Not a Man and a Brother? Protest Memory in Contemporary Antislavery Visual Culture." *Slavery and Abolition* 34 (2): 338–352. https://doi.org/http://dx.doi.org/10.1080/0144039X.2013.791172.

Tsutsui, Kiyoteru, and Alwyn Lim. 2015. *Corporate Social Responsibility in a Globalizing World*. Cambridge: Cambridge University Press.

Tuckman, Howard P. 1998a. "Competition, Commercialization, and the Evolution of Nonprofit Organizational Structures." In *To Profit or Not to Profit: The Commercial Transformation of the Nonprofit Sector*, edited by Burton A. Weisbrod, 25–46. Cambridge University Press.

———. 1998b. "Competition, Commercialization, and the Evolution of Nonprofit Organizational Structures." *Journal of Policy Analysis and Management* 17 (2): 175–194.

Turnbull, Nick, and Robert Hoppe. 2019. "Problematizing 'Wickedness': A Critique of the Wicked Problems Concept, from Philosophy to Practice." *Policy and Society* 38 (2): 315–337. https://doi.org/10.1080/14494035.2018.1488796.

Ucnikova, Martina. 2014. "OECD and Modern Slavery: How Much Aid Money is Spent to Tackle the Issue?" *Anti-Trafficking Review* 3: 133–150. https://antitraffickingreview.org/index.php/atrjournal/article/view/68 .

United Nations Global Compact, Ethical Trading Initiative, UK Department for International Development, and Verité. 2018. *Business: It's Time to Act*. United National Global Compact (New York).

United Nations Global Compact, and Maplecroft. 2013a. "Human Rights and Business Dilemmas Forum: Forced Labour and Human Trafficking Webinar." London.

———. 2013b. "Human Rights and Business Dilemmas Forum: Human Trafficking and Migrant Workers Webinar." London.

United Nations Global Compact, and United Nations Office of the High Commissioner of Human Rights. 2004. *Embedding Human Rights in Business Practice*. UN Global Compact (New York).

United Nations Global Initiative to Fight Human Trafficking, International Organization for Migration, International Labour Organization, and United Nations Global Compact. 2010. *Human Trafficking and Business: Good Practices to Prevent and Combat Human Trafficking*. United Nations Global Initiative to Fight Human Trafficking (UN.GIFT) (Vienna, Austria).

United Nations Office on Drugs and Crime. 2016a. "UN.GIFT.HUB: About." Accessed July 4, 2025. https://web.archive.org/web/20210415144929/https://www.ungift.org/about/.

United Nations Office on Drugs and Crime. 2016b. "UN.GIFT.HUB: Private sector initiatives." Accessed July 4, 2025. https://web.archive.org/web/20210415130929/https://www.ungift.org/business/initiatives

United Nations Voluntary Trust Fund for Victims of Human Trafficking. 2015. *Giving Hope to Victims of Human Trafficking*. United Nations Office on Drugs and Crime (Vienna).

———. 2019. *2019 Annual Report*. United Nations Office for Drugs and Crime (Vienna).

———. 2021. *2021 Annual Report*. United Nations Office on Drugs and Crime (Vienna).

———. 2022. *2022 Annual Report.* United Nations Office for Drugs and Crime (Vienna).

United States Department of State Office to Monitor and Combat Trafficking in Persons. 2021. *Trafficking in Persons Report.* United States Department of State (Washington, DC). https://www.state.gov/reports/2021-trafficking-in-persons -report/.

———. 2023. *Trafficking in Persons Report.* United States Department of State (Washington, DC). https://www.state.gov/reports/2023-trafficking-in-persons -report/.

Utting, Peter. 2008. "The Struggle for Corporate Accountability." *Development and Change* 39 (6): 959–975. https://doi.org/10.1111/j.1467-7660.2008.00523.x.

Van Buren, III, Harry J., Judith Schrempf-Stirling, and Michelle Westermann-Behaylo. 2019. "Business and Human Trafficking: A Social Connection and Political Responsibility Model." *Business & Society* 60 (2): 341–375. https://doi .org/10.1177/0007650319872509.

van den Anker, Christien. 2007. "Global Social Policy Forum: Global Ethics and Contemporary Slavery." *Global Social Policy* 7 (1): 6–10.

van Doorninck, Marieke. 2018. "Changing the System from Within: The Role of NGOs in the Flawed Anti-Trafficking Framework." In *Routledge Handbook of Human Trafficking*, edited by Ryszard Piotrowicz, Conny Rijken, and Baerbel Heide Uhl, 419–430. London and New York: Routledge.

Verité. 2019. *Assessment of Forced Labor Risk in the Cocoa Sector of Côte d'Ivoire.* Verité (Amherst, MA).

Vestergaard, Anne. 2013. "Mediatized Humanitarianism: Trust and Legitimacy in the Age of Suspicion." *Journal of Business Ethics* 120 (4): 509–525. https://doi.org/ 10.1007/s10551-013-2002-x.

Vogel, David. 2005. *The Market for Virtue: The Potential and Limits of Corporate Social Responsibility.* Washington, DC: Brookings Institution Press.

Walch, Angela. 2018. "Blockchain Applications to International Affairs: Reasons for Skepticism." *Georgetown Journal of International Affairs* 19 (Fall 2018): 27–35.

Walk Free Foundation, and University of Nottingham. no date. Modern Slavery: What Business Needs to Know. Walk Free Foundation.

Walker, Edward T., and Yotala Oszkay Febres-Cordero. 2020. "The Changing Face of Nonprofit Advocacy: Democratizing Potentials and Risks in an Unequal Context." In *The Nonprofit Sector: A Research Handbook*, edited by Walter W. Powell and Patricia Bromley, 507–520. Stanford, CA: Stanford University Press.

Walker, Edward T., and Christopher M. Rea. 2014. "The Political Mobilization of Firms and Industries." *Annual Review of Sociology* 40 (2014): 281–304.

Watkins, Susan Cotts, Ann Swidler, and Thomas Hannan. 2012. "Outsourcing Social Transformation: Development NGOs as Organizations." *Annual Review of Sociology* 38: 285–315.

Weil, David. 2014. *The Fissured Workplace: Why Work Became So Bad for So Many and What Can Be Done to Improve It.* Cambridge, MA: Harvard University Press.

————. 2019. "Understanding the Present and Future of Work in the Fissured Workplace Context." *RSF: The Russell Sage Foundation Journal of the Social Sciences* 5 (5): 147–165. https://doi.org/10.7758/rsf.2019.5.5.08.

Weisbrod, Burton A. 1997. "The Future of the Nonprofit Sector: Its Entwining with Private Enterprise and Government." *Journal of Policy Analysis and Management* 16 (4): 541–555.

Wells, Don. 2007. "Too Weak for the Job: Corporate Codes of Conduct, Non-Governmental Organizations and the Regulation of International Labour Standards." *Global Social Policy* 7 (1): (51–74). https://doi.org/10.1177/1468018107073911.

Whoriskey, Peter, Rachel Siegel, and Salwan Georges. 2019. "Cocoa's Child Laborers." *Washington Post*, 2019.

Wilhelm, Miriam, Alin Kadfak, Vikram Bhakoo, and Kate Skattang. 2020. "Private Governance of Human and Labor Rights in Seafood Supply Chains – The Case of the Modern Slavery Crisis in Thailand." *Marine Policy* 115. https://doi.org/10.1016/j.marpol.2020.103833.

Williams, Matthew S. 2016. "Strategic Innovation in US Anti-Sweatshop Movement." *Social Movement Studies* 15 (3): 277–289.

————. 2020. *Strategizing Against Sweatshops: The Global Economy, Student Activism, and Worker Empowerment.* Philadelphia: Temple University Press.

Wolf, Andrew B., Michael Piore, Hana Shepherd, Janice Fine, and Jacob Barnes. forthcoming. "Towards a Sociology of Labour Regulation and Enforcement in the Context of the Modern Fissured Workplace." In *Handbook on the Sociology of Work*, edited by Chris Rees, Ödül Bozkurt, Stephanie Limoncelli, and Jonathan Preminger. Cheltenham, UK: Edward Elgar Publishing.

Yaziji, Michael, and Jonathan Doh. 2009. *NGOs and Corporations.* Cambridge: Cambridge University Press.

Yaziji, Michael, and Jonathan P. Doh. 2013. "The Role of Ideological Radicalism and Resource Homogeneity in Social Movement Organization Campaigns Against Corporations." *Organization Studies* 34 (5–6): 755–780. https://doi.org/10.1177/0170840613479235.

Yea, Sallie. 2017. "Editorial: The Politics of Evidence, Data and Research in Anti-Trafficking Work." *Anti-Trafficking Review* (8): 1–13. https://doi.org/10.14197/atr.20121781.

Yea, Sallie, and Stephanie Chok. 2018. "Unfreedom Unbound: Developing a Cumulative Approach to Understanding Unfree Labour in Singapore." *Work, Employment and Society* 32 (5): 925–941. https://doi.org/10.1177/0950017017738956.

Yevgeniya, Dodina. 2007. "Relations Between NGOs and Trade Unions: The Case of Ukraine." *Development in Practice* 14 (1–2): 280–285. https://doi.org/10.1080/0961452032000170848.

Yu, Jianxing, and Kejian Chen. 2018. "Does Nonprofit Marketization Facilitate or Inhibit the Development of Civil Society? A Comparative Study of China and the USA." *VOLUNTAS: International Journal of Voluntary and Nonprofit Organizations* 29 (5): 925–937. https://doi.org/10.1007/s11266-018-9952-7.

Index

Nepal, 6, 30, 39, 53, 154
Nestle, 55, 80
Netherlands, 17, 27
new institutionalist theory, 10, 13, 130, 165, 182n10
niches, 63, 119, 120–24
Nigeria, 24, 154
Nike, 57, 71, 80, 90
Nokia, 95
Nolan, Justine, 3
Norway, 5, 171

Occupational Safety and Health Administration, 170
Office of the Special Representative and Co-ordinator for Combating Trafficking in Human Beings, 95
Ollus, Natalia, 32
Omidyar, Pierre, 6, 125
online content, 3, 17; AI used to gather, 101; anonymity of, 94; awareness campaign materials, 69; child sex trafficking video, 98; child trafficking rings, 117; data directory for activists, 110; INGO activities for sale, 137–38; INGO merchandise for sale, 150, 152; migrant workers' employer reviews, 114; photos of people in sex trafficking situations, 100; platforms, 96; promoting human trafficking, 92; sex industry ads, 99; sexual exploitation and trafficking, 96
online technologies, 93; activities monitoring, 94; Interactive Map for Business of Anti-Human Trafficking Organizations, 95
organizational actors, 3, 5, 7, 9, 10, 16, 46, 166; set and enforce labor standards, 54; working on labor rights, 23
Organization for Security and Co-operation in Europe (OSCE), 25, 95, 96, 186n8

outreach, 70, 168, 170, 172; awareness and, 97–99, 103–6; initiatives, 69; to migrant workers, 174; technological tools for, 94; technology initiatives, 97t
outsourcing, 20, 32, 51, 67, 69, 170; accountability, 87–89

Pakistan, 80
paternalism, 65, 135, 139, 141
people of color, 106, 167
philanthrocapitalism, 12, 156, 167
philanthropy, 138, 143, 182n10
Philippines, 39
political economy, 10, 137; framings of, 19; of "modern slavery," 168; of unfree labor, 18, 23, 32, 36, 37, 44
politics of rescue, 135
poverty, 29, 36, 145, 152, 162, 166, 167; global north companies contribute to, 31; in global south, 140; INGOs work against, 7, 153, 171; market-based solutions to fight, 154; trade agreements can exacerbate, 33; unfree labor an outcome of, 35
power differentials, 10, 19, 68, 79, 80
power dynamics, 165, 179
power relations, 10, 66, 118, 132, 145, 163, 179
precarity, 15, 155, 163
privacy, 20, 107, 114, 115, 118
private governance, 7, 12, 14, 151, 166
private regulation, 9, 10, 54, 167, 170, 184n10
private sector, 146, 166, 181n4; addressing "modern slavery," 164; beliefs about, 11; collaboration with, 3; Deloitte delivers services to, 63; develops technological tools, 95; funding from, 181n5; funding of, 5, 6; Harvard Kennedy School view of, 52; INGOs' criticism toward,

The authorized representative in the EU for product safety and compliance is:
Mare Nostrum Group
B.V Doelen 72
4831 GR Breda
The Netherlands

www.ingramcontent.com/pod-product-compliance
Lightning Source LLC
Chambersburg PA
CBHW030406270326
41926CB00009B/1292

9 781503 644823